PRIMA DONNA

INNER LIVES

SERIES EDITOR
William Todd Schultz

———

PRIMA DONNA

The Psychology of Maria Callas

Paul Wink

OXFORD
UNIVERSITY PRESS

Oxford University Press is a department of the University of Oxford. It furthers
the University's objective of excellence in research, scholarship, and education
by publishing worldwide. Oxford is a registered trade mark of Oxford University
Press in the UK and certain other countries.

Published in the United States of America by Oxford University Press
198 Madison Avenue, New York, NY 10016, United States of America.

© Oxford University Press 2021

Library of Congress Cataloging-in-Publication Data
Names: Wink, Paul, 1952– author.
Title: Prima donna : the psychology of Maria Callas / Paul Wink.
Description: New York, NY : Oxford University Press, [2021] |
Includes bibliographical references and index.
Identifiers: LCCN 2020027946 (print) | LCCN 2020027947 (ebook) |
ISBN 9780190857738 (hardback) | ISBN 9780197550861 |
ISBN 9780190857752 (epub)
Subjects: LCSH: Callas, Maria, 1923–1977—Psychology. | Sopranos (Singers)
Classification: LCC ML420.C18 W5 2021 (print) | LCC ML420.C18 (ebook) |
DDC 782.1092 [B]—dc23
LC record available at https://lccn.loc.gov/2020027946
LC ebook record available at https://lccn.loc.gov/2020027947

DOI: 10.1093/oso/9780190857738.001.0001

9 8 7 6 5 4 3 2 1

Printed by Sheridan Books, Inc., United States of America

In memory of Claire Zimmerman, a colleague and a friend.

CONTENTS

ACKNOWLEDGMENTS

Many friends and colleagues have contributed to the writing of this book. My biggest thank you goes to my wife, Michele Dillon, for her insightful comments, helpful suggestions, and unwavering support and encouragement. I would also like to thank Todd Schultz, the editor of the Oxford University Press's series on the study of lives, for his input, and the students in his seminar on the study of lives who read the manuscript as part of their class; their feedback was very helpful. I thank Jordan Burke for his strong editorial support.

During my sabbatical leave spent at the University of Verona, I profited greatly from the musical expertise and advice of Vincenzo Borghetti and Nicola Pasqualicchio and the hospitality of Renato Camurri. Farbrizio Cigni of the Scuola Normale in Piza contributed greatly to the manuscript. I would like to express my gratitude to Signora Giovanna Lomazzi, one of Maria Callas's last surviving friends, for meeting with me to discuss her relationship with Callas. I benefited greatly from my conversation with F. Paul Driscoll, Editor-in-Chief of *Opera News*, and from the editorial guidance and help of Abby Gross, Editor-in-Chief and Katharine Pratt, Assistant Editor at Oxford University Press. I am grateful to a number friends and colleagues who commented on the manuscript, including Jim Anderson, Jo Beatson, Jonathan Cheek, Lillian Cartwright, Alan Pollack, and Alek Silber. I benefited from comments and suggestions made by two anonymous reviewers of the manuscript. Thank you.

The writing of the manuscript was supported by funds from my endowed Nellie Zuckerman Cohen & Anne Cohen Heller Professor of Health Sciences chair at Wellesley College and from Wellesley College's Faculty Research Award and fund supporting the scholarly exchange program between Wellesley College and the University of Verona.

INTRODUCTION

I remember running frantically up the stairs of San Francisco's War Memorial Opera to secure the best possible standing-room spot, one that would provide an unobstructed view of the stage. Once firmly planted against the balcony railing—a prized spot for standees—I was captivated by this new-to-me art form, one integrating voices and music with the visual splendor of sets. I still have vivid memories of a shiver running down my spine listening to the Grand Inquisitor scene from Verdi's *Don Carlos* and the thrill mixed with bemusement of witnessing breast-plated Marilyn Horne, the famous American mezzo-soprano, pacing up and down the stage equipped with a shield and a spear singing the lead male role in Handle's *Orlando*. I identified with Rodolfo and his band of artistic friends in Puccini's *La Boheme*, in their poverty and disdain of bourgeois convention.

My interest in opera began while I was a graduate student at the University of California, Berkeley, in the mid-1980s. Jesus Mora, a Venezuelan graduate student in engineering and a Maria Callas fanatic, guided my forays into the world of opera. I recollect Jesus's enthusiasm as he loaned me this set of cassettes, a pirated live recording of Callas performing Bellini's *Norma*. "People in the know," he whispered excitedly, "say that this performance was Maria at her best." The recording was of Callas's 1956

Prima Donna. Paul Wink, Oxford University Press (2021). © Oxford University Press.
DOI: 10.1093/oso/9780190857738.003.0001

performance at La Scala, which showcases Callas at the height of her operatic career performing with a stellar cast that included Mario del Monaco and Giulietta Simionato. To this day, Bellini's *Norma*, of which I proudly possess seven of Callas's recordings, makes my list of top five operas of all time.

It was Jesus who introduced me to the intensity of debate concerning the merits of Callas's voice *before* she lost a massive amount of weight versus her voice *after* the transformation. It was also Jesus who informed me of the rivalry between Callas and Renata Tebaldi.

What attracted me most was the distinct nature of Callas's voice and the expressivity of her singing; in fact, hers was the only voice I could recognize after the first bar. I recall comparing Callas's and Tebaldi's versions of the aria "Un bel di vedremo" from Puccini's *Madama Butterfly,* an opera that brought Maria more notoriety off stage than on. I was wowed by her interpretive sensitivity. Tebaldi's vocal beauty, by contrast, left me cold. But in the operatic circles in which I moved, Callas was the one and the only one.

Many years later, my interest in Callas was reignited after I received the Henry Murray lifetime achievement award from the Society for Personology. The award acknowledged my contribution to the psychological understanding of individual lives, of how personality develops over the life course, and how it influences life outcomes. My research focused primarily on narcissism and its effects on everyday functioning in adulthood. It was based on two longitudinal studies, one of which followed a group of women from their college years to their early fifties, and the other traced the lives of men and women from adolescence until old age. Both studies included quantitative questionnaire data and qualitative in-depth interviews, allowing me to integrate statistical patterns with individuals' more personalized ways of being and meaning-making in everyday life.

My award came with the opportunity to address the Annual Meeting of the American Psychological Association in Washington, DC, in 2014. I chose the life of Maria Callas as the theme of my talk and did so because I wanted to demonstrate the complexity of narcissism as it unfolds in an individual life. One of my early contributions to the field of personality psychology was to show the dual nature of the narcissistic self—with personal vulnerability lurking behind a grandiose façade or, alternatively, a vulnerable self-presentation masking arrogance and a grandiose sense of entitlement.[1] The two faces of narcissism seemed to capture the disjunction between the self-assured and imperial *la Callas* the operatic diva and the vulnerable and insecure Maria the woman. In addition, Callas appealed to me as a subject of inquiry because she exemplifies a healthy aspect of narcissism—its association with creativity—something I had also documented in prior research but that appeared to be unacknowledged in scholarly research on the construct.

Since my initial work in the early 1990s, narcissism research has proliferated, deepening our understanding of the narcissistic personality and its family origins. This knowledge has advanced our understanding of the manner in which narcissism affects interactions with others and the sense of self, yet there was also a tendency to group narcissism with other personality types, including borderline and antisocial, both of which are characterized by impulsivity, volatility, and an unmitigated pursuit of the person's own interests. This trend appeared to belie the complexity of the construct. In particular, it appeared to disregard narcissistic perfectionism, a characteristic capable of motivating a relentless pursuit of excellence, even at the price of one's own well-being, as exemplified by Callas. Narcissists have a tendency to blur personal boundaries as a way of buttressing their fragile self-esteem, and current research has yet to fully acknowledge the capacity for deep-seated, albeit selective, empathy that emerges from narcissism. My analysis of Callas's personality is aimed to show the complexity of narcissism—a personality characteristic rather than a diagnostic category—as it unfolds in an individual's life.

Maria Callas's puzzling personal disintegration during the final years of her life also factored in determining her as a subject of inquiry. How could the most celebrated soprano of her era, if not the twentieth century, die in her early fifties in despair, addicted to drugs and socially isolated? Narcissism holds the key to understanding the latter years of Callas's life, especially the overt sense of vulnerability or hypersensitivity that masks the underlying imperial sense of self and explains her inability to negotiate the premature decline of her voice and Aristotle Onassis's abandonment. This book is in large measure an attempt to solve this puzzle. In my quest to unlock the mysteries of Callas's life, I draw broadly on contemporary research in developmental and personality psychology. Clearly, it is impossible to fully comprehend a life by reducing it to just one construct; nonetheless, narcissism provides the overarching theme for my inquiry.

Callas's narcissism evades a straightforward classification as being either grandiose or vulnerable. Chapter 2 considers how the dual nature of the narcissistic self is manifest in the split between

Callas, the self-assured, grandiose operatic diva, and Maria, who is vulnerable and hypersensitive. It also shows how her propensity toward merger with operatic roles and significant others enhanced the unprecedented power of her stage performances. As I will show in Chapters 3 and 4, family dynamics denied Callas the opportunity to express her own individuality: Her mother was self-centered and authoritarian while her father was emotionally absent, hence Callas was unable to shed the egocentrism appropriate to childhood. Instead, she ended up enacting her mother's inflated ambitions and aspirations. Callas's grandiosity and vulnerability were subsequently strengthened by both the hostility she encountered from fellow artists after launching her career in Athens and the ongoing negative dynamics in her family, as I discuss in Chapter 5. Consequently, Callas developed a bimodal persona characterized by grandiosity and feelings of vulnerability, depletion, and lack of efficacy or agency. "[T]here was Maria and there was Callas," writes John Ardoin, Callas's friend and music critic for the *Dallas Morning Star*. He goes on to assert that, being perceived as unattractive and unloved, Maria was widely jealous of the suave and universally adored Callas.[2]

The disjunction between grandiose Callas and vulnerable Maria did not preclude each of her personas exhibiting the complementary side of narcissism. Rather, as I show in Chapter 7, her public persona as the self-assured diva coexisted with personal insecurities and a perfectionism that undermined the affirmation she received for her professional accomplishments. The closeness of her intimate relationships was compromised by a sense of entitlement and distrust, a lack of empathy that spilled over from the public Callas to the private Maria. There were age-related changes as well: The confident and assured aspects of her personality, predominant in her early years, were gradually displaced by a vulnerability hardened by her loss of voice, then exacerbated following her breakup with Aristotle Onassis. Despite contributing to troubling aspects of her personality, Callas's narcissistic qualities enhanced her artistic power and the magic of her stage appearance by allowing her to merge with audiences and roles enacted on stage.

The most intriguing aspects of Callas's personality—the juxtaposition of her fierce independence and abrasiveness as a professional with the marked dependence of her personal life—stem directly from the narcissistic need of others. A tigress on stage and in public life where her needs were mirrored, she appeared incapable of functioning on her own outside of the operatic limelight. During the beginning of her career in Athens, Callas relied on emotional support from her mother, who attended all of her performances, helped her to dress, and acted as cheerleader (and confidence booster). Given what was an otherwise antagonistic relationship between them, one might have expected the twenty-three-year-old Callas to strike out on her own once she arrived in Verona in 1947, relishing the opportunity for her first Italian engagement. Yet, within a couple of days, she became involved with Meneghini who became her husband and full-time manager within two years. As discussed in Chapter 6, she quite willingly surrendered control over the financial aspects of her career to him. More surprising, she frequently looked to him to organize her daily activities, even to the point of choosing what clothes she should wear.

Callas moved straight from being with Meneghini to living with Onassis, as I will discuss in Chapter 8. Their relationship brought her a lot of joy and satisfaction, and it was a relationship characterized by devotion and care, at least on her part. But it also showed her striking subservience, her willingness to tolerate the many public humiliations he imposed. Although Callas's idealized relationships were successful in compensating for her psychological frailty, the potential loss of significant others and the vagaries of her voice left her highly vulnerable. These relationships failed to fulfill her hope of being accepted for her real self, thus she was unable to shed her narcissism and grow as a person in the process. After Onassis abandoned her for Jackie Kennedy, Maria completely fell apart. She spent the last decade of her life in despair, living a largely purposeless existence. She ended up secluded in a Paris apartment with her maid, a butler, and two poodles, a period that is the subject of Chapter 9.

What made Callas a tragic, narcissistic figure was her inability to carry over the vitality and purpose that was so evident in her most stunning operatic performances into the latter phase of her life, where her adjustment was undermined by envy and difficulty in accepting the limitations of aging. Thus, as I argue in Chapter 9, she could not withstand the devastating loss of meaning attendant on her lost voice and her lost love (Onassis) and, consequently, lost her desire to live. This vulnerability goes back to early childhood in New York City as the Callas family, after moving from Greece to New York City, faced the stress of adjusting to life in a foreign environment that exacerbated fundamental incompatibilities between Maria's parents. The psychological hardship experienced during adolescent years spent in Athens, notwithstanding professional successes, further buttressed Callas's fragile self.

Notes

1. Wink, P. (1991). Two faces of narcissism. *Journal of Personality and Social Psychology, 61,* 590–597.
2. Gage, N. (2000). *Greek fire: The story of Maria Callas and Aristotle Onassis.* New York: Knopf, p. 34.

21 | PRIMA DONNA ASSOLUTA
PSYCHOLOGICAL MYSTERIES

It is April 14, 1957. The Teatro alla Scala, Milan's world-renowned opera house, is filled to capacity. The stalls and lower balconies are occupied by the Milanese elite. The upper-most balcony is filled with the less affluent but fanatical *loggionisti* who know the scores of popular operas inside-out and stand ready to punish vocal missteps with jeers and whistles. Tonight is Donizetti's *Anna Bolena*, a rarely performed opera with, up to that point, only one other billing in Italy in the twentieth century. It is a brave choice, considering that it has no famous arias. Excitement centers on Maria Callas, who is scheduled to sing the title role this evening at the height of her operatic power.[1] Just over a year earlier, as La Scala's reigning queen, she mesmerized audiences as *Norma*. She brought down the house in Berlin with her performance in *Lucia di Lammermoor*, conducted by Herbert von Karajan, and, three months after *Anna Bolena*, she gave a legendary performance in Cologne as Amina in Bellini's *La Sonnambula*.[2] The thirty-three-year-old singer's voice is beginning to deteriorate, but its flaws are amply compensated by Callas's increased ability to inject nuance and drama into her performances. She is not only a brilliant singer but an exceptionally gifted actor as well.

The Milanese public is not disappointed. Although this April evening's production is more conventional than that designed by

Prima Donna. Paul Wink, Oxford University Press (2021). © Oxford University Press.
DOI: 10.1093/oso/9780190857738.003.0002

Luchino Visconti for Callas's La Scala performances of *La Vestale* and *La Traviata*, each set is greeted with warm applause. The black, white, and gray colors of Henry VIII's palace are meant to reflect the colors of London. They contrast well with the red dress of Jane Seymour and the chorus's scarlet and yellow attire. Callas's all-blue costume, sculpted to fit her figure, is based on Holbein's real-life portrait of Anne Boleyn. Perspective creates the optical illusion that the stage seems three times as deep as it is in reality, a sense of depth enhanced by a massive staircase filled with large portraits. The Visconti-Benois production "sets a new standard for interpreting opera of the early Romantic Era."[3]

In excellent voice that night, Callas seamlessly meets the demands of her audience. The final scene depicts Bolena locked in the Tower of London as she prepares for her death; it contains some of the finest music ever penned by Donizetti, and, as music critic Pierre-Jean Remy has noted, "[f]or these who saw her then Callas was never more beautiful than as the sorrowful queen."[4] The opera's ending not only focuses entirely on the soprano, something Callas always welcomed, but it also afforded her "dramatic opportunities, startling changes of mood, dazzling vocal pyrotechnics, music of melting lyricism, scorching passion and heart-rendering pathos"[5] to dazzle the audience. In essence, the opening night of *Anna Bolena* is a total performance: It is a perfect marriage of words, music, and action against the backdrop of memorable visual effects provided by the sets and costumes. Following the final curtain, the applause continues for nearly a half hour, a La Scala record for solo curtains that continues to stand even today. At a time when newspapers tended not to review operas that were staged internationally, both the *New York Times* and the *London Sunday Times* carried glowing reviews of Callas's performance. Both reviews were accompanied by her photograph. It is the apex of her career.

Callas was possessed at the height of her career, capable of making the audience completely lose itself in her performance. She was sublime. She mesmerized audiences with her special combination of vocal, artistic, and acting powers. And she did it by reviving forgotten operas that lacked the appeal of well-known tunes and arias, such as *Anna Bolena*. In doing so, she transformed the operatic repertoire for years to come. During the 1950s, Callas was sought by all the main opera houses in Europe and the United States. Her 1958 gala performance at the Paris Opera, broadcast internationally by French television and attended by royalty and the European jet set, was described as the greatest show on earth. As Wayne Koestenbaum has said, we love Callas "because she's the best."[6]

The adulation of her followers knew few limits. When, after a seven-year hiatus, Callas returned to the Met in 1965 for two performances of *Tosca*, the ticket lines formed a week in advance. National television broadcast the images of her devotees braving New York's winter cold in sleeping bags. Such was the hysteria surrounding the performances that, as a precaution, the tickets were locked in a vault until the day they went on sale.[7] Quite without precedent, *Les Temps Modernes*, Jean Paul Sartre's highbrow magazine, commissioned the renowned French musicologist Rene Leibowitz to write an article about Callas. She was the only soprano of recent times whose artistry and vocal range drew comparisons with Giuditta Pasta (1797–1865) and Maria Malibran (1808–1836), two legendary divas of the nineteenth century for whom the titans of the *bel canto* era—Gioachino Rossini (1792–1868), Gaetano Donizetti (1797–1848), and Vincenzo Bellini (1801–1835)—composed many of their operas.

Callas's charisma was enhanced by her public image as a willful, feisty prima donna who fought with opera directors over repertoire, canceled performances seemingly at a whim, and physically muscled her way past baffled tenors to get a greater share of the applause. She was an operatic diva par excellence, and, contrary to her denials, she acted like one. After her semi-retirement in 1959, at just thirty-six years old, she continued to make headlines as the glamorous companion of Aristotle Onassis, one of the richest men on earth and one of the most visible members of the international jet set. Her studio and live performance recordings continued to sell briskly. Her photos were splashed across the world. In his 1986 autobiography, Franco Zeffirelli, the renowned opera director and producer and Maria's friend, separates the history of opera into BC (before Callas) and AC (after Callas). This dividing line continues to resonate today.

Perhaps the best illustration of Callas's continued dominance in the opera world is the slew of international events organized to commemorate the fortieth anniversary of her death. In 2014, a newly remastered version of thirty-nine operas and recitals was released by Warner in anticipation of that anniversary—her complete studio recordings. That release was followed by a forty-two-CD set of selected live recordings in 2017 (Callas died on September 16, 1977). The anniversary was bookended with Callas exhibitions in Athens and Milan. *The Definitive Maria Calla: Life of a Diva: The Unseen Pictures* (2016) and *Maria by Callas: In Her Own Words* (2017) provide readers with her previously unpublished photographs. Articles devoted to her appeared in the *New York Times*, *Opera News*, *Gramophone*, and *BBC Music* among other news outlets. In 2017, the *New York Times* listed Callas's 1953 *Tosca* as the greatest opera recording of all times. Such is the continuing breadth of her appeal that the Irish seaside town of Bray, in County Wicklow, marked the anniversary of her death with a concert in its Arts Center titled *Grace and Elegance*, which included archival footage and artists' singing repertoire made famous by Callas. That same year, in Australia, a radio broadcast by Melbourne's ABC station of Callas's arias proved so popular that it led to a promise of an encore. Tom Volf's documentary film *Maria by Callas* (2018), a loving tribute to the *la Divina* includes previously unseen footage and unpublished excerpts from her letters. Anniversary recordings, articles in the press, documentary films, and the release of previously unpublished photographs indicate that public interest in Callas remains intense forty years after her death.

In examining people's lives, few things fascinate us more than puzzles and adversity. This is because it is hard to draw lessons from an unconflicted or clear-cut life, whereas an enigmatic one provides an opportunity to probe the mysteries of the human psyche. Our fascination with Maria Callas goes beyond her legendary status as opera's foremost prima donna. Her formidable strengths capture our attention: How did a poor girl from Manhattan rise to operatic stardom? Her frailties pique our interest even further: What contributed to her early demise? Callas's life is definitely an enigmatic one, and much has been written about her, including an insightful biography by Arianna Huffington (nee Stassinopoulos), Nicholas Petsalis-Diomidis's detailed accounts of her adolescent years spent in Greece, and Nicholas Gage's account of her relationship with Aristotle Onassis. Yet her life continues to puzzle.

Writing in 1960, George Jellinek, a music critic and early Callas biographer, predicted that her stage appearances would become less frequent and varied; more awareness would be given to the limitations of her voice. Jellinek made this prediction when Callas's career was at a crossroads, after her banishment from most of world's top opera houses and the beginning of her passionate affair with Aristotle Onassis—and it proved prescient. Jellinek also predicted that "the future will see a mellower Callas, an artist who can look back on an arduous road with the pride of accomplishment, and also with a retrospective view of content."[8] This second assertion seemed fully justified given Callas's stature as the foremost operatic diva of the post-World War II era and the financial security offered by sales of her eclectic and enormously popular recordings worldwide. Why did it fail to come true?

"A persuasive and revelatory intimate biography of Callas not only has not yet appeared, but is impossible" writes David Lowe, the author of an edited collection of commentaries on Callas. "The path taking us to the 'real' Maria Callas, the woman behind the legend is essentially a pitch-dark tunnel clogged with immovable obstacles and ending in a cul-de-sac."[9] Robert Sutherland concludes his book, *Maria Callas: Diaries of a Friendship*,[10] in a similar vein, calling for a brilliant young psychoanalyst to unravel the bewildering inconsistencies in Maria's life. Both Lowe and Sutherland correctly highlight the contradictory and puzzling

aspects of Callas's life. Some of this puzzle stems from her intimate relationships. What explains Maria's abrupt severance of
all contact with her mother when she was just twenty-seven and
experiencing great international acclaim? How are we to account
for Callas's abrupt break-up of her ten-year marriage to Battista
Meneghini only a few months after professing both an undying
devotion to him and a willingness to sacrifice her career for their
love? What are we to make of this proud and seemingly independent woman who incessantly deferred to her subsequent lover,
Aristotle Onassis?

Other puzzles pertain to her career as well. How did Callas's
vulnerabilities contribute to making her the great artist that she
was? Why did she have such a polarizing effect on her audience,
with some loving her, some hating her, and, perhaps most surprisingly, some flipping from love to hate and then back again? And,
most insistently, why did the greatest diva of her time, who died at
the age of fifty-three, spend the last four years of her life secluded
in despair in her Paris apartment? These psychological mysteries constitute the subject of this psychobiography. In contrast
to a biography that provides a detailed account of someone's life
from beginning to end, psychobiography aims to understand a life
through the systematic application of psychological theory. The
two approaches are not mutually exclusive as biographies inevitably rely on psychology and psychobiography interprets facts
from its subject's life. The difference is one of emphasis: A good
biography skillfully narrates a comprehensive life story while psychobiography focuses on interpreting selected life episodes using
methods and insights from the field of scientific psychology.[11]

Four Cancellations and a Triumph Wrested from the Jaws of Defeat

Milan's Teatro alla Scala is once again packed to capacity, April 9, 1958, and the audience is ready to hear Callas revive her 1957 *Anna Bolena* with an almost identical cast and production. Despite these similarities, the atmosphere inside and outside the opera house is strikingly different to what it was almost exactly a year earlier. "Such hate had been stirred up against her [Callas] that protesters were in the square outside La Scala, where an entire militia of armed police [200 in total] stood guard," writes Bruno Tosi, the Italian writer, journalist, and music critic who attended the performance. "It was like the Risorgimento. Inside the theater, plainclothesmen watched corridors, foyers, boxes. Backstage, more police. . . . To avoid an incident during Anna's entrance, Visconti hid Callas amid choristers." Tosi notes that, for two scenes, "the public reacted to her like ice" while at the same time they shouted "approval to the others—Cesare Siepie, Simionato, and Raimondi."[12]

Callas was visibly anxious and shaken before going on stage according to Gavazzeni, the same conductor as for the 1957 performance; she must have felt the same dread confronted by the real Anne Boleyn as she headed to the executioner's block. Yet adversity energized Maria, who thrived when challenged, and, in the opera's third scene, she managed to change the audience's mood entirely. As the two guards appear on stage to seize Anna and take her to the Tower of London on trumped-up charges of infidelity, Callas the actress cum queen pushed the guards aside.

She "hurled herself to the front of the stage, spitting her lines directly at the audience: 'Giudici? Ad Anna? Giudici? [Judges? For Anna? Judges?].' It wasn't theater anymore," writes Tosi, "it was reality." Callas was defending herself, all but saying "If this is my trial, judge me . . . but remember, I am your queen." The scene was one of confrontation.

> She dared her accusers and stared them down, dramatically surpassing anything she had ever done, singing with scorching brilliance. When the curtain fell, the audience went mad. An uproar, sheer lunacy. Then Callas swept forth for her bows, inflated with her power, her victory, her magnificence. And every time she came forth, she grew more, more, more. You could not dream what she did. It was a show within a show.[13]

After the performance, to the astonishment of the police patrolling outside the theater, Callas crosses the square linking La Scala with the Galleria, Milan's exclusive shopping and food arcade, surrounded by an adulating crowd of entranced admirers. She drives away to have dinner with the Earl of Harewood, an opera aficionado and cousin of Great Britain's Queen Elizabeth, yet the large crowd continues to linger outside the opera house. "[N]one of us could go home to sleep," recalled Tosi, "and we milled around for hours in a kind of shock and ecstasy."[14] That night Callas and her husband, Battista Meneghini, experience a shock of their own: They returned home from dinner to find the front of their house smeared with feces and vandalized with obscene graffiti, a stark reminder of the hostility Callas's behavior could provoke among some of the Milanese public.

In these two performances of *Anna Bolena*, we confront a vital Callas puzzle that, in many ways, holds the key to the other mysteries of her life. How could a singer so revered, as Callas was at the time of the first performance of *Anna Bolena* in 1957, elicit such virulent hostility just a year later? What accounts for the transformation of this complete adulation into hate and anger, if not utter disgust, at least during the first part of the 1958 performance?

The biographical explanation of the shift in the audience's mood between the two *Bolena* performances centers on the cancellation of four performances, which fueled negative publicity and made La Scala's audiences weary of Callas. The Vienna State Opera was the first cancellation, which occurred only a few weeks after the April 1957 performance. Negotiations between Callas and von Karajan, who was to conduct her performance of *La Traviata*, broke down over her demand for more money. Maria herself was not particularly mercenary; she was content so long as her fee was higher than what other singers, including the lead tenor, were getting. But her husband Meneghini, a businessman who acted as her agent, was notorious for driving a hard bargain. He miscalculated with Vienna, however. The opera rejected his demand for more money, which resulted in bad publicity for Callas: Maria was vilified in the press, portrayed as a greedy and inconsiderate diva attempting to profit at the expense of the impoverished Viennese, still recovering from the economic ravages of World War II.

In August 1957, Callas joined La Scala's forces in Edinburgh for four performances of *La Sonnambula*. Exhausted from her busy schedule, Maria was not in particularly good voice (as is evident from the available live recording).[15] Her mere presence intensified the demand for tickets, however, so an additional performance was scheduled. Callas became enraged that she hadn't been consulted, and she refused to prolong her stay in Edinburgh beyond the originally stipulated date. Despite pleading by La Scala's management, she left Scotland as scheduled on August 30, citing poor health due to nervous exhaustion. It was the second of four critical performance cancellations.

Three days later in Venice—on the very evening that the additional Edinburgh performance had been scheduled but Callas canceled—Maria was photographed sipping Bellini cocktails and singing "Stormy Weather" at an all-night gala party. The event was organized in her honor by Elsa Maxwell, an American columnist and socialite who hobnobbed with European and American elites on the strength of her smooth ability to organize entertainment for the rich and famous. Elsa had by that time developed a romantic crush on Callas. "I have had many presents in my life," Maxwell gushed in her column, "but I have never had any star give up a performance in an opera because she felt she was breaking her word to a friend."[16] Upon returning to Milan, Callas demanded that Antonio Ghiringhelli, La Scala's superintendent, corroborate her story, that her inability to sing in the unscheduled Edinburgh performance of *La Sonnambula* was due to a medical condition. Ghiringhelli agreed yet never fulfilled his promise. Callas stood accused by the press not only of willfulness in breaching her obligation but also of disloyalty to La Scala, her home institution at the time.

That fall, Callas attempted to postpone her singing engagement with the San Francisco Opera from September to October, citing health concerns. Opera director Kurt Adler was furious at yet another Callas failed appearance. It was Callas's third cancellation. And Adler's fury was magnified when he called Maria's home only to be told by the maid that Madame was out singing. (She was, in fact, rehearsing Cherubini's *Medea* in the recording studio.) He referred her cancellation to the Board of the American Guild of Musical Artists for arbitration. Based on her medical certificate—and the fact that she did not sing publicly during this time—the board censured her but stopped short of suspension. Nonetheless, the controversy did further damage to her reputation.

The series of cancellations reached a dramatic climax five months after her Edinburgh refusal. Well recovered from her health problems, Callas opened La Scala's 1957–1958 season in early December with a brilliant performance as Amelia in Verdi's *Un Ballo in Maschera*. After a quiet Christmas in Milan, she and Meneghini travelled to Rome. Maria was to prepare for a gala New Year's Day performance of *Norma*, to be attended by Giovanni Gronchi, the President of Italy. On December 31, after singing in a New Year's Eve concert broadcast on Italian radio, she was spotted dancing the night away at an exclusive disco. The next day she awoke with a painful sore throat, and, after being told that the Rome Opera was unable to secure a substitute, she reluctantly sang the vocally taxing role of Norma, as scheduled. Callas's singing of the opera's famous aria "Casta Diva" met with applause heard loudly on RAI's live broadcast of the performance, as did the end of the first act.[17] The performance also elicited jeers; calls to "Go back to Milan" from patrons who had paid unusually high ticket prices pierced the hall. Rattled by the vitriol and her obvious vocal problems, Callas decided not to continue, and, since there was no substitute, this meant the cancellation of the rest of the performance. The opera administrators appealed to her pride, her patriotism, her respect for the Head of State, and these appeals fell on deaf ears. The announced cancellation, which followed a forty-five-minute interval, caused pandemonium. The furious crowd congregated outside the opera house ready to physically assault Callas. It was January 2, 1958—a date forever enshrined in the annals of opera history—and only an underground tunnel linking the opera house with her hotel provided Maria with an avenue of escape.

In the following weeks, the Italian parliament debated the "case of Callas" in Rome. A fistfight erupted in Biffi Scala, a posh Milan restaurant, when a Callas devotee rose and attempted to speak in her defense. An article in the Rome newspaper *Il Giorno* reveals the extent of Callas's insult, published the day after her canceled performance.

This second-rate Greek artist. Italian by her marriage, Milanese because of the unfounded admiration of certain segments of the La Scala audience, international because of her dangerous friendship with Elsa Maxwell, has for several years followed a path of melodramatic debauchery. This episode shows that Maria Meneghini-Callas is also a disagreeable performer who lacks the most elementary sense of discipline and propriety.[18]

The Rome Opera's next performance of *Norma*, which took place a few days later with Anita Cerquetti replacing Callas, concluded with twelve curtain calls accompanied by fervidly patriotic cries, "Viva l'Italia!" "Viva le voci italiane." [Long live Italy. Long live the Italian voice.] These slogans targeted Callas, but they were also aimed at Maxwell, who described the Italian press as "a bunch of barbarians" in a column responding to the furor over the Rome cancellation. In view of these events, the icy cold reception that the Milanese public gave Callas three months later at the beginning of the 1958 performance of *Anna Bolena* is not surprising.

The general public interpreted Callas's behavior as that of a spoiled, entitled diva who couldn't care less about her audiences or contractual obligations. Though it is tempting to interpret Callas's behavior in this way, the true picture is much more complicated. For one, the frequency of her cancellations coincided with an exacerbation of her vocal problems. Her precipitous loss of weight—from 210 pounds in 1952 to 144 pounds in 1954, followed by additional weight loss—is widely seen as the main factor exacerbating preexisting difficulties that contributed to her loss of vocal power. From the outset, her voice had a wobble, and she had difficulty making smooth transitions between registers. Michael Scott, founder of the London Opera Society, argued that Callas was only a shadow of her former self by the late 1950s. Scott was Callas's strongest admirer and her harshest critic, yet he claims it was Maria's vocal problems (and the resulting insecurities) that explain the spate of cancellations in the year between her two *Bolena* performances.

Callas's behavior in the interval between the 1957 and 1958 *Bolena*s raises issues for a psychobiographer that go beyond the hostility generated by her overt behavior or the impact of her deteriorating voice. What stands out about the two *Bolena*s is the amount of polarization or splitting generated by her behavior. With splitting, the person lumps together their positive feelings and keeps them separate from their negative feelings; the person simultaneously projects negative emotions, including blame, onto the outside world.[19] Splitting tends to nurture the development of unstable personal relationships, typically because the person can instantaneously flip from adulating the other as flawless and all-good to a critically negative self-interpretation at the slightest sign of their imperfection. In some instances, this shift can result in others acting out the internal split, as happened with Callas's audience. In other words, our response to another person may reflect their own rather than our own perception of how things are. We unwittingly collude in acting out an imposed script prompted by its emotional intensity and centrality to the other's self-concept.

Parliamentary censorship in response to a canceled performance is extraordinary, even for the flamboyant world of opera. So is conduct that also results in angry fans smearing feces across a star's home. Such is the extent of Callas's polarizing nature. Her divisiveness is exemplified in public reaction to her cancellations but also by her feuds with other artists. Her legendary spat with Renata Tebaldi (1922–2004), a prominent soprano and rival, resulted in La Scala's audience being split into Callasianos and Tebaldistas long after Tebaldi departed the Milan opera house for New York's Met. From a psychological perspective, these polarizations reflect not only Callas's strong impact on others but also her own internal world. The radical shift in perspective that occurred between her two *Anna Bolena* performances, with the mesmerizing diva turned into a contemptible impostor in the La Scala audience's view, is entangled with the internal split in Callas herself.

It is Callas's fractured or split personality that accounts for many of her puzzling behaviors. In making sense of another person, we assume that they possess a cohesive and integrated self, making their actions predictable and easily comprehensible in terms of their underlying motives and intentions. This is not always true, however, especially in the case of highly creative and charismatic individuals like Callas, whose behavior frequently does not conform to conventional standards. Such personalities need to be understood using a more nuanced explanatory framework. Narcissism provides such a framework for Callas.

Narcissism: The Commonly Accepted View

The construct of narcissism echoes loudly in today's popular discourse. It has captured the public's imagination for two reasons: its purported increase among millennials and the election of Donald Trump as president. The narcissism of millennials is often linked to the self-esteem movement, particularly its influence on how American parents raise their children. The rise of expressive individualism is associated with how children are socialized, particularly two messages consistently conveyed to children during the past several decades. Robert Bellah and other scholars argue that messages such as "you're special" and "you can do anything you desire" promote the importance of self-esteem and feeling good about oneself over achievement and civic duty.[20] Consequently, millennials and ensuing generations are depicted as self-entitled narcissists who require special attention and accommodations in college and in the workplace. These young people lack self-discipline, according to this view, and they show little respect for authority. Social media encourages the posting of curated self-images that transform the self into an object whose value is measured by the number of "friends" and "followers" and "likes" and retweets one can garner. In fact, millennial culture *requires* this conduct, further enabling narcissistic vanity and exhibitionism. These same characteristics are prominent in descriptions of Donald Trump's personality, albeit with an acutely alarmist and negative tone that conveys that Trump's narcissism is malignant in form.

The claims both about narcissistic millennials and Trump's narcissistic personality have met their critics. Their veracity is not relevant to this book. What is important, however, is that the commonly accepted view of narcissism belies the construct's true complexity. The American Psychiatric Association (APA) depicts a unidimensional construct centering on the presence of a grandiose self and its corollaries: exhibitionism, entitlement, vanity, and impaired empathy. Rather than being one-dimensional, psychologists (unlike the APA) see narcissism as in fact having two faces: a grandiose side and a vulnerable side. The two faces reflect the fact that individuals become grandiose as a defense against underlying vulnerability or fragility. The narcissist's vulnerability stems from the desire to satisfy unmet emotional needs, specifically emotional needs unmet by the child's parents, and, in their struggle to satisfy needs, the narcissist feels unappreciated. Unless we appreciate the true complexity of narcissism, we risk mischaracterizing an entire generation of young people (millennials). We also risk mischaracterizing individuals like Donald Trump or, for that matter, Maria Callas.

The Narcissistic Split-Self

Narcissistic individuals fall into one of two categories, depending on which face predominates: either a grandiose type, as
reflected in the APA criteria, or a vulnerable type, characterized
by personal fragility and feelings of anxiety. The grandiose type
is invariably accompanied by vulnerability and a hypersensitive
prickliness. And the vulnerable type masks an underlying sense of
entitlement and expansive fantasies. Thus, the two contradictory
sides of narcissism are compartmentalized or split off from each
other—narcissistic individuals typically do not simultaneously
experience their grandiosity and vulnerability as part of their one
and the same personality (their reconciliation being psychologically too painful). Splitting differentiates narcissism from more
readily understandable behavior driven by healthy concerns about
personal adequacy. Most of us feel good and confident about ourselves in some moments and, at other times, less self-assured. In
non-narcissistic individuals, these attitudes are integrated into
the same persona rather than kept apart, as they are in the narcissist; this integration allows for shades of gray to creep into how
we evaluate ourselves and others. What differentiates narcissism is
the lack of integration between the positive and negative aspects
of the self. Rather than integrate—which would produce "shades
of gray" in our attitudes of evaluation—these aspects remain distinct, split apart in the exaggerated form of either grandiose superiority or vulnerable hypersensitivity. This split exposes the person
to instability in both interpersonal relationships and self-image,
negative consequences that may result from construing the world

in black or white terms. It also means that, continuing their family's legacy—many personality traits tend to be passed on from one generation to another—narcissistic individuals use others as tools for propping up their fragility and to deal with their unmet emotional needs (irrespective of whether grandiose or vulnerable).

Narcissistic Relationships: Quest for Admiration

Another key to understanding Callas is her dependence on others as a means of propping up a split self—a feature of both grandiose and vulnerable narcissism that is less well-known. In its broadest sense, narcissism implies that the person's interpersonal relationships are driven more by self-love than by love for others. Nevertheless, narcissism is not antithetical to an interest in interpersonal relationships; their interactions tend to be more self-focused and self-serving than in the case of non-narcissistic individuals who are more other-directed in their behavior, emphasizing intimacy, mutual cooperation, give-and-take, and dependability. Admiration from others plays a central role in the lives of narcissistic individuals, as does the tendency to merge one's personality with that of idealized figures. Callas's story exemplifies these traits. Her self-worth and initiative were inextricably tied to the adulation of her opera audiences, to the energizing effect of merging with idealized figures, primarily older men—including her husband, opera conductors, and stage directors, and, perhaps most importantly, her long-term lover Onassis. The need to be admired or gain confidence from identifying with an admired figure is not problematic in itself. We all engage in such behavior from time to time; the need for admiration only poses a problem when it becomes all-consuming, overshadowing the rest of one's life, as is the case with narcissism. Even when all-consuming, narcissism may have positive effects—it fuels a drive for acclaim and enhances creativity through merger with the creative object—but these gifts come at a personal cost, as we see in the case of Maria Callas.

Narcissistic Relationships: Twinship

Callas's relationship with her maid Bruna Lupoli and butler Ferruccio Mezzadri exemplifies *twinship*, a third form of narcissistic relationships in addition to those based on being admired or merging with someone admired. In twinship the individual gains a sense of well-being and cohesion from engaging in joint activities characterized by mutual affirmation and pleasure. Such relationships are exemplified by preadolescent "chumship," adolescent dating, and mature friendship or intimacy. Early in life, they are evident in the feelings of joy and pride that a child takes in "working" side by side with a parent, older sibling, or any significant other. From a developmental perspective, because twinship involves a sense of mutuality and interconnectedness, it originates later in life and results in healthier patterns of interaction than does mirroring or idealization. For Callas, twinship brought out her playful, spontaneous, and generous side, evident not only in interactions with Bruna and Ferruccio but also with several predominantly younger women including Giovanna Lomazzi in Milan and Nadia Stancioff (during the shooting of *Medea* and after it wrapped). Once again, however, these relationships were infused with too much dependence and fragility to allow Maria to shed her vulnerability as a result of the experienced mutuality and recognition.

Healthy Narcissism

A third point often misunderstood about narcissism is that, despite its negative connotations, it has positive aspects. Narcissism, as a personality characteristic, entails a continuum. Its positive pole is anchored by a healthy self-reliance, high aspirations, independence, and an emphasis on power and control. These characteristics are key components of the creative personality, especially in the arts. But the connection between narcissism and creativity goes further than this. Heniz Kohut, the psychoanalyst who revolutionized the way we think about narcissism, offers Enrico Fermi, the co-developer of the first atomic bomb, as an example of the link between narcissism and creativity. Upon witnessing the detonation of the first atomic bomb, Fermi threw bits of paper into the air intending to monitor the impact of the shock waves caused by the explosion—rather than ponder the moral consequences of his invention. His behavior, Kohut argues, vividly illustrates narcissistic self-absorption: both the narcissist's obliviousness to the impact of their behavior on others and their blurring of the boundaries between "I" and the creative object.[21] Extending Kohut's insights on narcissism, Elizabeth Lunbeck attributes Donald Trump's ability to impact his followers to two talents: "his direct access to the mind of the others" and an "uncanny ability to exploit, not necessarily in full awareness, the unconscious feelings of subordinates."[22] These powers, and the charisma associated with them, also characterized Callas on stage. The ability to lose oneself in the creative act resembles child's play, where the boundary between reality and fantasy is temporarily suspended. Callas's uncanny ability to psychologically merge with both her roles and her audiences goes a long way in accounting for the artistic power of her performances. This ability was yet again grounded in narcissism, but, in this case, it was a productive force in her life.

Responding to Adversity: Callas's "Long-Present Insecurity"

In using narcissism as the frame to understand Callas, my aim is not to pathologize her. Rather, my intent is to argue that Callas possessed little conscious control over her sense of superiority, her egocentrism, and her inability to construe the world in a nuanced way. Labeling her behavior as narcissistic does not exonerate the grandiose aspects of her personality. But it does allow us to view her behavior with greater sympathy and understanding, with an appreciation of her vulnerabilities. It also helps explain her strengths, including her meteoric rise to fame and the unprecedented impact she had on her audience. Neither is my intent to reduce Callas's life to a single psychological concept. Developmental psychology reaffirms the basic intuition that important aspects of behavior are learned, starting at infancy through interactions with others and immersion in one's social environment. Although these experiences are cumulative, personal growth is not linear or deterministic; rather, each phase of the life course provides turning points or opportunities for the individual to change, with varied consequences depending on the path taken or not taken. Callas's life, like most other lives, included its ups and downs, both in her career and in her private life.

Callas's personal deterioration during the last nine years of her life has been linked, on the one hand, to her trauma and shame over being abandoned by Onassis and, on the other, to the precipitous deterioration of her voice that prevented her from resuscitating a stage career. The latter view is articulated in a *New Yorker* article by Will Crutchfield. Callas's "tragedy is as simple as it seems, and as simple as the worshippers and psychobiographers don't want it to be," according to Crutchfield. "[S]he lost her voice, the most wonderfully musical voice we have ever heard."[23] This view is accurate in so far as no amount of psychologizing can every fully explain Callas's singing genius, her mesmerizing stage presence, nor the objective tragedy to the operatic world of her lost voice. But a psychobiographer has plenty to say about subjective personal factors that made it so difficult for her to preserve meaning and vitality at the end of life. Certainly, external successes and failures contribute to how we feel about ourselves and others. It is also almost certain that Callas's life would have turned out differently if she had stayed with Onassis. Similarly, her abandonment by Onassis is likely to have had a different effect if she retained her voice after their parting. The double loss of the love of her life and the voice that for so long constituted her raison d'etre was undoubtedly hard to deal with. Ultimately, however, it is not external events that cause misery or joy, but how we interpret them. Stated differently, life by itself has no sense other than the meaning we breathe into it.

In this regard, it is instructive to compare Callas to the American singer Rosa Ponselle (1897–1981), the only twentieth-century soprano whose performance of *bel canto* operas rivaled those of Callas in terms of artistry and vocal quality.[24] Ponselle's career came to an early end, when she was in her early forties, because of a deteriorating voice. Like Callas, this deterioration resulted in particularly negative reviews of her performance. In her case, it was Bizet's *Carmen* at the Met. Suffering the double loss of a singing career and a husband who had abandoned her for another woman, Ponselle had to be hospitalized in a psychiatric institution for several months. Nevertheless, she recovered from her adversity and spent the rest of her life in comfort, feted as the doyenne of the nascent Baltimore Opera. Renata Tebaldi had a long career, unlike Callas and Ponselle, but she, too, faced adversity resulting from the death of her mother, her ubiquitous travelling companion, and subsequent betrayal by an opera conductor with whom she fell in love. Like Ponselle, she, too, enjoyed her retirement, giving singing lessons, playing with her poodle, and finding satisfaction in the continued respect she received as a celebrated diva of the past. Equally, Louisa Tetrazzini (1871–1940) managed to retain her legendary joie de vivre right until her death despite squandering a fortune of five million dollars and becoming estranged from her husband. The question, then, is why Maria was unable to respond to adversity in a healthy manner, like other performers of her era.

Callas's inability to function independently of others is another characteristic that differentiates her from famous sopranos of the past. Not surprisingly, given the gender role expectations of the time, male opera singers did not experience problems in finding a supportive spouse, nor did they face the dilemma of whether to have children. The situation was very different for female singers who, since the beginnings of opera in the Italian cities of Mantua, Florence, and Venice in the 1600s, were stigmatized for engaging in a profession deemed inappropriate for "virtuous" women. Additionally, as Renata Tebaldi found out, "respectable" men (a medical doctor in her case) objected to the idea of having a wife who continued to pursue a career after marriage. Most of the prima donnas prior to the Callas era either married men who wanted them for their money (e.g., Maria Malibran, Adelina Patti, and Louisa Tetrazzini) or were forced to escape early marriage in order to launch their career (e.g., Nellie Melba). Others simply never married (e.g., Mary Garden, Renata Tebaldi). Left to their own resources, these divas were resilient women who fought with tenors for equal pay and, given opera's premium on high voices, were generally able to secure parity, if not higher fees.[25] Women singers learned to manage their own finances and forged meaningful lives with relatively little (if any) emotional support. Beginning early in her career, however, Callas was not able to manage on her own. In her personal relationships she relied heavily on the help of others to accomplish basic everyday tasks, as we will see.

It is not Callas's grandiosity and entitlement but her consciously experienced vulnerability that distinguishes her from her famous colleagues. Indeed, her vulnerability makes her more similar to Judy Garland (1922–1969), Marilyn Monroe (1926–1962), and Michael Jackson (1958–2009) than to operatic peers Adelina Patti (1843–1919), Nellie Melba (1861–1931), or Mary Garden (1874–1967), all of whom possessed unshakeable self-confidence. I argue that Callas's long-present insecurity is one of the keys to unlocking the devastation apparent in the last years of her life. In fact, the latter years of her life exemplify the particular difficulty that vulnerable narcissists have in negotiating losses associated with aging. Their ability to cope with loss is undermined by despair over lost opportunities. Vulnerable narcissists envy others and their accomplishments, accomplishments that are beyond the reach of an aging individual.

Notes

1. Callas's 1957 performance of *Anna Bolena* can be heard on an EMI Classics CD. It is also available on an Opera D'Oro release. A contemporary DVD version of the opera with Anna Netrebko in the title role is available on a Deutsche Grammophon Blue-Ray disc recorded at the Vienna State Opera with Evelino Pido conducting. A relatively uncut version of the opera is available on a London CD with Elena Souliotis in the title role.

2. Callas's voice can be heard in studio and live recordings. Not surprisingly, the studio recordings sound much better, but many Callas devotees agree that she sings better on stage where she can draw energy from the audience. Callas's legendary live performances include those of *Macbeth* (La Scala, 1952, EMI), *Lucia di Lammermoor* (Berlin, 1955, EMI), *La Traviata* (La Scala, 1955, EMI), *Norma* (La Scala, 1955, Instituto Discografico Italiano), *La Sonnambula* (Cologne, 1957, Myto), and *Medea* (Dallas, 1958, Myto). If you are undeterred by poor sound quality, then her performance of *Nabucco* (Naples, 1949, Opera d'Oro) along with those of *Aida* (Mexico City, 1950, EMI), *Il Trovatore* (Mexico City, 1950, Opera d'Oro),

and *Il Vespri Siciliani* (Florence, 1951, Testament) are good examples of Callas's early artistry. Callas's recordings of *Medea* (La Scala, 1953, EMI) and *La Sonnambula* (La Scala, 1955, EMI) with Bernstein conducting are also worth exploring. If you cannot find the 1955 La Scala performance of *Norma*, then the 1955 live recording from Rome (Opera d'Oro) is a good alternative. Callas's studio recordings have been recently remastered and are available individually or in a lush box set. Of the studio recordings, I recommend the set containing her first recordings from 1948 (especially the fragments from *I Puritani*) along with complete recordings of *Tosca* (1953) and *Norma* (1960). The collection of lyric and coloratura arias (1954) is also worth exploring. A remastered set of Callas's live recordings has been issued by Warner Classics in 2017. Of course, any recommendation of Callas's recordings is bound to be subjective.

3. Fitzgerald, G. (1974). Callas: The great years. In Ardoin, J. & Fitzgerald, G. (eds.), *Callas*. New York: Holt, Rinehart and Winston, p. 155.

4. Remy, P-J. (1978). *Maria Callas: A tribute*. New York: St. Martin's Press, p. 114.

5. Jellinek, G. (1986). *Callas: Portrait of a prima donna*. New York: Dover Publications, p. 183.

6. Koestenbaum (1993) makes this comment in *The Queen's Throat: Opera, Homosexuality and the Mystery of Desire*, Cambridge, MA: Da Capo Press to explain Callas's appeal to gay men, but it also explains her appeal to wider audiences. His book includes a provocative, thought-provoking, and highly insightful chapter on the cult of Callas.

7. This information was provided to me by F. Paul Driscoll, editor of *Opera News*.

8. Jelinek, *Callas*, p. 291.

9. Lowe, D. A. (Ed.) (1986). *Callas as they saw her*. New York: Ungar Publishing Company, p. 2.

10. Sutherland, R. (1999). *Maria Callas: Diaries of a friendship*. London: Constable.

11. Contemporary views and debates on psychobiography can be found in Schultz, T. (Ed.) (2005). *Handbook of psychobiography*. New York: Oxford

University Press. For an example of a recent (2013) psychobiography see his *An Emergency in Slow Motion: The Inner Life of Diane Arbus* (New York: Bloomsbury).

12. Fitzgerald, *Callas: The great years*, p. 156.

13. Ibid., p. 158.

14. Ibid.

15. See Bellini's *La Sonnambula*, recorded live at the 1957 Edinburgh Festival and conducted by Antonino Votto, released on Testament.

16. Jellinek, *Callas*, p. 195.

17. The RAI broadcast of the 1958 performance of *Norma* from Rome's Teatro dell'Opera is available on a Myto CD—Norma—Act 1 (Callas's famous Rome walk-out). Gabriele Santini conducted the performance.

18. Remy, *Maria Callas: A tribute*, p. 124.

19. The concept of splitting has two meanings in psychology. In the context of dissociative disorder or multiple personality disorder, it refers to alters or fully fledged alternative personalities that take over the psyche of an individual. This use of the term is exemplified in Robert Louis Stevenson's novel *Dr. Jekyll and Mr. Hyde*. In the context of narcissism, however, "splitting" refers to the fracturing of a single psyche that results in keeping opposing feelings (e.g., love and hate) or aspects of self-concept (e.g., grandiosity and vulnerability) apart. Thus an individual who uses splitting in this sense will tend to perceive the world in black or white terms because, when they evaluate others or the self positively, they tend to ignore any negative aspects and vice versa. Throughout this book, splitting will be used in its second meaning.

20. Bellah, R., Madsen, R., Sullivan, W., Swidler, A., & Tipton, S. (1985). *Habits of the heart: Individualism and commitment in American Life*. Berkeley: University of California Press.

21. Kohut, H. (1966). Forms and transformations of narcissism. *Journal of the America Psychoanalytic Association*, *14*, 243–272.

22. Lunbeck, E. (2017, Aug. 1). *The allure of Trump's narcissism*, https://lareviewofbooks.org/article/the-allure-of-trumps-narcissism/#!=

23. Crutchfield, W. (1995). The story of a voice. *The New Yorker*, November 13, p. 102.

24. Those interested in hearing Ponselle should start with a Nimbus CD titled *Ponselle* (make sure that you listen to the disc containing arias from *La Gioconda, Otello,* and *Norma*).

25. The opera world was arguably the first sector to embrace gender equality in pay.

3 | FROM OLIVE GROVES TO HELL'S KITCHEN

Marilyn Monroe never knew her father and spent part of her childhood in an orphanage. Judy Garland's mother fed her amphetamines and sleeping tablets from the moment the MGM studio identified her as a child prodigy. As a child, Michael Jackson lived in constant fear of his abusive father who, during the Jackson 5's rehearsals, stood with a belt ready to punish his youngest son's every misstep or missed note. There are many superstar performers whose tragic and untimely deaths have been linked to early childhood trauma. Their fate reinforces the perception that highly creative artists draw their inspiration from personal adversity and a conflicted self.

Many who knew Maria Callas claim that her vulnerabilities as an adult had their origins in early family experiences. Franco Zeffirelli, the renowned Italian opera director and producer, attributes Callas's craving for status to her difficult childhood. For example, Pia Meneghini, Callas's sister-in-law, explains Maria's tortured need for approval and her lack of diplomacy as consequences of a "sad childhood, little family affection, separated parents, and great poverty."[1] On one level, these assertions make good sense. Yet Callas's childhood is not marked by any single traumatic event or pivotal experience. Her family had to change Manhattan apartments many times due to financial pressures,

Prima Donna. Paul Wink, Oxford University Press (2021). © Oxford University Press.
DOI: 10.1093/oso/9780190857738.003.0003

and her parents quarreled frequently, finally separating when she was 13 years old. But such occurrences are not necessarily highly traumatic in a child's life. Callas's childhood differs in this regard from other superstars whose lives ended in tragedy.

The absence of a pivotal traumatic event in Callas's childhood means that we need to investigate the routine day-to-day interactions in the Callas family in order to discern their precise psychological impact on her early development. A good entry point into understanding her childhood is to contrast her early years with those of her older sister, Jackie. Jackie grew up in Meligala, a small Greek town located near the coastal trading center of Kalamata. She had fair hair and a complexion widely admired, and, in her journal, she recollects her childhood with fondness. Jackie recalls a staircase that "curved down from the first floor where we lived to the entrance hall," and at the bottom of the stairway was "a door that led through to the place where my father worked." Jackie evaded the cook and the housemaid, "whose most difficult task was to take care of her," and in those times when she managed to avoid them, she "would run to the top of the beautiful curved staircase and skip and jump up and down its long length."[2] As the excerpt conveys, Jackie (Yacinthy; 1917–1994), the first-born child of George and Evangelina (Litsa) Kalogeropoulos, enjoyed a happy, "normal" childhood. She grew up in a close-knit community where her family was well known and respected. She was surrounded by doting adults. She had plenty of opportunity to freely play on her own, and she frequently interacted with other kids, including the children of her family's servants.

As the local pharmacist, her father was well integrated into the fabric of the community. Jackie describes a father who adored her—and she adored him in return. Her description conveys a clear sense of her own personal warmth and kindness, traits well suited to the traditional gender role expectations of the time. In her book *Sisters*, Jackie narrates how one day she climbed up and opened her father's cash register, took out some change, and used it to buy ice cream and sweets for the neighborhood's poor children. This reminiscence is particularly illustrative of her nurturing and affirming environment. When she admitted to the theft, her father could only laugh, and, after they were left alone, he commended his daughter for being a good-hearted girl. His wife, Litsa, who even at this early stage of their marriage seemed frequently upset by things, was less impressed by this transgression. Litsa's negative disposition did not interfere with Jackie's well-being, however, because other members of the household served as a buffer—unlike in Maria's case. In addition, within three years of Jackie's birth, Litsa became preoccupied with the family's highly awaited newborn son Vassily and focused less attention on her daughters.

Jackie's early family interactions were different from Maria's experiences. Litsa's deficiencies as a mother were mitigated by the presence of other family members and servants in Meligala and, more generally, by the town's close communal ties. Jackie acquired a self-confidence that came from identifying with her father's high social status. Whereas Jackie's description of her childhood features many characteristics of a healthy upbringing, Maria's childhood was not nearly as idyllic. For her there will be no maid, no cook; there will be no grandparent, aunt, or uncle to provide the warmth and affirmation she was to miss at home.

New York's blustering wind whipped outside the Manhattan hospital in early December 1923. Mary, as she was known until age thirteen, was born six years after Jackie on a cold wintry day, her family having immigrated from Greece just four months earlier. The reason for the move to the United States is uncertain. It may have been an effort by the family to deal with their grief over the death of the three-year old Vassily from meningitis. Or it may have reflected George's desire to join his colleagues who found prosperity in New York City. In any case, the Kalogeropoulos's arrived in New York without knowing any English and without having many relatives who might have helped them negotiate a city that dwarfed in size the provincial Meligala.

Maria's Early Family Life

Emigration often presents significant challenges that may disrupt family histories. Relocation alters family relationships and brings upheaval to routines. In the case of Maria's family, relocation meant a new identity. The shortening of the family name from Kalogeropoulos to Callas is a point of rupture for her family's history. The Callas household was in disarray upon arrival in the United States, as illustrated by the uncertainty that persisted throughout Maria's life concerning the exact date of her birth. While her mother was convinced that she gave birth to Maria on December 4, her birth certificate states December 2, as does her passport. Maria favored the December 4 date because it is the name day of Saint Barbara, the feisty patron of artillery whose personality reflected Maria's own stage persona. As further evidence of the family's disarray, Maria, contrary to the Greek Orthodox tradition, was christened a full three years after her birth rather than the customary six months. The lack of family organization was rooted in issues that reached deeper than emigration alone. The move from Greece to America exposed marital tensions and incompatibilities between Callas's parents that were relatively dormant during the early years of their marriage in Meligala's secure and supportive environment. The seventeen-year-old Evangelina Dimitriadou (1894–1982) had married the thirty-year-old George Kalogeropoulos (1881–1972) out of love, despite her father's strong reservations. It took her only a few months to realize that her now deceased father was right and that she had made a wrong choice. Although well-respected as a pharmacist, George was not ambitious professionally; he held provincial attitudes and proved to have a roving eye. "[M]y husband ... was like a bee" Litsa "poetically" recounted later in her life, "to him every woman was a flower over which he must hover to sip the sweetness."[3]

George wasn't proficient in English, and he had difficulty establishing a career as a pharmacist in the United States, but he managed to pass the necessary exams. In 1929, he bought a pharmacy in the Hell's Kitchen district of Manhattan, at the time a run-down working-class neighborhood, but the timing of the purchase proved highly unfortunate. Shortly after its opening, George was forced to sell the business, a victim of the economic hardship that swept the nation during the Great Depression. Subsequently, he eked out a barely satisfactory income as a salesman selling cosmetics—even a self-produced ointment against gingivitis that he invented himself. The family's financial difficulties necessitated frequent moves around Manhattan in search of accommodation that would fit their fluctuating budget. This situation felt particularly demeaning to Litsa, who claimed to have grown up in a family of wealthy landowners that included among its members an army general and a personal physician to the King of Greece. Not unlike Rosamond in George Eliott's *Middlemarch*, Litsa found it impossible to forgive George for exposing her to the humiliation of financial strife, even though she contributed to it, and for destroying her ambitious aspirations for high social and economic status.[4]

Maria's infancy and early childhood, unlike Jackie's, was spent against a backdrop of family confusion, tension, and economic uncertainty. She was raised in a household aspiring to high social status—in Greece, pharmacists had a social standing almost comparable to doctors—yet her family was frequently forced to downsize apartments to afford the rent. At home, moreover, she witnessed her father being called "an animal" and "a peasant." Litsa constantly berated George for womanizing, for not providing his family with an adequate income. Maria was nurtured by a mother who loathed her life in New York City, who continued to grieve over the loss of her son, and who actively alienated her two daughters from their father. Litsa also prevented her and Jackie from playing with their classmates and other neighborhood children, a decision that further inhibited Maria's early psychological growth.

Litsa might have endured George's sexual affairs if she felt he provided the family with adequate income and social status; after all, in those days, it was not uncommon for Greek men to consider extramarital affairs their own private business with no bearing on family life. But because the move to America was not well planned, it soon plunged the family into financial strife. Although they arrived with considerable money from the sale of George's pharmacy in Meligala, the funds quickly disappeared.

Much of their money went in support of a lavish lifestyle, including Litsa's insistence on decorating their apartment in Astoria, Queens, with fancy furniture and carpets. Her desire for status and wealth began to affect Maria, particularly once Litsa realized that her young daughter was the only hope for improving the family's standing in life.

Litsa

Many people have argued that Maria's psychological development was detrimentally affected by her mother's initial rejection. Hoping to give birth to a son (a replacement for Vassily) and disappointed with the result, Litsa is purported to have refused to have anything to do with her newborn daughter. Litsa claimed, however, that following her initial disappointment she developed a solid bond with her newborn baby daughter, and there is little reason to doubt this claim. Jackie recollects her mother happily breastfeeding Maria and soothing her to sleep after she brought her home from the hospital. Maria grew up in a very controlling and sober family environment; it was not conducive to fun or play. Jackie recalled that, growing up in New York City, she and Maria were serious children who, given the tense family environment, hardly ever played with toys (what few they had). Yet, at the same time, Litsa was also a highly engaged mother who devoted a lot of time to cultivating her daughters' intellectual development with trips to museums and libraries and private music lessons.

Litsa prevented Jackie and Maria from playing with their classmates and other neighborhood children while in New York, which stifled Maria's development even further. This social isolation was driven in part by Litsa's desire to protect her daughters from what she perceived as an alien and threatening milieu. The decision to isolate her daughters also reflected Litsa's condescending attitude toward her neighbors and their children, whom she considered lacking in manners and of lower "class." Maria and Jackie were consequently deprived of the opportunity to dilute the hostile family environment with playmates and friendships that might have exposed them to warmer and more empathic family interactions. It is perhaps not surprising, then, that, as an adult, Callas was very reluctant to discuss her early life. In a 1957 interview for the Italian magazine *Oggi* she summarized her early experiences with a single sentence: "Turning to my childhood, I have no particular recollection, except the vague intuition that my parents were not suited to each other."[5] In another interview she commented that while she was growing up her home was not broken in the normal sense of the word—but it was not a very happy one. This early family experience instilled in her the conviction that her parents lacked good judgment. Maria learned at an early age to cope with tense situations by either misremembering, omitting to pay attention to, or even dissociating herself from the emotional turmoil. As I will discuss later in the book, many of her lived experiences show how her internalized negative images of family relations, in general, and her mother, in particular, had a detrimental effect on Maria's psychological growth.

Litsa was a handsome woman. She was also strong-willed, unlike George, and, in her family interactions, she was authoritarian and despotic, requiring complete obedience. She did not tolerate dissent and disregarded her daughters' psychological needs. If either Jackie or Maria failed to make their beds, their clothes were taken out of their drawers and thrown into the corridor. She would put pepper on their lips if she found them lying, a practice that she justified as an old Greek tradition. According to Jackie, her mother possessed a sixth sense: She could always guess when they were hiding a secret and could skillfully pry it from them. The family lived in fear of her "devilish temper," of mood swings that fluctuated with the "phases of the moon." Litsa's temper and need for control must have felt scary to young Maria who, as a child, sought comfort, security, and consolation from her sister, six years her senior. In the words of Jackie, "When neither parent was around Maria would come to me for company. She would cuddle up to me and I would try to give her the love we never seemed to get."[6] Yet, though frightening, Litsa's aggressive and controlling behavior was likely to have had the positive effect of sensitizing Callas to the moods of others. In doing so, it would enhance her empathy for the operatic roles of wronged and mistreated women she performed so intensely on stage.

Stelios Galatopoulos, one of Callas's few friends toward the end of her life, claimed that Maria's mother's "idea of maternal love was how much discipline she could impose upon her daughters to meet her own misguided snobbish standards."[7] Litsa was despotic and power hungry, characteristics she inherited from the male side of the Dimitriadou clan. If she had not been prevented by gender conventions, she would likely have had an outstanding military career, following in the footsteps of her father and grandfather. While these personality characteristics made her a poor caregiver to Maria, they certainly helped Litsa in launching Callas's career and assuring worldly success for a girl with humble origins and no connections to the world of opera.

Without consulting Litsa, it was George who made the decision to emigrate, and, in her defense, Litsa was confronted with a personally difficult situation after the move to New York. She found herself transplanted to a radically different environment against her will, stripped of family and communal support. Mothers also need care, not unlike their children, and this is something Litsa lacked in her new environment. The status-conscious Litsa also confronted the humiliation of a roving husband and a decline in family prestige; her realization that things were unlikely to change partially explains her feelings of depression. When Maria was six, Litsa took an overdose, most likely of belladonna, after observing George pay what she regarded as excessive attention to a female customer in his pharmacy. Although the suicide attempt seemed impulsive and designed primarily to elicit attention, it nonetheless resulted in Litsa's psychiatric hospitalization for a month. She entered the clinic, in part, to prevent a criminal investigation into the drug overdose (suicide was illegal in the United States at the time). It's likely that Litsa's depression exacerbated her anger, irritability, and lack of empathy, further undermining her ability to provide a psychologically hospitable environment for Jackie and Maria. Litsa's problem as a mother was not a lack of attentiveness but rather, as I will elaborate shortly, an inability to care for Maria in a way that satisfied her developmental needs.

George

George was a gentle, somewhat inadequate, and conflict-avoidant man. After selling the pharmacy, he worked hard selling his gingivitis ointment and trying to secure an adequate income for his family. But his personality was not well suited to the rough and tumble of life in America during the Depression, an era that required a much more "cut-throat" approach to life. George liked to listen to Greek folk music that reminded him of life in Meligala, though he never could listen for long. Litsa would whip into the living room, invariably changing the record on the gramophone to Puccini or some classical composer. For her, Greek folk songs were a sign of vulgarity she would not tolerate. According to Jackie, her mother pictured the entire Wall Street crash as a personal failure of her father. George's womanizing certainly did not improve his stature in the family. With family tensions and a job requiring constant travel, he spent less and less time at home; his wife and daughters ultimately came to consider him an outsider. Such a pattern of avoidance and disengagement is a common response of men in marital relationships marked by overt conflict and hostility.

There is no doubt that Maria was fond of her father. Reminiscing about her childhood, she claimed that "nobody loved me and I loved nobody, except my father."[8] It is easy to imagine both Jackie and Maria being fascinated by George's debonair figure, his good looks, and his habit of treating his two young daughters as adults. We get a glimpse of Maria's secure relationship with her father from her recollection of a time when, out on a walk, she stopped in front of an ice cream parlor and fixed her gaze on the shop's display, pulling her father's jacket without uttering a word. When asked what she wanted, the three- or four-year-old Maria gazed fiercely at her father, demanding he figure out for himself what she wanted. The memory of this incident suggests that Maria felt more comfortable and secure with her father than with her mother. It must, after all, have taken a certain level of assurance for an otherwise compliant young child to voicelessly insist on her will. Given Litsa's demand for obedience and control, it is hard to imagine young Maria using a similar communicative strategy with her. Only with her father could Maria assert the iron will, not unlike her mother's, that became a hallmark of her professional career.

The ice cream incident was significant in Callas's mind because it is one of the few childhood memories she recounted on several occasions later in life. The incident also reflects Maria's need to force her largely absent and emotionally disengaged father to show affection, understanding, and commitment, traits reflected in his willingness to read Maria's mind and to accept her—warts and all. In psychological terms, Maria saw in her father a means of getting the kind of emotional nourishment (ice cream) that was not forthcoming from her mother and which she badly needed for personal growth. The ice cream incident foreshadows Callas's later tendency to engage in dependent and highly idealized relationships with older men as a way for her to maintain a cohesive self. She was to marry an older man, Battista Meneghini, twenty-seven years her senior, and she subsequently had a long-term affair with Aristotle Onassis who was seventeen years older than her.

Despite Maria's fondness of her father, his psychologically marginal and tarnished status in the family prevented him from compensating for Litsa's despotism and curtailed empathy. There is no evidence that the introverted and conflict-avoidant George fought to assert his parental rights, nor that he showed any strong emotional or care-giving commitment to his daughters. He was no match for Litsa's authoritarian approach to their daughters. Litsa was the sole caregiver, having deposed George as head of family, and she had two options in relating to her daughters. She could allow her relationship with Jackie and Maria to compensate for a failed marriage. In such instances, the parent turns to the children for the approval and affection absent in the marital relationship. There is little evidence, however, that Litsa embarked on this strategy. If there were compensatory aspects to Litsa's relationship with her daughters, they largely involved her fantasy of improving her status by redemption, initially through Jackie's and subsequently Maria's artistic talents. This second compensatory strategy did not include any increased tenderness or attunement to their needs; rather, Litsa allowed the marital conflict to spill over into her interactions with them, which exacerbated rather than diminished her aggressiveness and controlling attitude toward her daughters.

Psychological Implications of Growing up in a Conflicted Family

What implications did living in a broken and hostile family environment have for Maria's psychological development? The simplest and most straightforward answer is provided by social learning theory, which argues that children learn to behave by observing interactions between parents and other influential figures. From this perspective, Maria was vulnerable because overtly hostile and controlling marital relationships frequently reflect spousal deficits in conflict resolution and in interpersonal skills. A mature and mutually responsive relationship between two adults assumes the capacity for concern, empathy, compassion, and the presence of positive feeling as a counterweight to negative emotions. (In a healthy marriage, the typical ratio of positive to negative interactions is highly skewed in favor of the former.) These characteristics, however, were in short supply in the Callas household. George certainly didn't exemplify them as he showed little concern for his daughters, whom he abandoned to Litsa's ministrations. Nor had he empathy for the pain Litsa felt due to his affairs with other women. He cared little that she had never wanted to move away from Greece. Mature intimate relationships were not Litsa's strength, either. Litsa's was a world inhabited by villains and victims, one where right and wrong were clear; this left little room for ambiguity or feelings of guilt that might prompt some form of reparation. Thus, rather than witnessing mutuality and responsiveness or respect for others, Maria learned a conflict resolution style marked by aggression, contempt, and absolutistic black-or-white thinking.

Early Personality

There is scant first-hand information on what Callas was like as a child, but an inherited disposition to negative affect and shyness would make her particularly vulnerable to Litsa's influence. While there is little doubt that Callas learned some of her notorious fierceness from Litsa, this process was also likely facilitated by Maria's own receptivity to her mother's disposition. Research comparing siblings raised in the same family suggests that early personality development is shaped by an interaction between the environment and the child's individual temperament. How children respond to their parents is partly determined by their own incipient, genetically influenced tendencies. Witnessing overt conflict between parents while growing up is likely to have a different impact on a calm, good-natured baby whose personality might dilute the surrounding negativity than on a temperamentally more hostile child who is likely to imbibe and amplify the effect of the hostility surrounding it. In this regard, Maria was a talented student of her mother's way of being. Litsa describes Maria as exhibiting a mind of her own long before she was weaned, and Jackie claims that her sister was a nervous child who blew up at times. Callas traced her renowned adult aggressiveness back to childhood. Maria was her mother's daughter, both in terms of anger and in the feeling of being cheated by life; conversely, Jackie inherited the placid and easygoing personality of their father. From very early on, Maria related to the world with anger and resentment. In fact, Jackie suggests that, despite the conflicted nature of their relationship, Maria and Litsa were both domineering and self-absorbed.

An exchange with the Papajohns, a Greek-American family whom the Callas's befriended while living in New York, sheds light on young Maria's negative disposition. Jackie and Maria were allowed to play with only a handful of other kids, and the Papajohn children were among them. Alexandra, the handsome and vivacious aunt of the Papajohn children, was visiting Litsa when she noticed that the hem of her skirt was undone. When Litsa went to another room to get a needle and thread, young Maria—only four or five years old at the time—ran after her mother frantically begging her not to give Alexandra any needle or thread. One interpretation of this incident is that it reflects Callas's precocious and unerring instinct, a talent evident in her operatic roles, because not long after this the same Alexandra became George's long-term lover and, following his divorce from Litsa in 1957, his second wife. Jackie, in her memoir, interprets the incident as an early sign of Maria's neurotic possessiveness. But what was this neurotic possessiveness about? It exemplifies Callas's hostile disposition and lack of empathy.[9] The absence of generosity is emblematic of someone who has not had enough goodness in their own life, and, as one Callas biographer suggests, Maria had no one—neither parents, grandparents, friends, nor companions—who gazed at her with admiration or took an interest in her development. It is easy to be generous, as exemplified by Jackie's buying treats for the poor children of Meligala, when one is psychologically well-nourished; it is much harder to be giving when the person herself is needy.

Steven Linakis, Callas's first cousin who grew up with her in New York City, recounts an episode that also illuminates Maria's negative disposition:

> Once when we both were about twelve years old, Maria said it was her turn on roller skates. I [Linakis] had made the mistake of telling her it was my turn. She knocked me over, yanking the skates right off my feet. The corner of my mouth was split open and later I had to have three stitches. She wasn't in the least sorry. It had been my own fault. It had been her turn.[10]

This behavior brilliantly foreshadows the temper and rage that the opera diva would frequently display in public encounters later in life, whether with journalists, court officials, or other opera stars. It also illustrates her tendency to lash out violently, without remorse or guilt, when provoked by a perceived slight or an encroachment on her rights. From an early age, her strategy for negotiating interpersonal conflict appears to have been to rage and ask questions later.

Litsa had a powerful influence on Maria's shy and introverted nature, her angry outbursts notwithstanding. Jackie and Maria were well-mannered and overly protected Greek girls who kept to themselves, according to a fellow student. Maria, or Mary Ann as she was known in school, was perceived as being stuck up; she was neither invited to other girls' houses nor encouraged by her mother to invite them back home. Maria's persona of an "uppity" loner was partially explained by Litsa's strict regulation of her daughter's social lives. Additionally, Callas herself was reticent in initiating social contact throughout her life, suggesting an ingrained personality characteristic. Maria's social isolation, irrespective of its causes, meant that she grew up relatively devoid of peer role models; hence, she was unable to learn more adaptive ways of interpersonal interaction than those she experienced in her immediate family. An intuitive individual tends to interpret external reality in terms of hunches and broad assessments—they pay scant attention to the everyday social minutiae in their surrounding environment. Maria's highly intuitive way of apprehending reality would have further undermined her ability to personally benefit from everyday lived experiences.

The distinction between authoritative and authoritarian parental style provides another clue to understanding Callas's personality development. Psychologist Diana Baumrind argues that authoritative parents combine a controlling manner with a warm and rational parental style, including receptivity to their child's needs and desires. In contrast, an authoritarian style is marked by absolute standards, the valuing of obedience, and punitive, forceful measures used to enforce "right conduct." Authoritarian parents emphasize respect for authority, traditional values, and insist on their word being right rather than encouraging verbal give-and-take.[11] Children raised by authoritative parents tend to be content, self-reliant, self-controlled, and explorative, whereas those raised in authoritarian families are likely to be discontented, withdrawn, and distrustful of others. Furthermore, being exposed to parental demands and expectations that are imposed without an appeal to reason fosters dependent, compliant, and passive behavior in the child. These characteristics are particularly true of girls, who typically find it more difficult to resist parental authority.

It is not surprising that Callas was to struggle throughout her life with independence and competence, especially given Litsa's authoritarian style. Maria's degree of obedience when dealing with individuals whom she respected, both as a child and as an adult, may come as a surprise considering her renown for assertive if not aggressive professional interactions. Yet there is an unmistakable tone of passivity in Callas's reminiscences about her childhood suggestive of a dutiful Greek daughter for whom any resistance to parental authority seemed inconceivable. Giulietta Simionato, a renowned mezzo-soprano and Callas's friend, recollects with surprise Maria's response to the suggestion that she damaged her voice by having sung opera too strongly and at too young an age: "But it was necessary! My mother made me do it and I obeyed."[12] In a 1970 interview with British journalist David

Frost, Callas offers a telling comment about the influence of her mother's authoritarianism on her own life.

> Has it occurred to you that life is a fight on who commands the other? Mother commands the child. Then, at school, everybody is trying to believe in doing what they want, and if you don't do what they want they get very angry and they accuse you and you are in fights all the time. I think that life is a struggle for independence. I have struggled lately [age forty-seven] to gain independence.[13]

Callas's dependence on others was to have a particularly strong and long-term negative effect on her ability to successfully negotiate emotional highs and lows, both personally in her relationships and professionally in her career.

While some of Callas's early childhood deficits are easily identifiable in her family relations, others are more difficult to discern because they derive from the very early stages of development that are hidden from memory. Yet these experiences form the bedrock of her adult personality and shed light on both her strengths and weaknesses. To develop a healthy sense of self, a child needs to experience two kinds of early relationships with its primary caregivers. One involves the parent mirroring or reflecting the child's behavior, which is particularly salient in the earliest stage of development when the child lacks the capacity to initiate its own goal-directed behavior. In traditional families like Callas's, mirroring is provided primarily by the mother, who has the closest initial bond with the infant. The second relationship involves idealization of the parent by the child. In the era in which Callas grew up, idealization typically involved the child's identification with the father—the family breadwinner who represented the excitement of work and a world beyond the family confines.

Inadequate Mirroring

The relationship between mirroring and narcissism provides an important clue to understanding Callas's behavior, both as a child and as an adult. In the initial stages of development, parents are tasked with treating their child as though it possessed an imperial, grandiose, or narcissistic self whose every need and wish must be satisfied. As many may know from experience, the infant's ability to delay gratification is limited, as is its sensitivity to the parents' own needs. Parents therefore tend to treat their offspring as a kind of royalty, not only by anticipating and fulfilling the child's basic needs but also by mirroring the child's gestures, vocalizations, and facial expressions. It is not accidental that "baby talk," the most easily identifiable type of mirroring, is a universal phenomenon: Parents affirmatively nod at their child, coo-cooing radiantly in exchange, because it satisfies a developmental imperative. The act of mirroring (i.e., feeding back to the child its own behavior) is vital to psychological development because it allows the child to feel understood, appreciated, and secure. It also enables the child to develop a sense of agency or efficacy by allowing it to have an immediate and easily recognizable impact on its environment. According to Heinz Kohut, the child sheds its grandiose or imperial self, somewhat paradoxically, not as a result of parents imposing early limits on its needs and wishes, but by indulging its grandiose self through mirroring.[14] This is the case, Kohut argues, because having its behavior adequately mirrored enables the child to develop necessary cognitive and emotional structures and feelings of security that, in turn, curb its narcissism. It is only by being immersed in a nurturing environment that the child is able to relax and profit from the inevitable failures in parental empathy. In other words, feeling good about itself enables the child to interpret the parent's lack of perfect attunement to its needs not as hostile acts or a lack of care but, rather, as indicators of the fact that parents possess an identity separate from the child and that they are fallible human beings. In this counterintuitive way, mirroring modulates the grandiose self and its associated egocentrism.[15]

Inadequate parental mirroring of the child's internal states has numerous consequences because it results in the continuation into adulthood of a narcissistic, childlike, self. It curtails empathy. It leads to the exploitation of others, who are perceived as existing primarily to fulfill the person's own needs, with little regard for the wishes and desires of other people. Both these characteristics will become evident in Callas's intimate relationships and in her relationships with fellow artists. Most importantly, inadequate parental mirroring inhibits the toddler's ability to transcend their egocentrism or the tendency to perceive the world solely from their own standpoint.

Litsa, confined to her own resources and without help from others, was likely incapable of providing Maria with the sort of adequate care and empathy (the mirroring) needed to transform her childhood narcissism into a more mature form of functioning. Although inevitably speculative given the lack of detailed accounts of Callas's early interactions with her mother, my contention regarding Litsa's deficiency in mirroring her daughter's early needs finds support in Callas's own insightful reflections about good mothering. "A mother must be a good mother to her children, yes or no?" Callas told John Ardoin in 1968, then the *Dallas Morning News*'s music critic and a friend in the later stages of her career. She goes on to claim that a mother should be wonderful without expecting anything in return or, otherwise, she should not have children.[16] In his account of Callas's adolescent years spent in Greece, Petsalis-Diomidis interprets this statement as indicative of Maria blaming Litsa for "giving her a shortsighted egocentric outlook on life, for which she, the daughter, had paid dearly."[17] Ardoin supports this view, claiming that a self-centered way of viewing the world was a key feature of the diva's adult personality.

> Callas literally and figuratively sees the world myopically and interprets everything—from news events to the weather—in terms of herself. Such ego is a means of insulation that every artist possesses to some degree. In Callas, it is as outsized as her talent, insecurities, and feelings. She tends to overreact, often to see things in an exaggerated manner.[18]

He goes on to suggest that although her myopia and self-centeredness might have helped her career, they proved a hindrance in her personal life. Ardoin illustrates Callas's self-centeredness by saying that, for example, if it rained, Callas would say: "Why is it raining? I wanted to go shopping. Why is God doing this to me?"

Anthony Montague Brown, Winston Churchill's last private secretary, provides another example of Callas's myopic, self-centered, and naïve view of the world. He recounts a cruise with Churchill, Callas, and her husband Meneghini on Onassis' yacht *Christina*.

> As we drove from the port of Naplion to the great Greek theatre of Epidaurus, the locals had erected a huge "V" of flowers in the middle of the stage [the V was meant to celebrate Churchill's role in defeating the communist uprising in Athens following the vanquishing of the Nazis]. Maria exclaimed: "Flowers for me! How kind! But why is it a V, Anthony?" I replied that it was undoubtedly meant to be an M for Maria, but that they had not had time to finish it. Maria's reactive smile was rapidly replaced by the sort of glance she should have remembered when she sang "Medea." When we reached Lesbos . . . the church bells were rung for WSC [Churchill], and Maria appropriated them as her own tribute.[19]

During the same trip, Callas did her utmost to create a good impression; nonetheless, she appeared oblivious to the ill-feeling her behavior generated among fellow travelers. Members of Churchill's entourage were revolted, for example, when she took it upon herself to spoon-feed Churchill with ice cream from her own plate. The only unperturbed person was the aging Churchill who, though he was quite capable of feeding himself, was well known to enjoy the attention of glamorous women.

Inadequate Idealization

As I have noted, the child's self develops within a matrix of relationships based not only on mirroring but also on idealization. Whereas mirroring entails a parent merging with the child, idealization involves the child merging with the parent. If, in the case of mirroring, the child's confidence and security can be captured by the child's implicit attitude "I am great because you admire me," in the case of idealization the underlying thought is "You are great and I am part of you." Idealization, just as mirroring, provides the child with comfort and security; but, with idealization, the assurance derives from identifying with an omnipotent figure: the parent. The security generated by idealization allows the child, just as in mirroring, to accept parental flaws without damaging the overall positive view of the mother or the father or undermining the perception of their goodness. This, in turn, enhances the child's ability to perceive other people and the world at large in a nuanced way rather than in an all-or-nothing, black-or-white perspective.

Maria's early relations with her parents suggest that she idealized her father but not her mother. In reflecting on her early childhood in Meligala, Jackie recounts how it was much easier for her to identify with her father's handsome appearance and his charming manner, how he elicited giggles from the young women who came in his store, especially in comparison to her moody mother. There is every reason to believe that the same characteristics appealed to Maria during her early childhood in New York. It was easy for George to acknowledge Maria for her true self without placing any demands on her—he was much less engaged in her life, after all. "Thanks only to your own efforts, your dreams [are] realized and your endeavors and desires fulfilled," he wrote her in 1949. "I take pride in being one of the happiest fathers in the world."[20] Of course, it was Litsa's engagement, even if ultimately overintrusive and lacking in sensitivity, that made Callas's rise to stardom possible. It is unlikely that Callas was able to truly merge with her largely absent father, even though she was emotionally close to him. It is also unlikely that she experienced him as an omnipotent source of confidence and security given his marginalized status and damaged persona. The strengths and limitation of their relationship are reflected in a comment she made to a friend in Athens: "I adore my father because he has always treated me right; and I also have a soft spot for him because we weren't living together for long."[21]

Ultimately, the limited opportunity for idealization further undermined Callas's ability to shed childhood egocentrism; it prevented her from aligning her ambitions with her ideals. Idealization also plays an important role in an individual's ability to value their own accomplishments. It is as though we first must identify and value another human being (and imbibe their sense of purpose) before we can develop the capacity to derive joy and meaning from our own achievements. One of the tragic consequences of narcissism is a mismatch between ambition—something Callas never lacked—and one's guiding values and ideals, a misalignment that ultimately challenges the subjectively experienced worthwhileness of one's efforts. It is noteworthy that, on numerous occasions as an adult, Callas claimed that she would gladly abandon her career for the roles of wife and mother. Given her enormous ambition as a celebrated diva, these proclamations may strike one as insincere. Nonetheless, they intimate an uncertainty in regard to her values or ideals in life, a lingering uncertainty further reflected in the ease with which she curtailed her operatic career after embarking on a relationship with Onassis.

Callas's experiences during early childhood appear to have left her with psychological vulnerabilities that would persist throughout her life. Having missed out on adequate parental input during a critical developmental stage in early childhood, and growing up in a family beset by conflict, Maria found it hard to compensate for her egocentrism and her lack of empathy and thoughtfulness later in life. She would also find it hard, despite tremendous operatic success, to derive true meaning and personal satisfaction from her remarkable accomplishments. As I will show, Callas's adult life can be construed as an unrelenting pursuit of the psychological bounties she was deprived of in childhood. Such uncompleted or interrupted tasks remain enshrined in our memories, and attempts at their completion motivate behavior. From this perspective, it is not accidental that Callas's strength as an opera performer lay largely in her insatiable need for adulation from the audience (mirroring) and that her relationships with the significant men in her life were characterized by idealization.

Notes

1. Meneghini, P. (2010). Seven years with Maria. In Tossi, B. (ed.), *The young Maria Callas*. Toronto, CA: Guernica, p. 121.

2. Callas, J. (1989). *Sisters*. New York: St. Martin's Press, p. 27.

3. Callas, E. (1960). *My daughter Maria Callas*. New York: Fleet Publishing Corporation, p. 13.

4. Throughout the book, I illustrate some of my psychological points with popular works of fiction and films. I do so in order to encourage the reader to seek psychological insights in their everyday lives.

5. Callas's *Oggi* memoirs 1957, in Lowe, *Callas as they saw her*, p. 114.

6. Callas, *Sisters*, p. 39.

7. Galatopoulos, S. (1998). *Maria Callas: Sacred monster*. New York: Simon & Schuster, p. 15.

8. Petsalis-Diomidis, N. (2001). *The unknown Callas: The Greek years*. Portland, OR: Amadeus Press, p. 65.

9. As evident from this paragraph, Callas was capable of exquisite empathy—in interpreting the behavior of others—while, at the same time showing scant concern for others' feelings and awareness of how her behavior impacted them. Such bifurcated empathy is found among individuals whose inhospitable childhood environment sensitizes them to the moods and actions of others but, at the same time, does not expose them to positive experiences necessary to develop caring for others or self-awareness.

10. Linakis, S. (1980). *Diva: The life and death of Maria Callas*. Englewood Cliffs, NJ: Prentice-Hall, p. 16.

11. Baumrind, D. (1971). Current patterns of parental authority. *Developmental Psychology*, *4*(1, Pt 2), 1–103.

12. Gage, *Greek fire*, p. 37.

13. Frost, D. (1970). Television interview on the *David Frost Show*, New York, December 10, 1970.

14. Kohut, H. (1977). *The restoration of the self*. New York: International Universities Press.

15. Recent research indicates that the mirroring process is complicated. In mirroring, the parent mimics the child's vocalizations or gestures, but the mimicking is not perfect. It is done, rather, with an almost ironic twist that communicates two things to the child: (i) I understand you,

but (ii) your physical or mental state is not mine despite my empathy for you. This subtle nuance in how the parent mirrors the child's behavior is developmentally crucial. Imagine a child crying "ouch" in pain. If the parent's "ouch" were to exactly replicate the sound, it would escalate the child's discomfort by conveying the impression that there are now two individuals—the child and the parent—who are in pain. It is the special twist in the vocalization that allows the parent to provide the child with feelings of comfort and understanding while, at the same time, begin to demarcate the boundaries between the self and the other. Current research thus confirms the fact that mirroring serves an important soothing function while simultaneously teaching the child to appreciate the parents as separate individuals with their own needs and beliefs and learning how to label their behavior (see Fonagy, P., Gergely, G., Jurist, E., & Target, M. (2002). *Affect regulation and mentalization: Developmental, clinical and theoretical perspectives*. New York: Other Press.

16. Ardoin, J. (1974). Callas: The art and the life. In Ardoin, J., & Fitzgerald, G. (eds.), *Callas*. New York: Holt, Rinehardt and Winston, p. 44.

17. Petsalis-Diomidis, *The unknown Callas*, p. 478.

18. Ardoin, Callas: The art and the life, p. 33.

19. Brown, A. M. (1996). *Long sunset*. London: Indigo, p. 253.

20. Petsalis-Diomidis, *The unknown Callas*, p. 530.

21. Ibid., p. 545.

4 | PRODUCT OF HER MOTHER'S IMAGINATION

Callas developed an ambition to become a celebrated artist, one that she pursued with fierce dedication and commitment. Yet throughout her life she maintained that her career had been imposed upon, that her mother compelled her to sing professionally, and this lingering view had a profound effect on her relationship with the world of opera. "She (mother) took no notice of me and never had a good word to say of me," Callas recalled. "To make her notice me, I began singing. I knew I had a beautiful voice and it did me good to arouse admiration when I sang. So singing gradually came to be the medicine for my inferiority complexes."[1] This perception was so ingrained in Callas's mind that she reiterated it in a number of interviews. "I didn't choose my career," she assured Lord Harewood in a taped television interview. At least in her mind, Maria Callas the opera diva was largely a product of her mother's imagining: "My program was set not by myself in life. From the very beginning it was set by my family, my mother mainly, who was commanding the family then. So, I had to act accordingly," she recalled in her conversation with Harewood. "The program was that, of course, I should become a singer; I should become an artist in any case."[2] These comments suggest the perception of coercion that would take away much of the joy and gratification Callas derived from her singing career.

Prima Donna. Paul Wink, Oxford University Press (2021). © Oxford University Press.
DOI: 10.1093/oso/9780190857738.003.0004

Without a doubt, Callas's discovery of her singing talent forever changed her life. Its immediate effect was to increase her status within the family, and, in the long run, of course, it brought her worldwide fame, wealth, and the acclaim of loyal audiences. Callas's recollection of how her career started is remarkable on two counts. The first is her contention that she started singing to get attention from her neglectful and critical mother. The second is that singing provided her with a way of overcoming an inferiority complex. These are unexpected claims. They suggest that Callas saw her career, at least retrospectively, as imposed by others and as serving external goals—getting her mother's affection and propping up her fragile self-esteem—rather than reflecting an intrinsic, self-generated passion for singing.

While the sense of being forced to appear on stage by a pushy parent is not uncommon in the performing arts, it is unusual among opera singers. Such grievances could have been legitimately voiced by artists such as Judy Garland, whose mother pushed her into an acting career as an antidote to her crumbling marriage, or by Michael Jackson, whose childhood was dominated by an ambitious, punitive father. Accusations of exploitation by an emotionally or financially greedy parent are relatively rare in the world of opera, however, because a career in opera is typically much less lucrative than that of a pop idol or movie star: the training of a soprano voice is time-consuming, which militates the promise of a quick return on the parents' investment of time and money. Two nineteenth-century opera prodigies who did have a grievance about being forced to appear on stage as children—Maria Malibran at age five and Adelina Patti at age eight—were raised in families deeply connected to that world. Malibran's father was a renowned opera singer and impresario. His use of physical punishment to mold her voice had a negative effect on Malibran's childhood, but it did not undermine her passion for singing. The same is true of Patti, whose mother and father were opera singers. Although Patti would complain later in life that she was exploited and stripped of her childhood (much like Callas), the experience did not diminish her love of the opera stage. Her early experiences, just as those of Malibran, were normalized by the daily routine of living in an artistic family.

The typical careers of renowned sopranos in Callas's generation were built on the bedrock of a musical talent nourished by self-motivated passion and a drive for success. And this self-motivation was typically augmented by a mentor who helped train the voice, groom the singer, and introduce her to the opera establishment. Callas's archrival Renata Tebaldi typifies this pattern. Born in 1922 to a musical family in the Parma region in Italy, her father was a cellist and her mother had a beautiful singing voice. Tebaldi was spoiled as a child due to having contracted polio and thus was subject to prolonged confinement at home. After finishing school at age thirteen, Tebaldi's mother gave her the option to either work with her grandparents in managing their general store or pursue her passion for piano. Choosing the piano, Tebaldi was undaunted by having to travel two hours each way, in sun, rain, or snow, from Langhirano where she and her family lived to the Parma Conservatory. The seventeen-year-old Renata eventually switched to singing, after one of her piano teachers discovered the beauty of her creamy soprano voice, and her career was subsequently nurtured by taking lessons from a renowned vocal mentor. Victoria de los Angeles (1923–2005), born to a family with no musical connections, exemplifies a similar trajectory.

Passionate about music from childhood, singing provided de los Angeles with an opportunity to gain visibility in her school's chorus and thus connect with other students. Following the great success of her performance at a benefit concert for the victims of the Spanish Civil War, de los Angeles became a popular performer. In 1936, she auditioned to sing for the prestigious Barcelona Conservatory, and, at fifteen, she gained admission. Throughout this process she received emotional support from her father who, as a janitor at a university, was not otherwise in a position to influence her career. Singing helped de los Angeles overcome her shyness, as it did for Callas, but her shyness was not related to an inferiority complex. Neither de los Angeles (nor Tebaldi) felt used by an overbearing parent. The ambition to sing was theirs and theirs alone. This allowed them the freedom to bask in the glory of their own accomplishments without any lingering resentment associated with the perception of being used.

In the pre-1960s era, if parents interfered in a daughter's singing career, it was typically done to block career aspirations seen as inappropriate for young ladies of good upbringing. The Brazilian-born singer Bidu Sayao (1902–1999) engaged in a prolonged fight with her family for permission to appear on stage. The mother of Giulietta Simionato (1910–2010), a mezzo-soprano who accompanied Callas in many of her legendary performances and recordings, unequivocally stated, "I would kill my daughter with my own hands rather than see her become a singer."[3] As a result, Simionato embarked on her career only after her mother's death. Nellie Melba had the strength of character to pursue an operatic career in defiance of her husband, who threatened to cut up her face with a sword if she continued to sing on stage. She also had to overcome her father's strong opposition to seeing his daughter on stage. Indeed, one of the reasons why Meneghini's mother objected to his marriage with Callas was that she did not want her son to be involved with what she described as "a stage harlot." Things were very different, however, in the Callas household. According to Litsa, Maria's initial response to her prophesy that she would become a great star was to think her mother crazy.

The Making of a Star

Callas was not a child prodigy. and her family had no personal connection to the world of opera or classical music, but she grew up in a home emphasizing culture and the arts. Her mother had artistic talent and came from a musically gifted family. Litsa's father had a fine singing voice, so good in fact that, according to family lore, he put to shame an Italian tenor who visited the port town of Stylis where Litsa's parents resided. As a girl, Litsa dreamed of becoming an actress but her aspirations were thwarted by the mores discouraging young women of "good families" from embarking on a stage career. When they lived in New York City, Litsa took Maria and Jackie to the library every week; she encouraged them to read classics and to check out opera recordings. Almost every Saturday, the family listened to matinee broadcasts from the Metropolitan Opera. They also owned a pianola (a foot-pedal instrument popular in the 1920s and '30s for playing music from perforated discs). Both Jackie and Maria enjoyed pretending they were admired concert pianists as they played. Music was particularly enchanting for Maria. As a four-year-old she rested on her knees and activated the pianola by pressing its pedals with her hands, a moment that astonished her mother. Callas demonstrated an interest in music from very early on, most likely the fusion of an internal passion combined with an external desire to grab her parents' attention. It is the latter considerations that would end up overshadowing and spoiling her self-motivated appreciation for music and singing.

Jackie recounts in her memoire *Sisters* how, from the time she and Maria were in elementary school, Litsa was already seeking personal acclaim from the success of an artistic daughter. Litsa's behavior was driven by two motives. She wanted her daughters to achieve the fame she had been denied, and, as argued by Arianna Huffington in her biography of Callas, for the highly ambitious Litsa, fame was an almost spiritual commodity. She desired public acclaim for herself, but if that was not possible, she was happy to partake in the glory of one of her daughters. Litsa saw artistic success as a buffer against economic hardship and an avenue for her daughters to escape being trapped in an unhappy marriage. Initially, she placed her dreams and hopes on Jackie's artistic potential. She sent her for ballet lessons, and, when dancing did not offer much promise, paid for her to have piano lessons. Maria took an active interest in all of Jackie's activities, joining her in piano lessons and singing duets at home.

A breakthrough occurred one summer's day when Litsa, coming home from shopping, noticed a crowd gathered outside the open window of their Upper West Side apartment. The source of the commotion was ten-year-old Maria singing to herself a popular song called *La Paloma*. This incident provided sufficient encouragement for Litsa to spring into action and dedicate all her effort to launching Maria's career. Although Jackie was a very pretty girl with a promising voice, she did not have the necessary drive for success nor, for that matter, the requisite talent. In contrast, Maria not only had a captivating voice, as vividly projected by *La Paloma*, but also hunger for acclaim. Though she may have initially disbelieved her mother's claim that she would become a great star, she had the right attitude and sense of destiny to fulfill her expectations.

Shortly after *La Paloma*, Litsa entered Maria into singing competitions and paid for lessons, overcoming George's objection, who thought that the money was ill afforded and ill spent. He interpreted the investment in their daughters' music education as yet another of Litsa's flights of fancy. Litsa made sure Maria practiced regularly, but her singing forays initially met with only moderate success. Her voice was appreciated by teachers and pupils in the elementary schools she attended, and every year, from age ten to thirteen, she was chosen to sing at graduation. Her repertoire included typical selections for a schoolgirl: excerpts from Gilbert and Sullivan's operettas *The Mikado* and *H.M.S. Pinafore*, and Kalman's popular *Countess Maritza*. At the age of twelve, she received a Bulova watch for being a runner-up (to a boy accordionist) in a radio contest hosted by Jack Benny. In the early days in New York City and later in Athens, Litsa's behavior suggests that she wavered between investing in Maria as a future opera star and trying to make her a child starlet, but a photograph of young Maria with a Shirley Temple-like bow in her hair and multiple entries into popular song competitions suggest the latter. As Callas recalled later in life, these attempts were emotionally painful and humiliating for her. She had neither Temple's easygoing temperament and charm nor her endearing looks. Temperamentally shy and with a powerful but unorthodox voice, Maria did not have the makings of a matinee idol.

Litsa's discovery of Maria's singing talent was undoubtedly a pivotal event in Callas's life, but its precise psychological impact isn't easily discerned, especially given the larger context of Maria's upbringing and her early relationship with her mother. Most biographers accept Callas's claim that she was deprived of a childhood by an overly ambitious and fame-starved mother who relentlessly drove her to practice and take part in singing competitions at the expense of playing with her friends and her sister. The bespectacled, obese, and pimply young Maria is also portrayed as feeling second-best compared to Jackie who, quite beautiful and socially poised, is assumed by Callas's biographers to have long monopolized Litsa's affection. This confluence of experiences—being pushed to perform and feeling emotionally and physically inferior—is further used to explain Callas's troubled relationship with both Litsa and Jackie, as well as the split between the highly assured and competent Callas the opera diva and Maria the insecure woman. Yet human relations are rarely this simple. In any family conflict, there are usually two sides to the story. And these sides are frequently equally compelling.

Bitter Conflict

Most of what we know about Callas's childhood and the beginning of her singing career is based on retrospective accounts provided by her mother, her sister, and Maria herself, all written after Callas's infamous breakup with her mother in 1950 and her consequent estrangement from Jackie. Callas's first public statement regarding her childhood was made in a 1956 *Time* magazine article. Litsa's account is contained in her memoir *My Daughter Maria Callas*, published in 1960 and clearly designed to portray Litsa as an innocent victim of her daughter's inexplicable cruelty.[4] Although Jackie's book *Sisters* was published in 1989, twelve years after Callas's death, her intent to portray herself as a wise and unjustly slighted older sister is transparent. In short, the recollections of Callas's childhood became public only when each of the three protagonists had a vested interest in skewing history in her own favor.

Callas's intense estrangement from Litsa and the vitriol expressed on both sides goes to the heart of their personalities. Having established herself as a promising young singer, the recently married Callas spent the summer of 1950 performing with a troupe of Italian singers at the Teatro de Bellas Artes in Mexico City. Then twenty-seven years old, she invited her mother to join her. Litsa was feted by Mexico's high society as the mother of a highly acclaimed diva. Her hotel room was replenished every day with fresh flowers provided at the expense of the management. She attended embassy and government receptions and dined at the homes of Mexico City's elites. It must have truly felt like the fulfillment of a long dream. Maria and Litsa parted on good terms, with Callas buying her mother an expensive fur coat and giving her a substantial sum of money on her return to New York. But it would be the last time the two saw each other, the final time they spoke.

The reasons motivating Callas's decision to sever contact with her mother are complex. Maria struggled to free herself from psychological dependence on her mother, and this desire was threatened when Litsa intended to live with her after she filed for a divorce from George. During the Mexican sojourn, Litsa slipped back into playing the role of Maria's supporter in chief, including washing her daughter's underwear blackened by the makeup required for the role of Aida. This resumed closeness—if not blurring of boundaries—must have felt threatening to Callas. Additionally, Litsa's attempts to get Maria to purchase expensive gifts for Jackie in Mexico City stoked smoldering feelings of jealousy and envy resulting from the deterioration in their relationship during their adolescent years in Athens. In 1962, New York's Welfare Department threatened to bar Maria from entering the United States if she failed to provide Litsa with a small monthly allowance. Maria's abandonment hurt her mother deeply, generating an enormous amount of ill will. Litsa would state publicly that she wished her short-sighted daughter would go blind or develop throat cancer, a shocking statement for any parent to make. Total severance of contact with a mother manifests an intensity of emotions that does not allow for shades of gray to moderate the experience of personal hurt, and such incidents are characteristic of emotionally exploited child prodigies (Judy Garland, for instance, also disowned her mother). I will discuss the reasons for the breakup between Maria and her mother more fully in Chapter 5.

The wider public only became aware of Maria's split with her mother in 1956, when *Time* magazine ran a three-page story on Callas featuring the estrangement—six years after it happened. Her portrait, painted by Henry Koerner, an artist renowned for his portraits for *Time*, graced the cover. Written by Pulitzer Prize-winning journalist George de Carvalho, the article appeared in anticipation of Callas's debut at the Met. Typical of Maria's difficulty in adopting the perspective of the other, she made little effort to ingratiate herself to de Carvalho. He had to wait for several days to conduct the interview, during which time she asked him to undertake a trip from Venice to Rome to fetch her new puppy. The dog was not toilet-trained and relieved himself on de Carvalho's lap, ruining the journalist's new suit. Callas rarely initiated a confrontation, but she held little back when feeling attacked. When de Carvalho asked Maria to justify the banishment of Litsa from her life, Callas did not hesitate to talk about her bitterness: "I'll never forgive her for . . . taking my childhood away. During all the years I should have been playing and growing up, I was singing or making money. Everything I did for them [Litsa and Jackie] was mostly good and everything they did to me was mostly bad."[5] Callas's grievance and rage is captured brilliantly in this statement. She was not only ruthlessly used for her talent; she was also stripped of the joys of childhood. "My sister was slim and beautiful and friendly, and my mother always preferred her," she added, during the same interview. "I was the ugly duckling, fat and clumsy and unpopular. It is a cruel thing to make a child feel ugly and unwanted." Thus, "I hated school. I hated everybody. I got fatter and fatter."[6] These are strong words and deeply felt assertions. So deep, in fact, that Maria felt she was "really loved" only when she sang, both at home and at school.

The *Time* article painted an unfavorable picture of the prima donna and resulted in the Met audience giving Callas a very cool initial reception (the image of a successful daughter who abused her mother offended deeply ingrained American values). Formal applause greeted her stage entrance in contrast to that elicited by her fellow singers Fedora Barbieri and Mario Del Monaco. Callas thrived on matching wits with "hissing snakes," as she called hostile audiences, and her performance that evening illustrates the magic of her artistry. She managed to turn a potentially disastrous performance of *Norma* into a Met triumph. After a shaky start singing "Casta Diva"—the opera's signature aria—Callas's confidence grew as she mesmerized the audience with the solemn passion of her performance. She was called out sixteen times after the end of the opera, each time acknowledging the thunderous applause in a studied way thus extending the stage performance after it had ended.

Although Callas launched a vigorous defense of her behavior toward her mother and sister, she didn't anticipate that Litsa herself had no inhibition in using the ace up her sleeve. For the same *Time* article, she provided de Carvalho with an excerpt from a letter Maria penned in 1951 in response to her mother's request that she send $100 for her "daily bread." "Don't come to us with your troubles," Maria wrote. "I had to work [bark] for my money, and you are young enough to work, too. If you can't make enough money to live on, you can jump out of the window or drown yourself." Though typically indifferent to the impression she made on others, Callas was stung by her portrayal in *Time*. In an interview filmed later, Callas asserted that she did not believe in "blood" relations.

In response to Litsa's accusation, Maria decided to present her own life story in a lengthy interview conducted by Anita Pensotti and published in 1957 in *Oggi*. Maria reiterated her accusations against Litsa, claiming that "as soon as she became aware of my vocal gifts," her mother "decided to make of me a child prodigy as quickly as possible. And child prodigies never have genuine childhoods." Callas claimed she did not have a special toy that she remembered, "a doll or a favorite game." For her, it was only the songs that she "had to rehearse again and again to the point of exhaustion."[7] Callas never deviated from these accusations. As late as 1971, she commented, "When I was young I longed so much" to go to the circus. "I used to dream about it," she recalled in 1971. "But I was never taken to see one. There ought to be a law against making children work and depriving them of childish memories—it's disgraceful."[8] In a conversation recorded in 1973, she declared, "I was made to sing when I was only four, and I hated it. That's why I've always had this love–hate relationship with singing."[9] The problematic nature of her relationship with singing was compounded by Callas never liking the sound of her voice.

Litsa consistently denied Maria's bleak assessment of her childhood and instead saw the accusations as evidence of her daughter's madness. "Only a crazy daughter would hold her mother to blame for things that never happened,"[10] she asserted many years after Callas's death. Litsa also denied favoring Jackie over Maria and disputed the charge that Maria was an ugly and obese child (though she did concede Maria was perhaps plump but not seriously overweight). She felt that Maria was overly dramatic in depicting her childhood as one of social isolation and incessant singing practice. Her bafflement may be partly due to Maria's tendency in her reminiscences to conflate her childhood experiences in New York with her adolescence in Greece.

Irrespective of its causes, this mother–daughter break-up had particularly bitter consequences. How are we to reconcile the two strikingly divergent views of Maria's childhood experiences and the beginnings of her singing career? It is certainly true that once she realized Maria's talent, Litsa pushed her hard. As Callas correctly recalled, Litsa did prevent her from continuing her education past elementary school. She enrolled Maria in numerous contests and singing competitions and paid scant regard to her stage fright, a feeling that persisted throughout her career. It is also the case that Litsa was a woman of tremendous drive; as argued by Stelios Galatopoulos, she wound up harming both herself and Maria with delusions of grandeur and a craving for fame. It is not true, however, that Maria was a pawn or an unwilling victim of her mother's machinations. Quite the contrary. Callas was renowned throughout her career for her ambition, exceptional work ethic, and a commitment to her artistry that started in childhood and only waned when her voice began its pronounced decline. As she herself clearly stated, "my mother wanted me to become a great singer. I was happy with that but only if I could become a great singer. All or nothing."[11]

The Drama of a Gifted Child

As an eleven-year-old listening with her family to the Met's Saturday matinee radio broadcast of Donizetti's *Lucia di Lammermoor,* Maria broke the spell of its famous mad scene by angrily shouting that the soprano was straying off pitch. When admonished by her parents to show more respect for its celebrated soprano, Lily Pons, Callas responded: "I don't care if she is a star. She sings off-key. Just wait and see, one day I'm going to be a star myself, a bigger star than her."[12] This incident encapsulates Callas's attitude toward singing; it illuminates her ambition, her sense of destiny. Singing had already become an integral part of her identity. Indeed, her school yearbook entries include comments by fellow students addressed "to a future great singer" and "to girl with the golden voice." No matter how we evaluate Litsa's ultimate impact on her daughter's development, it is undeniable that she played a key role in instilling in Maria the formidable work ethic and single-minded drive for success that were to constitute the bedrock of her career and her fame. Pierre-Jean Remy, Callas's French biographer, has argued, "If there was anything miraculous about Callas's childhood, it was her mother's extraordinary foresight. She saw beyond appearances and sensed her younger child's gifts. What was amazing was her relentless dedication to developing these gifts."[13] This is the irony in Maria's estrangement from her mother: Litsa's extraordinary gifts sowed the seeds that gave rise to her daughter's fame, but those same traits would doom her relationship with Maria.

In the 1957 *Oggi* interview with Anita Pensotti, Maria aired a second complaint regarding her education. "After grade school all my companions enrolled in high school," she recalled. "But I couldn't: my mother had decided that I should not steal even a moment from a day spent in studying singing and piano. So, at eleven years of age, I put my books aside and began to get to know the enervating anxiety and the waiting involved in contests for child prodigies."[14] Maria's accusation, reflected in her self-portrayal as a fat and ugly child marginalized by the family in favor of Jackie, may say more about her dissatisfaction with her physical appearance—something that originated during her adolescent years in Athens—than about the reality of her early childhood years. Contrary to her own later claims, Callas was not an obese child: Maria was 5 foot 3 inches tall at eleven years and she weighed 119 pounds. Though not as pretty as Jackie, she was, in fact, an attractive child. In photos from her early teenage years, she is tall and perhaps awkward but not obese. Maria needed glasses from the time she was five years old, which may have contributed to her negative body image, and the early onset of menarche (before she was eleven) was a second factor that may have influenced her self-image.

The fact remains that, as an adult, Maria felt deeply hurt and scarred by her childhood memories. When combined with her adolescent experiences in Athens, these recollections became, in a sense, deferred traumas. If it is not fully grounded in reality, what is the source of her grievance against her mother's treatment? Memory researchers argue that it is common for individuals to misremember or to compress autobiographical events.[15] Maria conflates childhood experiences while living in New York with events that happened during her adolescence in Athens, and this tendency reflects the personal salience of the material that is misremembered. Although framed in terms of objective neglect, the real source of the grievance is psychological deprivation. What appears to be lurking behind Callas's perception of exploitation is resentment: She is hurt because she grew up without feeling loved, without feeling accepted for her intrinsic self. Though Litsa celebrated her daughter's voice, this is very different from celebrating a daughter simply because of who she is. Litsa's involvement in promoting Maria's talent left no time for love and affection, as perceptively noted by Petsalis-Diomidis, yet this is something that Litsa never fully understood.

It is not that Litsa failed to mirror Maria's impulses and desires; rather, she selectively affirmed those aspects of her daughter's personality that suited her own needs. Maria had a ruthless ambition and single-minded dedication to music, personality traits that suited Litsa's own personality—and her agenda. All parents selectively reinforce aspects of their child's personality or talent, and there is nothing wrong with this, so long as the relationship also includes warmth and care. Litsa failed to devote attention to other aspects of her daughter's life, other talents she might develop, and this selectivity left Maria with little evidence that she was loved for anything other than her singing. Total unconditional regard is obviously an ideal never to be expected or experienced; nonetheless, the positive glow of parental admiration seems to have been particularly scarce for Maria. Litsa could not fathom the nature of Maria's grievance against her precisely because the whole idea of celebrating her daughter as a person—and not merely for her voice—was so far removed from her consciousness. In fact, as we saw, the whole idea struck her as crazy. As we recall, she publicly interpreted Maria remembrances as those of a "crazy daughter."

Callas's craving for acceptance is easy to understand. The universality of the human desire for unconditional acceptance is well illustrated by a scene from *Notting Hill,* in which Julia Roberts plays the role of Anna Scott, a rich movie star, and Hugh Grant portrays the character of William Tucker, an unassuming owner of a small, specialized travel book store. After a series of misunderstandings, Roberts stands in front of Grant and says, "I am just a girl standing in front of a boy asking him to love her."[16] This story line is not particularly original; it is found time and again in movies where a rich young man (e.g., Elvis Presley in *Clambake*) or a wealthy young woman (e.g., the character of Laurel in Presley's *Girls, Girls, Girls*) hide their identity to test whether a partner will be attracted to them as a person rather than to their wealth. The emotional power of this plot line lies in the yearning to be loved simply because of who one is, a seemingly basic desire yet one not easily fulfilled. Callas was not immune from this longing, nor is anyone.

Although the discovery of Maria's precocious vocal talent elevated her place in the family, it did little to help her develop healthy self-esteem. It served, instead, to consolidate her narcissism. In *The Drama of the Gifted Child,* Alice Miller describes a pathway to narcissism that involves a parent's use of a gifted child for the gratification of their own unfulfilled personal needs and ambitions.[17] Being used in this way leads the child to develop two contradictory personas or selves: a grandiose self and a vulnerable self. The grandiose self emerges from the child's internalized absorption of the parent's high expectations and unfulfilled aspirations, and it's clear that Callas possessed a sense of superiority already evident at age eleven in her disdain for Lily Pons going off key and in her belief that she herself would surpass the fame of the well-established Met star. "From the time [Mary] was born, she always wanted to be conspicuous, to stand out from the crowd," Litsa claimed. "'Mother,' she said to me once, 'I'm going to be the greatest opera singer of all time! The whole world's going to be talking about me.'"[18] Of course, many children believe that they will grow up to be famous. But Callas's sense of superiority persisted unchanged well into the mature stages of her singing career. This grandiosity constitutes a false self—to use Miller's language, an "as-if" personality that never feels quite real—the roots of which can be traced to early interactions with her parents that failed to satisfy the mirroring and idealization needs critical to the development of healthy self-esteem, as discussed earlier. Such failures result in an adult grandiose self that reflects an insufficiently modified egocentrism and omnipotence. These characteristics are developmentally appropriate in a young child, but they denote narcissism when continued into adulthood.

The origins of Callas's superiority reside in early childhood experiences, but the internalization of her mother's own expansive ambitions and expectations consolidated the development of her grandiose self. Litsa's sense of grandeur was reflected in her expansive claims about her family's social status, the beauty of her mother, the singing prowess of her father, and by her contempt for her husband's humble origins. Jackie and Maria experienced their mother's grandiose self on occasions when Litsa captured their imagination by transporting them to a magical land of make believe. Litsa and her two daughters gathered each week for dinner at a local Chinese restaurant, and, with a single gesture and a few words, Litsa would transform the humble setting and a simple dish of chop suey into a pretend sumptuous banquet consumed in the dining hall of a Renaissance palace. Similarly, when they were a little older, she amused the girls and one of their friends by dancing with them in the sitting room of their Riverside Drive apartment, converted in the dancers' imaginations into a palace ballroom with a Prince Charming undoubtedly hovering in the wings. In those moments, according to Jackie, Liza appeared to possess magical powers. Maria inherited her mother's magical sense, powerfully mesmerizing audiences with a single gesture, glance, or phrase.

It is easy to imagine how the early signs of Maria's vocal talent fueled Litsa's grandiose fantasies of riches and fame and how, in turn, these fantasies buttressed Callas's own ambitions. Her identification with her mother's expansive aspirations was further facilitated by the fact that grandiosity defended her against feelings of vulnerability. Singing allowed Callas to gain her mother's acceptance, but, as John Ardoin argues, it also provided an antidote for her shy, introverted personality. In other words, Maria had a vested interest in exaggerating her specialness as a singer for it enabled her to compensate for the feelings of inadequacy she experienced growing up in a discordant and impoverished family, having to compete with a prettier, more outgoing, and more likeable sister. It must have felt satisfying for her to look at her peers and think that while they may have been richer, prettier, more popular, or more loved at home, she was the one with a special voice, with a great destiny that made her far superior to them.

Alice Miller has argued that a sense of superiority derived from being celebrated for a special talent is a double-edged sword: While it causes a child to feel good about herself, it simultaneously reinforces feelings of vulnerability. The vulnerable self, in contrast to the grandiose self, emerges from the child's realization of not being celebrated for their intrinsic worth but for their exceptional abilities or talent. It reflects two questions that nag the gifted child: "What is wrong with me that I cannot be admired simply for whom I am?" and "why am I essentially unlovable?" In Callas's case, this concern was expressed by the feeling, persistent throughout her life, that she was loved—noticed, even—only because of her voice. As she aptly expressed in this chapter's opening quote, "To make her notice me, I began singing. I knew I had a beautiful voice and it did me good to arouse admiration when I sang. So singing gradually came to be the medicine for my inferiority complexes."[19] Her feelings of being unloved and inferior were further exacerbated by Litsa's favoring of Jackie and the emphasis placed on good looks in the Callas household; though she possessed a great voice, she could not compete with Jackie when it came to physical attractiveness and "feminine charm." For the highly competitive Callas, this must have been an additional blow to her self-esteem, a narcissistic injury that would become more prominent during their time in Athens, especially given a weight gain that further undermined her confidence as a woman.

Notes

1. De Carvallo, G. (1977). Der einsame Tod der Maria Callas. *Neue Revue Illustrierte*, 40(26 Sept.). As quoted in Petsalis-Diomidis, *The unknown Callas*, p. 61.
2. Television interview with Lord Harewood for the BBC "Maria Callas talks to Lord Harewood." Paris, 23–26, 1968. Available on EMI Classics.
3. https://www.theguardian.com/music/2010/may/07/giulietta-simionato-obituary
4. Callas, *My daughter Maria Callas*.
5. De Carvallo, G. (1956). The Prima Donna. *Time*, 1956, October 29.
6. Ibid.
7. Pensotti, A. (1957). Callas speaks. Reprinted in Lowe, *Callas as they saw her*, pp. 114–115.

8. Remy, *Maria Callas: A tribute*, p. 18.
9. Both quotes come from Petsalis-Diomidis, *The unknown Callas*, p. 40.
10. Ibid., p. 58.
11. Pensotti, Callas speaks, p. 115.
12. Stassinopoulos, A. (1981). *Maria Callas; The woman behind the legend.* New York: Simon and Schuster, p. 29. (Note that this book has been republished under Huffington, A.)
13. Remy, *Maria Callas: A tribute*, p. 17.
14. Pensoti, *Callas speaks*, p. 115.
15. Conway, M. A. (1990). *Autobiographical memory: An introduction.* Maidenhead, UK: Open University Press.
16. Notting Hill, Universal Studios, 1999.
17. Miller, A. (1981). *The drama of the gifted child.* New York: Basic Books.
18. Petsalis-Diomidis, *The unknown Callas*, p. 59.
19. De Carvallo, Der einsame Tod, p. 61.

5 | AN ATHENIAN INTERLUDE

Callas's move from New York City to Athens was a major turning point. In Athens, she experienced poverty, personal humiliation, and, during the World War II years and subsequent communist uprising, threats to her life. But her singing benefited from the strong mentorship she received, which helped launch her operatic career. Her experiences during these years also exacerbated the split between Callas, the self-assured artist, and Maria, the vulnerable young woman. Alice Miller has shown how a parent's use of their child's gift for the gratification of their own unfulfilled personal needs and ambitions presents a possible pathway to narcissism.[1] This kind of exploitation may result in the development of two contradictory personas: a grandiose self and a vulnerable self. For Maria, the consolidation of a grandiose, yet vulnerable self undermined her ability to manage her often dueling desires for operatic stardom and a fulfilling personal life.

Litsa's desire to promote Maria's singing career led her and her two daughters back to Greece in the spring of 1937. Her decision was prompted by a need to separate from her husband—a wish George seemingly shared for, upon hearing of her decision to return to Greece, he fell on his knees in gratitude. Litsa hoped that her own mother and her five surviving siblings, several of whom were musically talented, would support her in helping to launch

Prima Donna. Paul Wink, Oxford University Press (2021). © Oxford University Press.
DOI: 10.1093/oso/9780190857738.003.0005

Maria's career, but these hopes were quickly dispelled. Litsa's family members proved less wealthy and well connected than she had assumed. Litsa's mother, Frosso Dimitriadou, lived together with five other members of her family in a house located on the rural outskirts of Athens's city center at that time. The six of them were supported by Frosso's pension and the meager civil servants' salaries of her two daughters. The Dimitriadou clan, many of whom were musically gifted, did not share their newly arrived sister's conviction that the socially awkward Maria, with her heavy and somewhat manly voice, had the talent to become a star.

Nonetheless, for the first time in her life, Callas experienced the joys of family. She lived with her warm and fun-loving grandmother, who presided over a traditional protracted Sunday lunch that included improvised theatrical and musical performances by Maria's three aunts and two uncles. Yet this emotionally gratifying interlude ended abruptly, within a few months of Callas's arrival in Athens. That winter, Litsa and her brother Doukas clashed with bitter acrimony. The quarrel, most likely over money, escalated and led Litsa to sever contact with her entire family. Neither Maria nor Jackie were to see their grandmother again until she became seriously ill in 1944. Around the same time, the quick-tempered Litsa also broke off relationships with a cousin whose four daughters were friendly with Jackie and Maria. On learning that Maria disobeyed her and met with one of the girls, Litsa threatened to chop off her feet. As a result, for Maria (or Marianna as she was known then), life in Athens ended up replicating the pattern of social isolation that characterized her childhood in New York. Matters were then made worse. Maria found out that Jackie had become a mistress to the son of a wealthy Athenian, and an emotional distance developed between the two sisters.[2]

Although Litsa failed to provide Maria with an emotionally rewarding and supportive environment, she believed in her daughter's talents and sought to cultivate them. Undeterred by her family's skepticism, Litsa featured Maria's vocal talent wherever possible; in fact, Maria often sang in taverns despite her protests that performing in such venues was personally humiliating for a budding opera star. Litsa also managed to obtain the high-quality training and education needed for her daughter's operatic success, a task that proved easier in small and parochial Athens than in larger, more impersonal New York. Less than six months after her arrival, Callas became a pupil of Maria Trivella, a well-regarded singing teacher. Then thirteen years old, Callas was soon falsifying her age to meet the sixteen-year-old minimum requirement of the National Conservatory of music. Maria gained admission with a scholarship, and, after recognizing the true potential of her voice, it was Trivella who helped guide Maria through the Conservatory's admission process. After a year of studying with Trivella (dates unknown), Callas began taking lessons from Elvira de Hidalgo (1891–1980), a prominent member of the more prestigious Athens Conservatory, where she would transfer as a student following a couple of well-received concerts. During the next five years, both before the invasion of Greece by Italian forces and during the subsequent Italian and German occupations, Maria took on leading roles in a number of successful opera productions. And as a member of the Greek National Opera, she gained significant recognition singing important female roles, including in Puccini's *Tosca*, d'Albert's *Tiefland*, and Beethoven's *Fidelio*.

A prodigious musical talent such as Callas's is largely innate, a gift offered by a chance combination of genes. It cannot be acquired merely by hard work or perseverance, nor does possession of such a talent guarantee an artist a successful career. It requires a combination of strong mentorship, personal dedication, a desire to succeed, and a modicum of luck. There is no doubt that the training Maria received from de Hidalgo played an influential role in her rapid development as an artist; indeed, it was de Hidalgo[3] who taught Callas the intricacies of *bel canto* singing. She drilled young Maria using a comprehensive set of exercises aimed at the development of breath control. She introduced her to the art of ornamentation, embellishment, and sequencing of notes. And she chose the right kind of music to suit Maria's vocal capabilities. Callas learned roles that would later bring her worldwide fame while training with de Hidalgo: Norma, Lucia, Aida, Gioconda, Turandot.

Maria's initial encounter with Elvira de Hidalgo, which occurred during a 1938 audition, exemplifies the contradiction between Callas's singing talent and a personal neglect that characterized the early stages of her career in Greece (and, subsequently, in Italy). "The very idea of that girl wanting to be a singer was laughable! She was tall, very fat, and wore heavy glasses," says de Hidalgo, recalling the moment she first met Maria. Behind her heavy glasses were "huge, starting, feverish eyes." Meekly, she "sat in a corner, not knowing what to do with her hands," recalled the instructor, so she "began biting her nails." Maria wore a "loose-fitting schoolgirl's overall" to the audition, and she "walked heavily, with a swaying gait." Her face was "spotted with pimples." "I'm not going to get anywhere" with this girl, de Hidalgo recalled thinking to herself. But without a word, Maria started to sing: "All at once I was alert, full of tension," de Hidalgo remembers. "That voice was the voice I had secretly been waiting for; in fact, I had been looking for it for years." A tear escaped her eye, and de Hidalgo quickly shielded her face. Maria's voice had a "certain individuality" that "moved me deeply,"[4] she recalled.

Maria proved to be de Hidalgo's model student. Her rapid progress in mastering the art of operatic singing was greatly aided by her unrelenting drive, her dedication to her studies, and her perfectionism. It was not unusual for Callas to spend more than ten hours a day in de Hidalgo's studio. She was among the first students to arrive and the last to leave. She spent her time practicing as well as listening to other students, convinced that she could learn from hearing the progress made by others. Despite warnings by her teachers at the Athens Conservatory that Callas's conceit would cause her trouble, as a pupil there was nothing stuck-up or superior about her. Quite the contrary, Maria was open to criticism, humble, and rarely satisfied with her progress. She strove constantly to improve her performance so that she would meet her own lofty standards. Maria's perfectionism spilled over to rehearsals both in Athens and later in Italy: conductors and fellow artists experienced first-hand Callas's interminable appetite for perfecting every aria and every scene through practice. Before the first performance of *Tosca* in Athens, dissatisfied with the routine rehearsals at the opera house, Callas asked the conductor to continue practicing at his home. The conductor's widow later recalled her husband's frustration with the nitpicking Maria who pestered him with trivial detail and insisted on seemingly never-ending retakes when her peers would look at their watches the moment the word "rehearsal" was mentioned.

Perfectionism and the Grandiose Self

Perfectionism is frequently a manifestation of a grandiose self, and the high standards associated with perfectionism often reflect the narcissist's high self-regard. In short, a grandiose self is a perfect self, and because grandiose individuals demand perfection from their own accomplishments and from those of others, even a small blemish threatens to undermine the entire effort. It is easy to imagine how this can lead to self-paralysis and chronic dissatisfaction with one's achievements, and it is this darker underside of narcissism that will become fully evident in the later stage of Callas's career. In the early years of her career in Athens, however, those high standards motivated her to work hard and be her best.

Maria was infatuated with de Hidalgo, which aided the teacher's ability to shape her pupil's vocal performance. De Hidalgo worked hard to extend the high ranges in Callas's voice, smoothing out the transition between its three registers and trying to eliminate the vibrato or wobble that crept into her high notes. This wobble would plague Callas throughout her career and became particularly prominent after her weight loss in the early 1950s. De Hidalgo became both a valuable mentor and a surrogate mother. Maria impressed her with the power and range of her voice and with her musicianship and acting ability. As a model student, Callas extended her perfectionism to include de Hidalgo who, in her eyes, became a flawless object of idealization.

Maria's perfectionism and drive for achievement helped her master the art of singing. It also allowed her to turn personal adversity into an asset. By the time she arrived in Athens, Callas's vision had deteriorated to the point where she could not see the conductor or confidently locate the stage props. Contact lenses were intolerable, and so she wore thick glasses. Undeterred by her poor vision, Maria resorted to memorizing the entire opera score to ensure that she would not miss her entry points. In doing so, she uncovered an almost photographic memory that allowed her to learn an entire opera score in just a few days. After she became concerned about her ability to locate props and her positioning on the stage, Maria recreated the entire scenery of *Cavalleria Rusticana* at her home in preparation for her first operatic appearance in Athens. Callas's short-sightedness meant that, during a stage performance, she did not see the conductor or the audience—she was enveloped in a cocoon of sound without much visual input. These characteristics enhanced her sensitivity to rhythm, sharpened her ability to enter into the role of the characters performed on stage, and greatly added to the magic of her performances. "Maria can't see very far," declared Luchino Visconti, a prominent Italian film and opera director. He suggested that this was a big asset because, being in an aquarium of sorts, it allowed Callas to totally immerse herself in a world of her own.[5]

To become an opera star requires a sense of destiny, a self-confidence that propels the artist to transcend obstacles and get ahead in a competitive, cut-throat environment. What is unusual about Callas is that her grandiosity and many of the less appealing characteristics of a stereotypic diva were evident during her adolescent years, in Athens, hence preceding her rise to fame.

Following her triumph in the opera *Tiefland*, for example, a class-mate's mother praised Maria by saying "Mary, you were wonder-ful." "Oh, yes, I was," responded the twenty-year old. "And tell me, Mrs. Mandikan," Callas asked, "who else in the world today can sing Marta as I can?" In 1945, just before her departure from Athens, Callas issued the following boastful, albeit prophetic, warning to her fellow singers at the National Opera: "I'll make sure they never forget me and spend their lives dreading the day I come back," Callas declared. "I'll make them eat their words and remember me for many years to come."

Some of Callas's adolescent grandiosity can be attributed to the exuberance of youth. Her question to her uncle Doukas, uttered shortly after arrival in Athens, whether he would go to hear her at La Scala in Milan, or her assertion to Litsa that she would be the world's greatest prima donna, capture her youthful ambition. Such claims, however, persisted unabated right until Callas's departure from Athens. When told by a sympathetic colleague that part of the hostility she encountered from other artists was due to the fact that there existed an ascribed pecking order and that other sing-ers ahead of her could not just be brushed aside, Callas responded "Yes, but I'm the best! I can't wait that long because I know what I'm worth."[6]

This adolescent grandiosity clearly differentiates her from past prima donnas of the operatic stage, such as Adeline Patti or Nellie Melba, whose sense of entitlement and self-centeredness grew proportionately as adulating audiences led to the acquisi-tion of immense personal wealth and success. Melba, whose early career was fostered by the patronage of prominent members of the British aristocracy, including Lady de Grey, had "the patience and inexhaustible capacity for forbearance of the successful courtier."[7] When interviewed, at age nineteen, for the *Le Figaro*, Patti stated, "My papa arranges everything." Though known to have tantrums on occasion, Patti asserted, "As for me, they tell me I must start, and I start, they tell me to sing and I sing."[8] In other words, although Patti and Melba were each supremely confident in their abilities, their self-absorption and imperial self were fueled by their operatic successes. Callas, on the other hand, wielded a supreme confidence long before she ever reached fame on the stage. She lacked the savviness and compliance that characterized Melba and Patti at the onset of their careers. Instead, her relationships with staff and fellow student at the Athene's conservatory were characterized by disdain and irreverence.

Lack of Reverence for Status

In the play *No Exit*, Jean Paul Sartre conceives of hell not as a subterranean space full of fire and brimstone but a room with three people who, barred from exit, mercilessly dissect and exploit each other's weaknesses, creating their own hell. Maria's egocentrism and lack of basic social skills led to troubled relationships with artistic peers and, at home, with her mother and sister. It was her own private hell, a *"No Exit"* environment created by Maria's self-absorption and personal interactions marked by jealousy, envy, and a lack of care on the part of Callas, her operatic colleagues, and her family. The key to understanding Callas's narcissism during her Athenian years, set against the backdrop of war-torn Europe, is provided by her hostile and troubled relationships.

During her adolescence in Athens, Callas had the habit of saying whatever came into her mind without considering the implications, as documented by Petsalis-Diomidis. She showed scant regard for what other people might think of her and had little empathy, as evidenced by her relationships with superiors. As early as her days at the National Conservatory, the fourteen-year-old Callas was expelled for being rude to the principal after he allegedly ignored her singing and commented on her size. She was reinstated after an apology. The same situation occurred at the Athenian Conservatory. After finding out that the Conservatory's principal criticized her, Callas marched into his office, banged her hands on his desk, shouting, "Look here, Filoktitis, I won't have you sticking your nose into my business." The principal, shocked equally by the tone of the remarks and by being called by his first name, managed only to roar, "Get out!"[9] A couple of years later, while attending a small reception held in the office of the Director of the National Theatre, Maria blurted "Come on then, Niko, get up from there and let me make a few phone calls."[10] As recalled by one of the attendees, what was astonishing about Callas's behavior was not only the presumed familiarity implied by using the director's first name, but also the total disregard for age and status difference. A fellow student recalled meeting Maria on a streetcar around the same time; quite shamelessly, Maria told her that even though one of the teachers informed her not to come to the conservatory because she hadn't "theory and rudiments," the teacher, in Callas's word, "can take a running jump." Yet another example of Callas's lack of respect for age or status occurred after the conductor of Beethoven's *Fidelio* doubted her suitability for the role of Leonora: "Listen, Maestro, whether I'm any good or not is none of your business. But I tell you, one day you'll be grov-eling to conduct me!" Later in her career, Callas was well known for adversarial relations with opera directors, fellow singers, and conductors who dared to cross or criticize her, but such insolent and egocentric behavior exhibited by a still teenage girl is unusu-ally precocious.[11]

The Greece years exacerbated Callas's egocentrism. The envi-ronment certainly did not enhance her ability to take on the per-spective of others or to consider the impact of her words. As we saw in the previous two chapters, Callas's early childhood experi-ences were not conducive to the development of empathy for oth-ers or gaining a perspective on her own behavior. These deficits, resulting in part from her social isolation in New York, were now compounded by her mother's estrangement from her extended Greek family. Maria was deprived of yet another opportunity to develop social skills and to modulate her impulsivity by interact-ing with others. Callas lived in "a fool's paradise," similar to the mental state of Baron Charlus, the highly narcissistic character from Marcel Proust's novel *In Search of Lost Time*. Charlus is quite oblivious to the impression his behavior makes on other peo-ple, particularly those he considers beneath him. He is "like the fish that thinks that the water in which it is swimming extends beyond the glass wall of its aquarium which mirrors it, while it does not see close beside it in the shadow the amused stroller who is watching its gyrations, or the all-powerful keeper who, at the unforeseen and fatal moment . . . will extract it without compunc-tion from the environment in which it was happily living to fling it into another."[12] Proust's description applies equally well to the young Maria Callas. She lived not only in a physically but also in a personally and emotionally myopic world that prevented her from recognizing the impressions she created on others.

Universally Disliked

Not surprisingly given her contemptuous and intimidating manner, Maria was universally disliked, and even feared, by fellow students at the Athens Conservatory and the Greek National Opera. Her peers were taken aback by her rudeness, her bluntness, her aggression, and her disdainful attitude. She developed the reputation of being cocky—a big talker obsessed by the notion of her own greatness. In 1943, Maria and two other singers were nominated to sing for the occupying forces at a concert at Casa d'Italia. After the concert rehearsal, one of the other two performers commented on hearing Maria sing a love duet from *Madama Butterfly* that she had learned in one day: "Hey, that's fantastic! You're really going to be a great singer," she said. "I am [already one]," Callas quickly retorted before walking out of the room, leaving all of the others thunderstruck.[13] Apart from her insolence and bluntness, Callas was known for being aloof and reserved, someone who kept to herself and who, moreover, would storm in and out of the Conservatory with a scowl on her face. She did not help her reputation by stealing scenes and applause from other singers, as her mother noted. Yet she did not belong to any cliques, and she avoided gossip and kept her distance from any of the theatrical intrigue. She showed the aggressive part of her personality only when she perceived that she was being attacked or unfairly criticized. When scorned, however, her rage knew no limits. So much so, in fact, that she got into fistfights with other singers. She sang the opening night of *Fidelio* with a black eye, the result of an encounter with the husband of a jealous fellow soprano. In the encounter, Callas gave as good as she got. On a different occasion, she got into a physical fight with another singer; the two rivals ceased their hostilities only to search for an earring displaced during the battle. Physical fights between singers, even on stage, are an integral part of opera's history, however. The custom dates back to the infamous melee between Francesca Cuzzoni (1696–1778) and Faustina Bordoni (1697–1781) and their respective partisans during a performance of Bononcini's *Astianatte* at London's Haymarket Theatre in the 1720s.

Callas's grandiosity and self-absorption contributed to her unpopularity among fellow artists, but it does not fully account for the intensity of the hostility she encountered. Rather, a victim of her own success, she generated envy, particularly among older and more sophisticated female singers at the Athens Conservatory and the National Opera. As early as 1940, at a very early stage of her career, the sixteen-year-old Callas heard the negative comments of her peers during rehearsals for *Boccaccio*: "That American bitch that's come in, what right has she got to be here, the fat cow taking our performances away from us?" And after her success in that same opera, her peers declared, "Kick the American out! A foreigner's got no business in our opera company. She'll ruin the performances with her accent."[14] Callas achieved her first operatic triumphs and became a regular lead singer before her twentieth birthday. Here was a teenager, an upstart with only an elementary school education, who spoke and sung Greek with a foreign accent, who was poor, shabbily dressed, myopic, and indifferent to her appearance. And it was this upstart who was taking jobs away from much older, more sophisticated, and well-established artists. She was usurping their fame and glory, so it is not surprising that, under these circumstances, Callas provoked a lot of envy and hostility from her colleagues.

Many people find pleasure in knowing that their achievements are met with affirmation and good wishes from others. But as Tolstoy perceptively notes in his novel *Anna Karenin*, success frequently elicits feelings of jealously or envy in others. Alexy Karenin had been overlooked for a promotion and now "he could not repress a feeling of hatred, comprehensible to anyone in an official position, from one who had suffered a set-back in the service for one who had received promotion."[15] In contrast to jealously, envy denotes a feeling of resentment aroused by someone else possessing qualities or achieving success that is clearly beyond our reach. Thus, as argued by Melanie Klein, envy is a much more destructive feeling than jealousy. Callas's two personal flaws, her neglected physical appearance and her noticeable vocal wobble, provided her fellow artists with a convenient justification for their feelings of both jealousy and envy. In other words, Callas's "feet of clay" allowed her colleagues to mask their resentment behind the veil of a sense of injustice or lack of fairness.

Operatic stars are expected to take care of their appearance (the opera scene is an artistic one, after all, where esthetics and elegance of dress and manner all matter).[16] Yet, it is precisely these expectations that Callas violated, seemingly with obliviousness and disdain. Upon arrival in Athens, 5'8" Maria weighed around 140 pounds. Her weight increased to 200 pounds before stabilizing at around 175 pounds during the last two years of her stay there.

Her weight gain made it hard for her during rehearsals to bend, kneel, and fall down, impediments to anyone performing in opera where the heroines routinely swoon and collapse in spasms of agony or death. Furthermore, Callas's weight gain coincided with the famine among Athenians induced by World War II and made her stand out all the more relative to her famished and emaciated peers. Making matters worse, Callas dressed poorly in clothes of dubious freshness and, as reported by her sister Jackie, was allergic to deodorant and perfume, a considerable handicap in the hot Athenian climate. An admirer who did not wish to be rude compared Callas to "an elephant that had swallowed a nightingale." More derogatory descriptors included "whale," a "full-sized cow," and even "monster." Some referred to her as "repulsive."[17]

One can imagine the fury and resentment generated among her colleagues as Callas effortlessly shed all her vulgarity on stage, turning, as if by magic, from an ugly duckling into a swan. Her artistry, musicality, and the sheer power and range of her voice overshadowed the wobble that crept into her singing. Many individuals on hearing Callas for the first time found the timbre of her voice memorable, yet also distinctly unpleasant. Her voice lacked the crystal clarity of Patti, Melba, Tetrazzini, or Amelita Galli-Curci (1882–1963). Despite its extensive range, spanning almost three octaves, its upper, middle, and lower registers were different enough to give the semblance of three different voices.

From the earliest years of her career, Callas had the capacity to captivate her audiences and grab their undivided attention with her performance. An audience member witnessing Maria's early triumph as a nineteen-year-old singing Tosca recounted that when she came on stage, she compelled the audience to hear her, almost "as if she took" hold of them physically. According to a music critic commenting on her performance in *Tiefland* (at age twenty-one), Callas appeared on stage in a way that caused all eyes to be turned on her alone. She intuitively knew how to use her hands and body to express the emotions inherent in her roles. On stage, she could easily hide the obese lower part of her body and draw attention to her attractive torso and face. Commenting on Callas's first professional appearance in 1940, in the minor role of Beatrice in von Suppe's *Boccaccio*, de Hidalgo told her that, although she herself was an acclaimed actress, she could not help but admire the originality of Maria's hand and body movements.

The stark contrast between Maria the aggressive, arrogant, and inelegant youth and the miraculous Callas the actress fueled her colleagues' resentment and vindicated their attempts to derail her career, at least in their minds. Following Callas's success in *Tiefland*, her fellow female singers stopped talking and congratulating her or even saying hello when they met, according to a fellow singer at the National Opera. Callas confided to one of the male students that because she was such a hit in the opera, the other singers could not stand her and behaved as though she had done something terribly wrong. Her fellow singers' spite was intensified by their partly conscious awareness that they might be dealing with a God-given talent, an awareness conveyed in a comment by a fellow soprano, made half in jest and half in earnest: Was there something divine in Callas they had all overlooked? Vindictive spitefulness, fueled by the perception of vulnerability in someone otherwise unusually gifted, is not as preposterous or as uncommon as might first be thought, and a similar scenario is depicted in the film *Amadeus*, which portrays Mozart's relationship with Salieri.

The film, an adaptation of Peter Schaffer's play, is narrated by Antonio Salieri, a highly celebrated composer at the court of the Austrian Emperor Joseph II, but in reality quite mediocre. While Salieri is the only person to recognize Mozart's true genius, he is, at the same time, appalled by the vulgarity of his personal life (given poetic license in the film as there is no archival evidence that Mozart had crude personal habits). It is this disjunction between Mozart's musical genius and personal inadequacies that disinhibit the envious Salieri, who ends up poisoning him. Here, the physical act of murder should be interpreted metaphorically as the ultimate manifestation of envy destroying something that the other admires and desires but can never possess. Similarly, Callas was also a victim of a literal and figurative assassination when, after Greece's liberation from German occupation, an intervention by her colleagues resulted in her being denied a prima donna's contract at the National Opera. It is easy to imagine how the hostility and envy experienced by Callas in her professional life reinforced her narcissism; it is an understandable response to the hurt, shame, and vulnerability she felt in light of her colleagues' behavior toward her.

Individuals are programmed to thrive psychologically given a modicum of support, goodness, and care in their lives. It is highly likely, therefore, that the adolescent Maria could have withstood the hostile environment confronted in her professional life if it was counterbalanced by warmth and support at home. Unfortunately, this was lacking. Indeed, Callas's strained relationships with her mother and her sister contributed to her personal vulnerability and her self-absorption.

Trouble at Home

Although the move back to Greece fulfilled Litsa's dream of launching her daughter's operatic career, it was otherwise disappointing. Litsa's belief that she would be surrounded by wealthy and socially well-connected family members did not materialize, and Maria's early operatic triumphs proved less glamorous and certainly less financially rewarding than Litsa fantasized. The promised monthly checks from George arrived only sporadically. Litsa, Jackie, and Maria moved five times during the first two years of their stay in Athens, and, at one point, they even found themselves sleeping on the floor in an unfurnished flat. Within three years of their arrival, they were caught up in the chaos of World War II and its imminent threats of starvation and death. These experiences contributed to Litsa's lapses in judgment and a self-destructive short-term hedonism.

The first lapse in judgment involved Litsa's cynical encouragement of Jackie to become a mistress of Milton (Miltiadis) Embirikos, the son of a wealthy ship owner. A considerate and likeable young man, Milton did not have the strength of character to go against his father's opposition to what was considered a socially inferior marriage, however. In encouraging this relationship, Litsa must have realized that she was tarnishing the reputation not only of her older daughter but of the whole family. In New York, she forbade her daughters from socializing with boys, and yet now she was favoring an arrangement whose main value was providing relief from financial hardship with only a distant hope of Jackie ever marrying Milton (the couple stayed together unmarried until Milton's death from cancer in 1963). The highly moralistic Maria felt betrayed by Jackie's behavior, and their relationship never recovered from the strain.

Litsa's second lapse in judgment was her fraternizing with Italian and German army officers during the occupation of Greece. The war years brought enormous hardship to the population of Athens, with many thousands dying of starvation and related illnesses such as tuberculosis. Despite these adverse circumstances, most Athenians refrained from befriending the occupying forces and foraged for food as best they could. Litsa showed no such inhibitions, and, capitalizing largely on the popularity of Maria's singing in military circles, she began what became a long-term romantic relationship with an Italian officer. Her behavior was motivated, in part, by the desire to obtain food, but it also reflected her fondness for male company and her need for affirmation. A young male lodger living in Callas's apartment on Patission Street recalls that Litsa "spoiled me and continued to do so whenever I went back" to visit with his aunt, who lived in the building. Then forty-six years old, Litsa, was typically heavily made up, smoking, talking loudly, and telling jokes. "Come here," she said to me one day. "Everyone in this house makes fun of me. Tell me who do you think is the best-looking of the three of us?"[18] The young man's affirmation that she surpassed in appearance both Jackie and Marie earned him Litsa's admiration from that point forward.

In addition to her own flirtatious relationships, Litsa also insisted that Maria go out with Italian and German soldiers in exchange for food. This was a great source of humiliation for Maria, so much so that several years later she confided to Giulietta Simionato that, during the Occupation, her mother forced her essentially into prostitution. Although Maria succeeded in getting food from members of the military, she insisted that she did so without granting any sexual favors. Nonetheless, her willingness to sing at events organized by the Italians and Germans raised eyebrows among her colleagues at the Conservatory and at the National Opera. In 1944, when she was offered the lead role in *Fidelio*, Callas said that one of her colleagues called her a "wh--- and said that I ----ed Italians and Germans, and that was why I had the highest salary in the company."[19] She was also called a dirty slut. The mantra of a whore who had sexual relations with Italians and Germans was subsequently picked up more widely by Callas's colleagues.

In truth, neither Litsa nor Maria could ever be branded as collaborators. In fact, they and Jackie risked their lives by sheltering two English airmen shot down over Greece. The day after the two men left, the Patission Street apartment was raided by Italian soldiers looking for the fugitives. The soldiers would have undoubtedly discovered incriminating evidence if it was not for Maria's quick presence of mind: She distracted them by quickly singing excerpts from *Tosca*. Nevertheless, neither Litsa nor Maria ever realized the ill-will that their behavior generated among their Greek compatriots. Litsa's obliviousness to this concern is underscored by her decision to include a picture of her occupying Italian lover as well as one of Maria's German admirers in her 1960 memoir. In the photos, the men look undoubtedly handsome in their uniforms. Such photos, however, would surely give pause to

American readers of Litsa's book, many of whom lost family members fighting the Axis forces.

Maria's Weight Gain and Traditional Gender Ideology

The war years coincided with Maria's weight gain, placing her in stark contrast to operatic colleagues who were reduced to skin and bones during this period of severe societal starvation. There are many puzzling aspects to Callas's weight problems and her general physical appearance during the Greek years. The most obvious is the question of what caused her rapid and expansive weight gain. The suggested factors include her tense relationship with her mother and sister, her loss of contact with her much beloved father, and hormonal changes. One also cannot exclude the simple possibility of gluttony, especially since Maria had a particular fondness for calorie-rich food including eggs and soft cheese, stewed meat and potatoes, and macaroni drizzled with her mother's special tomato sauce. But Callas also began menstruating at age ten, an unusually early onset for the 1930s. Until recently, early menarche was thought to cause psychological problems, the result of having to negotiate what many experience as embarrassing bodily changes ahead of their peers. New findings reverse this causality by suggesting that early menstruation can be precipitated by childhood stress. In other words, any adjustment issues associated with early menarche may reflect antecedent psychological problems rather than being the consequence of subsequent discomfort with bodily changes. This hypothesis is particularly interesting in Callas's case for two reasons. First, it directs attention to the potentially negative impact on Maria's well-being of living in a conflict-ridden and unsupportive family. Second, because early menarche has, in turn, been associated with a subsequent propensity toward obesity, this may explain why Maria was the only member of her family to experience weight problems in adolescence and adulthood.

Irrespective of the reasons for her weight gain, the more psychologically intriguing question is why did Callas, who worked so hard at perfecting her artistry, choose to neglect her physical appearance, making so little effort to present herself in the most favorable light physically? That she failed to do so is vividly demonstrated in de Hidalgo's description of Callas's first audition with her, quoted earlier, in which she noted her untidiness and hefty gait. Even if little could be done about Maria's need to wear thick glasses, there was plenty that she, or her mother, could have done about how she dressed and presented herself in general.

It is easy to attribute Maria's indifference to her appearance to her young age and inexperience. She was a mere teenager after all, much younger than the other female singers at the National Opera. Family role status and age differences notwithstanding, Litsa saw Maria (and Jackie) as her competitors. She compared her physical appearance to that of both daughters and had no hesitation in competing with Maria for the attention of a young Italian solider whom Maria had befriended. And, while pushing Maria to fraternize with the military in order to secure scarce food, she nonetheless insisted on dressing her in shabby clothes, owing to her fear that her singing career would be derailed in the event of a marriage proposal. There may also have been a defensive aspect to Callas's behavior, reflecting a desire to ignore aspects of her persona that seemed beyond control. According to her sister Jackie, while in Athens, Maria plaintively asked, "mother why have you given me such big ears that stick out, such a big nose and these awful, fat legs!"[20] Yet it remains surprising that Litsa, though she controlled many aspects of Callas's life in Athens, failed to recognize the importance of self-presentation for an aspiring diva. What about advice from Jackie, a young woman of impeccable taste and appearance? It is hard to pinpoint from existing sources the exact nature of family dynamics in the Callas household, particularly the negative undercurrents. Yet there is merit to Maria's retrospective claim that her mother and sister treated her like Cinderella during their time in Greece—in other words, with derision and contempt.

Jackie's memoir leaves no doubt that she, too, used the vast disparity between their physical appearance and social poise as a tool against her professionally successful sister. Discussing their time in Greece, Jackie recollects walking with Maria along an Athenian boulevard and hearing them called Oliver and Hardy by a street beggar. She further recounts an imprinted memory of Maria "bent double, reaching for handfuls of figs or nuts, her fat backside filling the doorframe."[21] The feeling of contempt, if not gleeful revulsion, contained in these memories is quite transparent. On another occasion, Jackie recalls, with some "regret" how, at a party, she deliberately flirted with a boy that Maria was interested in. The message in Jackie's behavior seems clear: Maria might have a better voice than her sister and not carry the stigma of being a mistress, but she is no woman when it comes to feminine charms. Both mother and sister appear to have had a vested interest, more or less consciously, in undermining Maria's confidence in her appearance and thus contributing to her feelings of shame and humiliation. In turn, Maria's envy of her sister and generally belligerent demeanor at home were not particularly conducive to receiving care and attentiveness from either of them. As in any family, each member tries to maintain and enhance her self-esteem, and, especially if there are negative dynamics, such esteem-building efforts are frequently at the cost of others.

Yet another related puzzle is why Maria let her self-image as a woman be defined by her mother and sister. Maria's emphasis on the importance of physical attractiveness and traditional gender roles is seen in exchanges Jackie recounts between her and Marina, a lodger at the Patission Street house and Callas confidant. According to Jackie, Maria barraged Marina with questions about how to be more attractive, about what accounted for her sister's popularity. Maria insisted on getting married and having a family. In response to Marina's reminder that she had a wonderful voice, Maria allegedly responded angrily, "What is a voice? I'm a woman, that's what matters." This exchange illustrates Callas's ambivalence regarding gender roles that would resurface later in her life. Callas reaffirmed these teenage sentiments in an interview conducted during the last year of her life. "Where did I fail?" she asks. "Why, I failed to fulfill myself as a woman, because what I always wanted, even more than success, was to be a mother and have lots of children. If I could start out all over again," she insisted, "I would have at least six children, four boys and two girls. We Greeks put our family life before everything else."[22] Was Callas really ready to sacrifice her career for marriage, family, and fulfillment in a traditional feminine role? The answer is a definite no.

Callas had several marriage proposals while in Athens, including one from a rich industrialist. She rebuffed all of them, knowing that marriage would interfere with her operatic career. How are we, then, to interpret her statements? Were they made only in jest? Their true significance lies in Callas's acceptance, on some level, of her family's traditional social values, particularly the notion that a woman's primary role is as wife and mother. Jackie never married her long-term lover, and this remained a source of deep regret, both for her and her mother. Isolated from interactions with others, Callas's attitudes toward what makes for a fulfilling and successful life were inevitably shaped by her family relations. And here the message was a confusing one, with Litsa, on the one hand, extolling the virtues of operatic success, but, in her own day-to-day behavior, emphasizing the importance of being attractive to men as a determinant of self-worth. Callas thus exited adolescence without a coherent sense of identity. On the one hand, she identified with her operatic career, but this choice was in tension with her (and her family's) traditional view of what it meant to be a woman in the 1940s. This was not an inevitable tension. Many other operatic singers prior to Callas did not experience such a conflict. In their cases, however, the operatic career tended to reflect either their own choice (e.g., Melba, Garden, Ponselle) or, alternatively, a continuation of a family tradition in which such choices were normalized (e.g., Malibran, Patti). Callas's role confusion was to have a particularly negative effect later on in life, but it did not prevent her from experiencing positive aspects of adolescence, including romance and generosity of spirit.

Positive Aspects of Life in Athens

So far, I have emphasized how Callas's experiences in Athens consolidated her narcissism and increased her personal vulnerability while at the same time enhancing her artistic stature and confidence. It is undoubtedly the case that young Maria was exposed to many negative events during her time in Greece, yet she also had a swath of positive experiences and interactions. In fact, despite her projected arrogance and disdain, she was quite capable of considerable generosity when feeling good about herself and not threatened. In one such instance, Callas not only shared a large amount of food with members of the National Opera (given to her by Italians following a concert performance), but she also carried some of the provisions on foot to distribute them among her colleagues.

Some of Callas's most joyous experiences during the war years involved her relations with men. She enjoyed flirting with men, many of whom found her not only personally magnetic but also physically attractive. Her companions included a well-established baritone at the opera, a dentist, an industrialist, and, shortly after the end of the war, a British office and the son of a lord. The depth of these relations remains uncertain, with Litsa claiming that Maria was still a virgin when she met Meneghini in 1947, even as some other evidence suggests otherwise. What is important here, however, is that the adolescent Callas was quite capable of sustaining interpersonal relations that were characterized by playfulness and warmth, qualities lacking in her family and professional life. Maria's popularity puts in perspective some of Jackie's negative comments about her physical appearance. Nonetheless, they provide valuable insight into the home atmosphere surrounding Callas's years in Athens.

Perhaps the most illuminative was Callas's relationship with Takis Sigaras, the clever, well-mannered, and popular son of a wealthy industrialist. This is a relationship that would foreshadow Maria's life-long psychological search for personal support and growth through close relationships with men. During 1943–1944, Maria and Takis met almost daily, spending time in restaurants and bars or going to the beach where, on one occasion, Maria entertained her partner by singing an operatic aria as their car slowly sunk into the sand. Takis protected Maria from his many women acquaintances who treated her with condescension. He never offered her money or jewelry but, on one occasion, gave her a fancy two-piece bathing suit only for it to be appropriated by Jackie who had it altered to suit her own measurements. Takis acknowledged Callas's plumpness, but he felt that her personality well compensated for it. In particular, he was impressed by the impact of her personality and joie de vivre that, in his eyes, trumped Jackie's beauty and attractiveness. Although the two never became lovers, evidence suggests that Maria and Takis were in love and that, after the death of his father, Takis proposed marriage. The offer was refused by Callas, who correctly perceived that marriage would have undermined her operatic career. According to one witness, Callas responded to Takis' proposal by saying "I don't belong here . . . I am cut out for greater things."[23]

In summary, at the end of her Athenian interlude, Callas consolidated healthy aspects of her personality that would serve her well in the future. She was ambitious, driven, determined, hardworking, and conscientious. She was receptive to feedback from mentors and strove relentlessly to develop her artistic talent and skills. At the same time, her dominant operatic persona reflected a grandiose self, a precursor to the awe and fear-inspiring *la Callas* of the early La Scala years. This persona, characterized by an inflated sense of self-importance, perfectionism, contempt for others, and rage in response to perceived slight or psychological injury, reflected Callas's identification with her mother, who failed to adequately mirror her early emotional needs and who subsequently fueled her grandiosity after the discovery of her singing talent. In adulthood, Callas's grandiose self would be nourished by the adulation of her adoring audiences and fans. The vulnerable self, however, became split apart from its grandiose counterpart; it housed Maria's feelings of being used for her talent, of being celebrated without actually being appreciated or admired for who she really was as a person. This included her sense of physical ugliness and of being unlovable as a woman. Callas's narcissistically bifurcated grandiose and vulnerable selves hid a true yearning for self-actualization through relationships where her true self would be acknowledged and where she would gain confidence by merging with an idealized—perceived as all-powerful—other. Because of early family dynamics, Maria would seek such a relationship primarily in the arms of older men who, like her father, offered her the prospect of love uncontaminated by a concern that they were using her for their own personal gratification.

Notes

1. Miller, *The drama of the gifted child*.
2. I am in debt for many of the facts concerning Callas's life in Athens to Petsalis-Diomidis's detailed and well-researched book, *The unknown Callas*.
3. Born in Spain, de Hidalgo forged a successful career as a coloratura soprano specializing in such *bel canto* roles as Rosina in Rossini's *Il Barbiere di Siviglia* and the eponymous heroine of Donizetti's *Lucia di Lammermoor*. Although not a star of first magnitude, de Hidalgo performed at the Met in New York and La Scala in Milan opposite celebrated singers Enrico Caruso (1895–1920), Beniamino Gigli (1890–1957), and Feodor Chaliapin (1905–1992). Given her Spanish ancestry, de Hidalgo traced her musical heritage to such influential exponents of *bel canto* as the singer and music teacher Manuel Garcia (1775–1832) and his two famous soprano daughters: Maria Malibran (1808–1836) and Pauline Viardot (1821–1910). The latter's career extended well into the second half of the nineteenth century.
4. De Hidalgo as quoted in Tosi, B. (Ed.). *The Young Maria Callas,* Toronto, CA: Guernica, p. 138.
5. Petsalis-Diomidis, *The unknown Callas*, p. 373.
6. All quotes in this and the preceding paragraph come from Petsalis-Diomidis, *The unknown Callas*, pp. 89, 375, 490, and 489.
7. Heatherington, J. (1995). *Melba: A biography*. Melbourne: Melbourne University Press, p. 82.
8. Cone, J. F. (1993). *Adelina Patti: Queen of hearts*. Portland, OR: Amadeus Press, p. 60.
9. Petsalis-Diomidis, *The unknown Callas*, p. 180.
10. Ibid., p. 311.
11. The preceding two quotes come from Petsalis-Diomidis, *The unknown Callas,* pp. 94 and 419.
12. Proust, M. (2003). *In Search of Lost Time*. New York: The Modern Library, *vol. 4*, p. 609–610

13. Petsalis-Diomidis, *The unknown Callas*, p. 314.

14. Ibid., p. 221–222.

15. Tolstoy, L. (1979). *Anna Karenin*. New York: Penguin, p. 404.

16. Compared to Hollywood and the film industry in general, the opera world has always been much more tolerant of imperfections in bodily appearance. This was particularly true before the advent of video recordings that emphasized close-up shots of the singers. Rosa Ponselle, for example, who was feted for her beauty as an opera singer, had to be fitted nonetheless with a prosthetic nose when she tried to embark on a film career.

17. Petsalis-Diomidis, *The unknown Callas,* p. 268.

18. Ibid., p. 227.

19. Ibid., p. 411.

20. Stancioff, N. (1987). *Maria Callas remembered: An intimate portrait of the private Callas*. Cambridge, MA: Da Capo Press, p. 40.

21. Callas, *Sisters*, p. 79.

22. All three quotes come from Jackie Kalogeropoulou [Callas] discussion with members of the Maria Callas International Club, London, October 8, 1991.

23. Petsalis-Diomidis, *The unknown Callas*, p. 354.

6 | A MARRIAGE OF MUTUAL CONVENIENCE

On June 30, 1947, Maria Callas arrived in Verona, Italy, contracted to sing at the Arena, newly reopened after the end
of World War II, in the title role in Ponchielli's *La Gioconda*.
Verona's summer opera festival was renowned for staging large-
scale productions in an open-air Roman amphitheater dating back
to the first century and capable of seating an audience of 15,000.
Reflecting its international stature, the opening season included
the soprano Renata Tebaldi, a rising operatic star, and the highly
esteemed conductor Tulio Serafin. Both would play an important
role in Callas's life; Tebaldi as a rival to be vanquished and Serafin
as a mentor who would help to launch her operatic career.

Upon leaving Athens in 1945, Callas spent two years in
New York City living with her father. The move back to the States
was not a success. She auditioned for the Metropolitan Opera
with the outcome uncertain. According to Callas, she was offered
the title roles in Puccini's *Madama Butterfly* and Beethoven's
Fidelio but rejected both. She declined the role in *Fidelio* because
it was to be sung in English rather than the original German. The
role of *Madama Butterfly* did not appeal because, as a "fatty," she
considered herself ill-suited to playing the title role of a diminu-
tive adolescent geisha. Callas's account is contradicted by evidence
from the Met's archives suggesting that, while judged to have a

Prima Donna. Paul Wink, Oxford University Press (2021). © Oxford University Press.
DOI: 10.1093/oso/9780190857738.003.0006

good voice, she was encouraged to continue working on it in lieu of a contract. Her interview with Gaetano Merola, the founder of the San Francisco Opera, was also a fiasco. Merola's assurance that he would hire her after she made a career in Italy met with a curt retort from an angry and dejected Maria: "when I've made my career in Italy, I'm certain that I will no longer have any need of you."[1] On top of her professional setbacks, Callas was further distraught by her father's public relationship with Alexandra Papajohn, the same woman who several years earlier had provoked Maria's ire by asking Litsa for a needle and thread to sew the hem of her skirt.

While in New York, Callas struck a friendship with Eddie Bagarozy and his wife Louise Caselotti, a relationship which occurred at an opportune time for young Maria. Bagarozy, a lawyer with a life-long interest in opera, was mustering a troupe of Italian singers to stage a performance of Puccini's *Turandot* in Chicago, and he designated Callas to sing the title role of the icy princess. His wife Louise Caselotti, a mezzo-soprano and voice teacher who made her career in Hollywood musicals, became Maria's friend and would accompany her on her first trip to Italy. Although Bagarozy's venture collapsed due to a lack of funds, Maria managed to network with other singers in the failed project and received a contract to sing in Verona. This proved to be a lucky break as Callas's chances of launching her career in America looked bleak. The terms of the Verona contract were not generous, however: Callas was paid the equivalent of $80 (approximately $1,000 in today's dollars) for each of the four scheduled performances, and she had to pay her own travel expenses. Maria was further disadvantaged by having had her luggage stolen at the port of Naples, resulting in her arrival in Verona with little money and no spare clothes.

On the first day in Verona, Callas was introduced over dinner to Battista Meneghini (1896–1981), an affluent local industrialist who owned several brick factories. Although not musically gifted, Meneghini, a bachelor and a local "Romeo," mixed in Veronese operatic circles because of his love of opera and romantic interests in female performers. Meneghini recalls finding Callas's "plump face, sweet features, and commanding presence" immediately attractive, although he was shocked by her disfigured ankles swollen to the size of calves. Callas felt warm and secure in Meneghini's presence. "I knew he was it five minutes after I first met him,"[2] Maria claimed. Despite the immediate attraction, Maria hesitated about initiating their relationship due to shame over not having more than one blouse to wear. She did not want Battista to think that he could take advantage of her because of his money. Nonetheless, within a few weeks, following trips in Meneghini's Alfa Romeo to Venice and Brescia, the two became a couple. They did not seem well matched, with the short Battista overshadowed by the tall Maria who, at age twenty-three, was twenty-seven years his junior. Nonetheless, throughout the twelve years they spent together, both Callas and Meneghini maintained they had fallen in love at first sight.

Subsequently published materials paint a somewhat different picture of the courtship. During her first months in Verona, Callas continued her correspondence with Eddy Bagarozy. The letters indicate that Maria was torn between her feelings for Battista and Eddy, who appears to have in fact been her lover, based on their correspondence. The infatuation with Maria waned for Meneghini after she failed to obtain new contracts following her debut at the Arena, which met with positive but not overwhelming reviews. Yet the relationship strengthened toward the end of 1947, despite initial hesitancies, after Maria obtained a contract from Venice's La Fenice to sing the title role in Wagner's *Tristan und Isolde*. From then on, Maria and Titta, as Battista was known among his close friends, developed a strong bond. The couple did not marry until 1949, partly due to the hostility of Meneghini's family—his mother and his brothers felt that Maria was a Greek gold digger— and partly because of Titta's own hesitancy. Their marriage proved to be good and devoid of conflict although lacking in true passion.

There is no doubt that Maria felt deeply grateful to Battista for his early help and support in launching her career. Shortly after meeting her, and even before hearing her first performance of *La Gioconda,* Titta offered Callas financial support for a six-month trial period. The money was designed to give Maria time to launch her career, and it came at a critical juncture; it certainly would have been hard for the cash-strapped Callas to stay in Italy other-wise. Having faced financial hardship throughout her childhood and adolescence, she appreciated Battista's willingness to buy her clothes and trinkets, but she never lost her frugal streak. Even at the height of her career, in possession of fabulous jewelry and high fashion, one of Callas's favorite pastimes was to browse and shop at Rinascendi, the Italian equivalent of Macy's. While Maria and Battista's relationship changed over the years, Callas's sense of gratitude remained strong until the couple's separation. There is also little doubt that Callas was deeply infatuated and in love with Meneghini, at least at the beginning of their relationship, once initial hesitancies were brushed aside.

The Nature of Love

Love is blind. The sentiment conveyed in this aphorism refers to two distinct aspects of the emotion. First, mate selection and mutual attraction are typically not governed by reason alone but by irrational impulses, an intuition captured when we say there is positive chemistry between two people. In one of his early novels, Johann Goethe uses the chemical term *elective affinities* to draw an analogy between the blind forces driving the bonding of molecules and the mystery and unpredictability of human love. After all, sex and mating are as close as we get to the biological and evolutionary underpinnings of our personhood. The proverb's second meaning reflects a more psychological aspect of love. It refers to the fact that, in its initial stages, love has frequently less to do with the actual characteristics of the beloved than with the wishes, dreams, and desires that the lover projects onto the beloved (of course, some congruence between the actual and the projected is required to maintain the illusion). To put it more extremely, when we fall in love we tend to do so largely with ourselves or with our own image of the other. This aspect of love accounts for why, once the initial bloom wears off, romantic partners face a new reality as they begin to perceive each other in more realistic ways. This "awakening" almost always results in anxiety over the need to reconcile the positive and negative emotions felt toward one's partner, and, inevitably, some disenchantment occurs. Callas's mother, Litsa, provides a good example of this phenomenon. As we saw in Chapter 3, she fell madly in love with George, whom she married against her father's wishes, only to find out six months later that her husband was a very different person than she had imagined. Similarly, Maria felt strongly drawn to Meneghini from the start, attracted by a sense of comfort and security in his presence. Their relationship offered her a sense of acceptance and admiration that she yearned for while growing up in New York and Athens, or—at least—this reflects Callas's feelings about the marriage before her voice deteriorated.

Personal projections may not be consistent with the actual characteristics of the individual being loved but, to adapt Freud's famous dictum, love offers a royal road to understanding the lover's own internal working model of relationships and intimacy. Analyzing the attitudes and behavior of a person in love sheds light on their positive expectations, but it also reveals fears and anxieties over abandonment. From a developmental perspective, love provides a window into the early patterns of attachment between the person as a child and their primary caregivers owing to the fact that early childhood experiences provide a blueprint for adult intimacy. This was the case for Callas, whose attachment to both Battista Meneghini and Aristotle Onassis provided her with an antidote to early childhood insecurities. These romances tantalized with the promise of personal growth.

Patterns of Attachment

John Bowlby, a British psychiatrist who studied children separated from their parents during the Nazi bombing of English cities, was the first to highlight the importance of early attachment for subsequent functioning. Bowlby documented the negative emotional impact of ruptures in attachment after observing the surprising difficulties mother and child encountered in reestablishing their bond following reunion. Mary Ainsworth, an American-Canadian developmental psychologist, investigated Bowlby's theories more formally using a laboratory procedure called the Strange Situation. In this procedure, young children and their mothers were brought into a laboratory; after a short time of joint play, the mother exited the room, leaving the child alone with one of the researchers. As expected, children reacted differently both to separation from their mother and the subsequent reunion. After showing initial concern, children who were securely attached with their parent resumed playing in the presence of the researcher. Upon the mother's return, these children acknowledged her presence and proudly shared their accomplishments. Ainsworth elicited two different patterns of less secure attachment. Whereas some children became highly agitated when left alone and found it hard to be comforted when rejoined by their mother (fearful attachment), others tended to ignore both being left alone and then being reunited with the mother (dismissive or avoidant attachment).

Since Ainsworth's era, attachment theory has been extended to investigating relational patterns not only among children but also among adults, generating a wealth of new research. Secure infants have been found to grow up into adults who are more confident, socially skilled, and open in expressing their feelings. Understandably, the Strange Situation, while highly appropriate for research with children, is not easily adapted for adults; it is difficult to credibly engineer a separation between grown-up individuals. Consequently, studies of adult attachment largely use self-report questionnaires, a procedure with its own methodological problems. However, in trying to understand Callas's attachment pattern and her internal model of relationships, we face no such obstacles: Maria's career required frequent trips away from Battista, particularly in the early stages of their relationship, before he became her full-time manager, and these separations provide a naturalistic proxy for the Strange Situation. Serendipitously, many of Maria's letters written to her husband during their time spent apart are reproduced in his memoir *My Wife Maria Callas*, published after her death.

Maria and Battista's first separation occurred in December 1947, exactly four months after their initial meeting. Callas was spending a week in Rome preparing for her role of Isolde, under Tulio Serafin's direction, to be sung in Venice at the Teatro la Fenice. The letters written to Battista suggest a woman deeply in love and visibly distraught by the separation. "Last evening was the first time that I have eaten alone since we met. I cannot tell you how unhappy I was," Maria writes in her first letter. "Since I left you I've only managed to eat green salads and eggs. I just don't have appetite. We've only been apart a couple of days and I'm miserable," she confesses, only to ask, "what will happen tomorrow and the next day?"[3] Maria would write ten more letters over an interval of six days conveying similar feelings. "Don't leave me here. I'm very alone," she writes in one of the letters. In another, she writes, "Dear, this is the third letter I'm writing to you today. I must be crazy, you're saying." And in another, "Now, my love, how shall I make the return trip? Will you arrange it for me? . . . I hope you're not displeased to see me so soon."[4] The intensity of Callas's distress over her separation from Meneghini is remarkable. The dependence she conveys at such an early stage in their relationship is particularly striking, and it is all the more noteworthy given that she was accompanied to Rome by Meneghini's sister Pia, a fact not mentioned in her letters. A second noteworthy separation between Callas and Meneghini occurred just a year later, in December 1948, when she was hospitalized for an appendectomy. Maria suffered great loneliness and found the ten-day hospital stay difficult, according to Meneghini. She pleaded with Battista to stay with her, not wanting to be surrounded by strangers, including the nurses. He spent the nights sleeping in her room on a fold-out bed. The couple was not yet married at the time.

What are we to make of Callas's need for closeness and her lack of tolerance for being left alone? Given that her adolescence in Athens and her early adult years in New York were spent trying to distance herself from her domineering and overpowering mother, one might have thought she would appreciate some time on her own. Yet, soon after she first arrived in Verona, she quickly became dependent on Meneghini, though she was accompanied by Louise Casoletti (Bagarozy's wife), who likely offered practical and emotional support. Maria found it impossible to function effectively without a secure base provided by the affirming presence of the other.

Maria decided almost instantly that not only would she engage in a romantic relationship with Battista—she would also completely surrender to him the responsibility for launching her career. It was he who arranged her singing lessons, and it was he who approached various impresarios trying to secure her a singing contract. With Meneghini busy with all these arrangements, Callas appeared happy to stay in the background, exuding confidence in his ability to succeed on her behalf. When Louise Caselotti tried to give Maria some suggestions for improvement after the first performance of *La Gioconda* in Verona, Callas declared she would do as she pleased. She expressed confidence in Battista's ability to make her an international superstar, telling Caselotti that he was going to arrange for her to perform in all the world's theaters. During those first months in Verona with Battista, Callas differs quite markedly from the fiercely independent Maria we saw in Athens. Perhaps the shift in Callas can be attributed to the newfound confidence derived from merging her identity with that of Meneghini who, in her eyes, seemed to exude omnipotent power. The secure emotional base he provided may have blunted her need for self-promotion and control and, unlike with her mother, elicited feelings of trust, care, and dependence. There are two plausible explanations for Callas's trusting reliance on Meneghini. Either Callas's actions indicate her total devotion to Battista, or, alternatively, her behavior is contrived play-acting aimed at securing the affections of a wealthy benefactor who proved to have cold feet when it came to marriage.

One could argue that Maria was put in a particularly vulnerable position in having to negotiate the demands of establishing a career in a new environment with very limited financial resources. But Callas was not only a great actress on stage. She could also put on a performance in her daily life when it suited her. The persona Callas presented to the media following her abandonment by Onassis provides a vivid example: though totally heartbroken, she would routinely pretend that Aristo's marriage to Jackie Kennedy did not perturb her in the least. Callas's sister Jackie, who visited Maria in Verona in March 1949, provides support for the play-acting hypothesis.

We set off for his [Battista's] sister Pia's house far too early, so impatient was she [Maria] to see her man again. While we waited for him to arrive the two women talked together. I had noticed that on entering the house Mary had adopted a rather miserable expression, almost as if she were in pain, but when I'd started to ask her what the matter was she'd hissed at me to keep quiet. Now Pia enquired if she was feeling unwell and to my amazement Mary went into a long litany about how distressed she was because I, her sister, had come all this way and had found the two of them in bed although they were not married.[5]

Pia provides a somewhat different twist on Callas's effusive letters to Meneghini. She speculates that perhaps her brother forged the letters to demonstrate to the world, and maybe to himself, that Maria truly loved him during the time they lived together. She justifies the claim by arguing that Maria never put pen to paper, and, if she needed something, she would always call Battista. Although Pia's conjecture seems to be just that, what her and Jackie's accounts have in common is shared incredulity that the feisty Maria they knew so well was capable of such deep infatuation and dependence on Battista. Yet the claim that Callas manipulated her true feelings to trap Meneghini into marriage is doubtful because her love letters continued to exude passion even after several years of marriage. Moreover, her apparent devotion to Meneghini throughout their marriage is corroborated by a variety of sources.

A second explanation of Callas's early relationship with Meneghini is offered by attachment theory: Callas's behavior may be construed as a prototypic example of fearful or insecure attachment. Characterized by concern over abandonment and the resulting need for reassurance, insecure attachment entails the subjugation of those needs and desires that might threaten the relationship. Somewhat counterintuitively, longitudinal research on children at risk for psychopathology suggests that problems with sustaining independence in adulthood are particularly characteristic of children who suffered emotional deprivation in the early stages of their development. In other words, it is children who were emotionally deprived who are prone to be clinging and dependent later in life, not children who had an emotionally close relationship with their primary caregivers. Insufficient coping skills and a lack of self-worth, characteristics frequently associated with emotionally deprived children, may impede the ability to function independently. Such individuals are particularly vulnerable to the threat of abandonment. The speed and intensity of Callas's attachment to Meneghini and her fear of being alone is congruent with the early emotional deprivation she experienced while growing up in New York. Yet her "fearful attachment" behavior does not align with other aspects of her relationship with Battista; in fact, there is little evidence from her subsequent correspondence to support the view that fear of abandonment or insecurity about her self-worth were the main motives for her behavior. The fear driving Maria's attachment had deeper, narcissistic roots, reflecting her largely unconscious concern over disintegration rather than the more commonly experienced anxiety over the emotional consequences of being left alone. This attachment also illustrates her equally unconscious desire to heal her fractured self through an idealized relationship with an older man, a father substitute whom she uses to buttress her fragile self.

Maria and Battista married in April 1949, shortly after Jackie's visit. The ceremony was delayed because Battista needed a dispensation from the Catholic Church to marry Maria, who was Greek Orthodox. The Church's final approval was also delayed due to the machinations of Meneghini's brothers, who had long opposed the relationship. Battista continued to drag his feet, and the tension culminated when, the day before Maria's scheduled departure to sing in Buenos Aires, she calmly announced that she would only go as a married woman. Just a few hours before the ship departed from Genoa to South America, Maria became Maria Meneghini Callas at a ceremony attended by only four people: herself, Battista, and two witnesses. The newlyweds would then be apart for the next three months, from April to July 1949, their longest separation in the two years since they had known each other.

Maria "was crying like a child when she left Meneghini," recalled Nicola Rossi-Lemeni (1920–1991), the Italian bass who accompanied Callas to Buenos Aires. "It was perhaps the only moment when I saw Callas really moved, really sincere, really caring for somebody. She was desperate leaving Meneghini. He was not only her husband, he was her father, brother, the security she found after rather a difficult life that she had had as a child and a young woman."[6] Callas's emotional turmoil and the intensity of her feelings during the separation are evident in the letters she wrote to Battista from Buenos Aires.

April 24th: How aware I am of your absence, the absence of your thoughtful gestures, your caresses, the tiny bell with which you awake me in the morning. . . . *Remember that I am alive only when I am with you*, my husband.

May 2nd: I adore you, I honor you and I respect you, and I am so proud of my Battista! Even though I'm well known for my singing, most of all I have the man of my dreams!

May 14th: Dear, is it possible for my love to grow? It seemed to me that I had given you everything but I understand that your every word, your every gesture of tenderness increases the paradisiacal love I feel for you.

June 20th: *If I lost you,* or were deceived by you, *I would lose all my faith in life.* . . . I am so proud of being called Meneghini.[7]

The letters not only exude passion, but they are also written with great care and attention to detail. This is perhaps best exemplified by the varied ways in which Callas addresses Meneghini in the opening line of each letter: "Dear, Dear, Dear"; "My dear adored one"; "My dear beloved Titta"; "My dear Titta, my love"; "My great eternal love"; and "My adored and sublime love." Callas's letters indicate a strong emotional dependence on Meneghini and her concern regarding what might happen should the relationship end (i.e., "If I lost you, or were deceived by you, I would lose all my faith in life"), but there is little evidence of anxiety over the threat of abandonment. The dominant theme is Callas's pride in Meneghini, in the specialness of their relationship.

The pride that Callas appeared to derive from what she perceived as the extraordinary nature of their marriage is evident in several instances. "I adore you," she writes, "and am so proud of my Battista." In another letter she gushes, "You have made me the happiest, proudest most loved woman in the world." "We must be proud of having a love so pure so extraordinary, and rare" she reminds her husband. "I am so proud of being called Meneghini."[8] Rather than fear, Maria's letters convey the sense that their love is a special relationship between two equally worthy partners. On May 27, for example, she writes, "I'm not jealous because no woman would ever be able to love you, nor would she ever be able to give you the understanding I have given you, and continue to offer."[9] And on July 3, shortly before her departure back to Italy, she warns Battista: "You will find me perhaps a little fatter: I was feeling so poorly that I ate like a horse to get back on my feet. So, if you don't want to see me look like Caniglia [a reference to an Italian soprano from the 1930s and '40s], you must help me eat little and only grilled meat and raw vegetables. You'll be in trouble if you don't help me."[10] Though somewhat diffident about her weight gain, this last statement hardly reflects a vulnerable woman fearful of abandonment or concerned about being worthy of her partner's love.

If, as I argue, Maria's behavior does not fit the standard pattern of fearful attachment, how are we to account for her unusually strong need for closeness with Meneghini? There are two key phrases in the quoted letter excerpts: *"I am alive only when I am with you,"* and *"If I lost you, or were deceived by you, I would lose all my faith in life."* Her words are not meant merely to assuage an overtly felt anxiety over abandonment, lack of self-worth, or uncertainty about what to do if left alone; rather, they illustrate that the comfort and security Maria derives from her relationship with Battista is deeply felt. Callas's psychological merger with Meneghini provided a buffer against feelings of emptiness and disintegration, feelings that reflect the presence of a fragile, fragmented self in need of the other to maintain a sense of cohesion and vitality. It also provided her with meaning in life and restored hope undermined by past experiences with her mother and sister during the time spent in Athens. Her declaration that she is "alive" only when with Battista should be treated literally rather than metaphorically because narcissistic individuals frequently merge or fuse their identity with another person whom they treat as an extension of the self. In Kohut's terminology, Meneghini became for Callas a *self-object* or a source of cohesion and security. Absence of age-appropriate mirroring and idealization prevents narcissistic individuals from developing a mature self that is capable of meeting the demands of adulthood unaided. As noted in Chapter 3, this was true of Callas.

Mirroring and Idealization Revisited

The significance of relationships based on mirroring and idealization is central to my psychological analysis of Callas. Although such relationships are common, understanding their real significance is complicated by the fact that they occur primarily outside of conscious awareness. It is hard to acknowledge feeling real only when in the presence of the other or the use of someone else to buttress one's own self-esteem. Let me further illustrate these phenomena with vignettes drawn from two films. A good example of the use of the other as a narcissistically fused self-object is provided in *The Night of the Shooting Stars,* a film by the Taviani brothers set in World War II Italy. One of the film's scenes depicts a fifteen-year-old boy, dressed in a military uniform, taunting local villagers trying to escape from the fascists. As the boy hurls insults at the escapees, he keeps referring to his dad: "Right Dad, am I right, Dad?" The young man derives his strength, power, and venom from a merger with his idealized father, a merger that will cost both the son and dad their lives. Like the boy in *Night of the Shooting Star*, Callas derived strength from merger with predominantly older men, including Meneghini, Serafin, and, subsequently, Onassis.

A more extreme but psychologically powerful example is provided by the film adaptation of Tennessee William's play *Suddenly Last Summer*. The film centers on three characters: Violet Venable, a wealthy Southern dowager; her son Sebastian; and her niece Catherine Holly. Violet and Sebastian are locked in a symbiotic union, using each other to maintain their respective psychological equilibrium. In the words of Mrs. Venable "we were a famous couple; they said, 'Sebastian and Violet. Violet and Sebastian.' We were the center of attention." For Violet, nothing mattered other than "the special [idealized] love" between her and her son. The couple traveled together each summer for Sebastian to write his yearly poem, until suddenly, one last summer, Sebastian chose Catherine as his travelling companion rather than his mother. Mistaking his gesture in selecting her to accompany him on the annual trip for love, Catherine is horrified to realize that Sebastian needs her only as a replacement for his aging mother whom he used as bait to attract young male lovers. Catherine is nothing but a tool and a decoy. Neither Sebastian nor Violet survive being separated from each other (his death and Violet's ensuing madness are not surprising because of their fused identities). Violet points out the poignancy in the name "Venus flytrap," "a devouring organism aptly named for the goddess of love." In this instance, it is the goddess of narcissistic love that consumes the other in a vain attempt to satisfy a personal void. Although extreme, the relationships depicted in *Suddenly Last Summer* shed light on Callas who—like Sebastian—failed to survive the rupture of her psychologically fused relationship with Aristotle Onassis. In turn, Mrs. Venable's use of her son for personal gratification resonates with Litsa's treatment of Maria.

Battista's sister Pia provides a cross-reference to buttress my argument that Callas's intense attachment to Meneghini was driven largely by her narcissistic needs. Maria was "irascible, capricious and obstinate," according to Pia, the kind of woman who "wanted everything and immediately."[11] Maria's difficult character helped account for her brother's hesitancy in proposing marriage. She was "a woman who could cause lightning to strike from a clear sky," Pia recalled. "I can't remember how many times my brother would repeat, 'You have to be very careful how you behave around her. A mere trifle can turn the most idyllic situation into a disaster.'"[12] These assertions put Callas's effusive letters from Buenos Aires in a new light. Behind Maria's deep and sincere affection for Battista, so aptly captured in her correspondence, lurked a sense of entitlement and the quintessentially narcissistic assumption that he will behave in an expected way without allowance for deviation.

It is not easy to convincingly capture the self-serving nature of a relationship based on idealization. Indeed, the propensity to merge with one's partner and the tendency to hold them in high regard can be a perfectly healthy and natural manifestation of early love, and this is certainly true in Maria's relationship with Battista. The narcissistic aspects of Callas's relationship with Meneghini would become more evident as their relationship unfolded over time, as it evolved from one based on idealization to one of mirroring. Maria's narcissistic use of Battista for self-serving purposes is illustrated in Battista's account of the morning ritual they developed while living in Milan (1954–1959). Reading the excerpt from Meneghini's memoir, one cannot help but note his obliviousness to the real significance of her behavior:

Life between Maria and me was blissful in our Milan home. . . . Maria would not allow me to leave her alone. I always woke up early and I could go for the newspaper, but I was expected back by nine because, even before the maid brought her coffee, she wanted to see me. After her "good morning," she would ask: "How are you today? What should I wear? Do you have any plans for us to go somewhere?" I would run down the schedule for the day and she would select something suitable for the appointments. It was I who always helped her dress. I brushed her hair and even did her pedicures.[13]

Bruna, Callas's long-serving maid, sheds additional light on the significance of their ritualized mornings in a conversation with Jackie following Maria's death. Maria "really loved him," Bruna explained. "If she woke up late and he wasn't in bed beside her she'd go crazy, running around the house demanding to know where her Titta was. He'd come back and explain that he'd only gone to buy his paper, but it would take ages to calm her down again."[14] Bruna's description brilliantly illustrates the narcissistic use of another person. Here is Maria, after several years of marriage, expecting Battista to be present the moment she wakes up. No consideration is given to his wishes, and no allowance is made for his tardiness. Furthermore, even the slightest deviation from the ritual is met with rage, which is exactly what is meant when narcissistic individuals are described as treating the other as an extension of their self or as a psychologically fused self-object: They are literally treated as part of the self and thus subservient to the desires and needs of the (entitled) self. The fact that it took Callas ages to calm down when her expectation was violated is also significant. Her lack of capacity for self-soothing, or simply getting on with her morning, demonstrates the extent of her rage and the fragility of her psychological make-up. Rage is not only a manifestation of narcissistic entitlement or an imperial self; it also reflects fright associated with an underlying sense of insecurity and vulnerability.

Imperial Self

Callas's propensity to fits of rage was not limited to her interactions with Battista, either. Her very public outburst with a US Marshall who was serving her with a summons to appear at court in Chicago, exemplifies this tendency: "I will not be sued! I have the voice of an angel! No man can sue me!"[15] she shouted. Because the incident occurred on the premises of the Lyric Opera after a performance of *Madama Butterfly*, a photographer was present to capture Callas's face twisted with rage at the affront of being treated as a mere mortal subject to the rule of law. The photo made the pages of newspapers across the globe. It was Eddy Bagarozy, Maria's old friend, who filed the lawsuit demanding that Maria honor a contract she signed in 1947 nominating him as her agent. Although Bagarozy had never actually managed Callas's career, he now, six years later, demanded $300,000 in back payment. The case was ultimately settled out of court after Bagarozy threatened to make public the love letters Callas wrote to him from Verona.

Maria's sense of narcissistic entitlement and her lack of empathy is evident in other areas of her life beyond her relationship with Meneghini. As part of her contract to perform at the Met, Callas was reimbursed for a first-class airline ticket from Rome to New York, but Meneghini was not. Upon arrival in New York, a journalist noticed that while she travelled first class, Meneghini flew tourist. When told by Walter Legge, the legendary EMI producer responsible for most of Callas's studio recordings, that this was not the kind of publicity she needed before her first appearance at the Met, the irate Callas responded: "If those stinkers [Met officials] won't pay for him to travel first-class, I won't pay either. Anyways I always order a second portion of whatever I eat and drink, put it in a vomit-bag and send a stewardess to take it back to him."[16] In another instance, following Callas's 1959 recital in Amsterdam, Maria accidently dropped something while surrounded by rapturous fans. "While smiling round she rudely hissed at sixty-three-year-old Meneghini to bend down and retrieve it,"[17] according to Michael Scott, who attended the performance. What is striking about both incidents is not only Callas's imperial persona and disregard for Meneghini as a person, but also her obliviousness to, or, perhaps, disregard and disdain for, what others might think of her. She did not seem to be perturbed in the least by how Legge might interpret her rationalization of having Battista fly tourist while she enjoyed the luxury of first class, nor did she seem to care about the prospect of humiliating her husband in public.

A further illustration of Callas's egocentrism and imperial self is provided by her encounter with Pope Pius XII. In 1953, after Maria shed about fifty pounds, a newspaper advertisement for the Pantanella Company attributed her weight loss to the fact that she ate its pasta. The ad included a statement certifying the claim from Callas's personal doctor and a Meneghini family friend. Callas sued the Pantanella Company, demanding an immediate and clear retraction because she never ate pasta. She was infuriated by the advertisement and by her doctor's betrayal, but her case stalled in the courts. Pantanella's president was the Pope's nephew, who was well-connected politically, so it was in this context that the Meneghinis received an unexpected invitation to meet Pius XII. Although Maria prayed dutifully, believing God to be on her side, she remained Greek Orthodox after her marriage, hence she did not have the same feeling of awe and respect for the Pope as did Battista. On the day of the scheduled visit, Callas announced, to Battista's utter surprise, that she did not feel like going to see the Pope. Wearing black—the required color for women's attire at a papal audience in the 1950s—would only irritate and depress her on an already gray day. "We'll go some other time," she pronounced. Meneghini pointed out, in vain, that a papal audience was very different from an appointment with one's dentist or lawyer and that, for most people, it was an opportunity of a lifetime if they were to be so fortunate. His pleading failed to persuade the intransigent Maria.

Following a second invitation, the Meneghinis, including Battista's mother, did eventually attend a private audience with the

Pope. Callas was totally oblivious to the significance of the event to Battista, and especially to his mother, for whom the Pope represented God on earth. She promptly engaged in a heated argument with the pontiff. After conveying that he was extremely moved by Callas's performance of Kundry in Wagner's *Parsifal*, a performance at the Rome Opera that was broadcast on the radio, Pius XII expressed regret that the opera was sung in Italian and not the original German. "I do not agree at all," was Callas's bold challenge to papal infallibility. Battista intervened to prevent further escalation of the argument. He still recalled vividly an incident in Brazil when Maria, during an argument with an impresario, kneed him in the groin. Not surprisingly, following the visit, Maria expressed no intention to adhere to the pope's wish for a quick resolution of the Pantanella lawsuit. Although her behavior during the papal audience was insensitive to social convention and, more immediately, to Battista's and his mother's feelings, it also captures the vitality in Callas's personality that contributed in no small way to her operatic success. As reflected in her confrontation with Pope Pius XII, Callas showed no fear of anyone or anything, not unlike young Siegfried, to continue the Wagnerian theme. It is this fearlessness and spunk that allowed her, as we will see in the next chapter, to redraw the map of the operatic world.

Love Is Complex

Maria's self-serving use of Battista should not overshadow the positive aspects of their relationship. There is little doubt that, in the early stages of their liaison, Callas loved and idealized her much older, more experienced, and well-respected Veronese husband. To the not-yet-twenty-four-year-old Maria, raised in poverty and having had relatively few experiences with men, Meneghini, "the industrialist," must have appeared as a knight in shining armor. He was not only prepared to risk money on the off-chance that Callas would make it in the competitive world of opera, but he also plied her with compliments, bought her clothes, and took her on romantic car trips. There is something endearing indeed in the image of Battista waking her up with the ring of a little bell, feeding her sweets. Her hopes and fears regarding their relationship find expression in a letter she wrote from Rome during their first separation in 1947. "Sometimes you too are in love with Callas the artist, and lose sight of the person," Maria writes, a fear rooted in her family experiences as a child. "Your letter was very beautiful, so sweet, but I wanted to find more 'Battista and Maria' in it, and less 'Meneghini and Callas,'" she chides. "Let's see if I find my Battista in your other letters."[18] The letter, penned by a twenty-four -year-old woman to her fifty-one-year-old lover strikes one as unusually mature, insightful, and forthright. It expresses in the clearest possible terms Maria's yearning to be loved as a woman (Maria) and not just as a potential celebrity (Callas) or cash cow. The strength of Callas's infatuation with Meneghini resided in a fusion of her hope for psychological growth—of having her "true" self reflected back in the admiring gaze of her man—and her various dependency needs. Her wish, unfortunately, was not to be realized; after the break-up of their marriage, Callas became convinced that Meneghini was just as exploitative as was her mother. Thus, in Callas's eyes, her marital relationship ended up repeating her childhood trauma.

It would be unfair to construe Meneghini's initiation of his relationship with Callas as being purely mercenary. After all, no one could have predicted that the physically awkward singer with an unusual and somewhat disconcerting voice would become the superstar that she did when he first offered Maria financial support for six months. Meneghini was truly smitten by Maria's charisma, the same magnetism that enchanted Takis Sigaras in Athens, but this was not enough; the aging provincial brick manufacturer who had thrived on short-term flings with ballerinas and chorus girls was poorly equipped to fulfill Callas's need for an emotionally fulfilling and mutually enriching relationship. Furthermore, according to Pia Meneghini, her brother "did feel a genuine affection for her [Maria] and in a way considered himself her Pygmalion, her guardian angel, but was not in love with her."[19] While Meneghini undoubtedly felt affection for Callas throughout their marriage and was deeply wounded when she abandoned him, their relationship evolved into an overtly instrumental one, at least from his side, as reflected in a retrospective comment made in 1981.

As a singer, Maria was in my eyes a *valuable product*. Instead of selling bricks, as I had done successfully for years, I began to market a voice. The most important prerequisite was that the product be of a first-rate quality, and since Maria's voice was not only first-rate but unique in the world, I did not hesitate to demand the highest fee possible.[20]

As the comment suggests, both Battista and Maria ended up using each other; he for financial gain and she for support of a vulnerable self.

Maria's early infatuation with Meneghini gradually wore off, his once idealized image tarnished as Callas transformed into an international celebrity. In this new reality, the interpersonally gauche Battista, who displayed few intellectual or artistic interests and spoke only Italian (and with a thick Veronese accent to boot), must have struck Maria as a diminished choice for a partner. Mary Carter, a woman Callas befriended during her singing engagements in Dallas in the late 1950s, offers a sign of Maria's cooling affection. When Callas spoke of her husband, she gave the impression that though she respected Battista, she was not crazy about him. This attitude was reflected in her comment to Carter that, as Carter was aware, they had to "perform wifely duties" from time to time. Anita Pensotti, the Milanese journalist who interviewed Callas for the 1957 autobiographical article in *Oggi*, asked her why she married Meneghini. Known for her honesty when talking off the record, she answered, "Who would have known that I was to become Callas?"[21] Callas was terrified of widowhood, according to Pensotti, and erroneously presumed that she would outlive her much older husband. Accordingly, she had composed a list of possible replacements that, to Pensotti's surprise, included men who were already married and with children. The disjunction between Callas's outward moralism and private behavior would only deepen later in life.

Nonetheless, having grown up in a family fractured by parental conflict, Callas placed great emphasis on the sanctity of marriage. She never forgave her parents for separating and, at least in public, took a dim view of divorce and infidelity. According to Renzo Allegri, an Italian journalist who collaborated with Meneghini in writing his memoir, for Callas, her home was an impregnable fortress. Maria never considered the possibility of betraying Battista. Having experienced her parent's divorce, she emphasized the importance of the marriage vows. She broke off her relationship with Ingrid Bergman when the latter separated from the film director Roberto Rossellini.

During their years together, Maria made considerable effort to make their relationship live up to her middle-class, bourgeois values. She enjoyed cooking elaborate, though frequently inedible meals for Battista (after starting to diet in 1953, she restricted her own menu to steak, preferably raw, and salads). And she insisted that, befitting the man of the house, Battista be seated at the dinner table before her. She habitually left little love notes for him around the house and used to give him three flowers or three bunches of flowers, with a meaning that only the two of them knew about. When they moved into their own apartment in Verona, Maria spent countless hours decorating its rooms and interminably changing the placement of paintings on the walls. She paraded from one room to another with a toolbox containing a hammer, "playing house" because the tools were never actually used.

In his essay on the cult of Callas, Koestenbaum partly attributes Callas's popularity among gays to making the improbable and highly stylized world of opera—where characters sing rather than recite their woes—believable and vivid. He argues that "by importing truth into opera, an art of the false, she gave the gay fan a dissonance to match his own."[22] Callas's inversion of truth and falsehood in opera also applied to her everyday life, including her marriage, where the real became make-believe. Having grown up in a family rife with conflict, and yet full of determination to make her marriage work, Maria injected operatic unreality into her daily interactions. The love notes scattered throughout the house are a case in point. Maria's tendency to import make-believe into the reality of everyday life is perhaps best exemplified by the Rules of the House, which governed the behavior of servants in the Meneghini's Milan home. They required the staff, among others, to wash and iron their intimate garments, knock and ask permission between entering rooms, and address the master and mistress of the house with respect devoid of annoyance. All of this was to be accomplished without the nonsense of saying "Yes, sir," "Yes ma'am." These rules blend a stylized view of courtly behavior with a democratic insistence on informality in how the servants should address their masters.

Apart from the make-believe aspects to Maria and Battista's relationship, another characteristic that helped them stay together was Callas's low sexual desire during their marriage. As suggested by Stelios Galatopoulos, at the height of her operatic career Maria tended to channel her sexual energies into singing.

> Even though Callas did not admit it in so many words, it became clear to me as I got to know her better that her capacity of love for her art had been stronger than for human beings. When, as a young girl, she became aware of her talent she pursued its fulfillment with unmitigated devotion; it was her only weapon of self-preservation.... Her sexual impulses found an emotional outlet in her art.... She was content with what her rather elderly husband had to offer.[23]

In this regard, Callas differed from many other singers whose sexual exploits added to their diva status. Psychologists argue that the arousal of feelings of power, of having impact on others, whether during a performance on stage or addressing an audience from a lectern or a pulpit, increases a person's sexual appetite. It was purported that the soprano Luisa Tetrazzini, for example, would demand a man in her dressing room during the intermission between the opera's second and third acts so that she could have sex before singing the famous "Mad Scene" from Donizetti's *Lucia di Lammermoor.* This may be an extreme example of sexual arousal through music; nonetheless, many other female opera singers of that era were known to engage in multiple sexual relationships, showing a healthy sexual appetite unconstrained by traditional expectations of women's sexual behavior.

Callas's relative lack of erotic desire (things changed when Onassis appeared on the scene) might have made it easier for her to stay married and faithful to Meneghini, but it was her emotional neediness that ultimately held the marriage together. Maria derived both moral support and strength from the marriage, which allowed her to "proceed with her career and life regardless of the inevitable obstacles,"[24] according to Galatopoulos. During the time they lived together, Maria and Battista did not socialize much, spending most of their time alone in their apartment in Verona and subsequently in their house in Milan. Battista, who might have been an important figure in Verona, was regarded as parochial and unsophisticated by the Milanese cultural elite, and Maria felt shy and ill at ease in social situations. Their relative social isolation allowed Callas to devote all her energies to her highly demanding operatic career. "My best hours are in bed," Callas stated in a *Time* interview, "and my best work [studying opera scores] too, with my dog cuddling beside me and my husband asleep." The Meneghinis "had a life based on Spartan domestic economy, rigorous self-discipline and hard work," notes John Dizikes in *Opera in America*. "For decades, her [Callas's] ambition, willpower, and passion for self-improvement were focused on her art. Nothing interfered with it."[25] It might be tempting to argue that, in her relationship with Battista, Maria sacrificed erotic desire for the bounty provided by her singing career, not unlike Alberich in Wagner's Ring cycle. The truth is more prosaic: it reflects the fact that Callas's sexual appetite remained dormant until ignited by Onassis.

The Meneghinis formed an almost symbiotic unit. According to Battista, the two were so close together that Maria never went to bed without him, even if it meant waiting late into the night. This is yet another example of Meneghini's tendency to interpret psychologically problematic behavior as a sign of healthy mutuality. It was not simply choosing her clothing and grooming; Maria depended on Battista for scheduling daily activities and she also required his presence at her performances. In 1955, for example, Callas's famous Berlin performance in *Lucia di Lammermoor* was jeopardized because Meneghini's flight from Milan had been delayed due to bad weather. In another sign of dependence, Maria gave Battista total control over her finances and business arrangements. It was he who negotiated all of her singing engagements, contracts, and fees for her performances. Unlike other famous prima donnas of the past, such as Melba, Patti, or Garden, who were all shrewd businesswomen, Callas did not know or care about how much money she had. "What almost everything written about Miss Callas fails to catch," notes Rudolf Bing, the long-term General Manager of New York's Met Opera, "is the girlishness, the innocent dependence on others that was so strong a part of her personality when she didn't feel she had to be wary."[26] This insight applies to her equally as both a singer and as a marriage partner.

Twinship

In Milan, Callas's relationship with the young and glamorous socialite Giovanna Lomazzi revealed a girlish and playful side to her personality. They met in 1952, when Maria was twenty-nine and Giovanna, the daughter of a wine producer and opera buff, was twenty. Callas never wanted to be alone; she always needed someone to provide company, love, and admiration. The two became almost inseparable, with Giovanna driving Maria shopping and escorting her to restaurants. They were like sisters, according to Lomazzi, who accompanied Callas on her three trips to the United States, including the first one, where Meneghini flew tourist class while the two women enjoyed the comforts of first-class travel. Lomazzi interprets Callas's tendency to surround herself with young people as reflecting a desire to lead a normal life combined with a naïveté and lack of preparedness for the elegant lifestyle of Milan's high society. In this regard, Lomazzi compared Callas to Ava Gardner (1922–1900), who experienced similar difficulties following her abrupt transition from life in poverty to becoming a Hollywood mega-star. At Savini's, a chic Milanese restaurant near La Scala, Callas felt compelled to leave a tip nearly as large as the price of the meal, behavior which struck Lomazzi as gauche.[27]

From a psychological perspective, Callas's relationship with Lomazzi and other glamorous women is yet another manifestation of her inability to meet the demands of everyday life without the help of others. In the case of Lomazzi, the relationship entailed elements of idealization (i.e., the admiring gaze of a young woman infatuated with a famous opera star) and mirroring (i.e., the insecure opera stars' gratification from being seen in the company of a glamorous young woman), yet the unconflicted nature of their relationship, devoid of angry outburst, pretense, or posturing, highlights its *twinship* nature. As will be evident in her subsequent relationship with Nadia Stancioff, Maria and Giovanna drew strength and experienced joy and pleasure from the sheer mutuality of their interactions, a hallmark of strong friendships frequently found among teenagers. Callas's gratification from twinship reflects her deep-seated insecurities; it was in her relationships with younger women, especially, that Maria became playful, capable of lowering her guard only when she felt in a position of power. The uncomplicated mutuality of twinship may have also reminded her, at a visceral level, of the times she and her sister Jackie spent cuddled, consoling each other during the early days in New York City.

Although reflecting different psychological mechanisms, Callas's relationship with Meneghini and Lomazzi, as well as her subsequent liaison with Onassis, exemplify both healthy and less healthy aspects of her personality. In psychotherapy, client–therapist relationships based on mirroring, idealization, and twinship provide a stepping stone for personal growth. For Callas, however, none of these relationships resulted in lasting change that could buffer her against the adversities of the last decade of life. The difficulties in functioning independently and an inability to draw firm personal boundaries were to persist for the rest of her life.

Polarized Relationships

Maria's intransigence in dealing with her mother brings up another aspect of her relationships: Her tendency to view the world in dichotomized black or white terms. The last time Maria had any direct contact with her mother occurred in Mexico City in 1950, when Maria was twenty-six. She looked forward to Litsa's calming influence as she prepared for a demanding singing schedule while trying to adjust to Mexico City's high altitude. At the same time, she felt trepidation about her ability to negotiate a mature relationship with her mother. In letters to Meneghini penned from Mexico, Callas conveyed her conflicting emotions between wanting to help her mother and once again becoming the victim of her will. The letters also reflected an understandable desire to live alone with Battista without having their happiness compromised by her mother's presence. Not too long after their meeting in Mexico, the matter came to a head. Litsa, now divorced from George, announced she would come and live with Maria and Battista in Verona. Maria's refusal led to an angry exchange of words—and her infamous suggestion that her mother either go work or jump from a bridge. Throughout her life, Callas blamed their breakup on her mother's treatment, both during her childhood in New York and her adolescence in Athens, and, as we saw, Maria had many good reasons to bear resentment toward Litsa, whose insensitivity, authoritarian intrusiveness, and favoritism of Jackie demeaned Maria. The main reason for the breakup, however, as underscored by the preceding quotes from her letters to Meneghini, was Callas's inability to maintain a healthy sense of independence from her mother, a difficulty compounded by an inability to inject shades of gray into her relationships with others.

Maria and her mother had difficult emotional histories, and, given Litsa's domineering personality, it is not surprising that Callas found it hard to negotiate a mature adult relationship with her mother. Yet the extremity of Maria's ultimate solution is still striking. One could argue that it simply replicates Litsa's own break with her mother. Even so, one might expect that she could have found an alternative solution, a compromise that might involve allowing her mother to live with them for a time, yet not permanently, rather than severing all future contact. Callas's refusal even to give her mother money so that she could live in comfort displayed the depth of her emotional harshness. It also stoked the negative publicity attendant on her mother having to ask for handouts from others. Greek government officials even felt compelled to ship Litsa and Jackie off to America before Callas's arrival in Athens in 1960 for a series of concerts, a fact that conveys the intensity of the negative feelings involved but did little to soften Maria's public image.

Maria's tendency to construe relationships in black-and-white terms was evident also in her relationships with most of her operatic colleagues. Her first prolonged separation from Meneghini, during the 1949 tour of Latin America, sheds light not only on her emotional dependency but also on the black-or-white way in which she perceived the world at large. The early letters penned to Meneghini from Buenos Aires reflect the perception of a hostile and envious environment. "Not one of my colleagues came to see me when I was sick. They were all overjoyed because I wasn't singing. They're afraid, the poor things. They know they're overshadowed when they're on stage with me [letter dated June 8]. And, "a hostile wind is blowing! ... They [fellow singers] know I'll give them a run for their money. Well, they can say what they want. The important thing is for me to be in good health: then they will see. I enjoy making then uneasy" [letter dated June 12]. Callas appears to treat her fellow singers and colleagues as a largely faceless and undifferentiated group of individuals, each of whom is envious and fearful of her talent. This attitude leaves her with little choice but to contemplate retaliation meant to cut down her colleagues to size. "They've had a triumph and now they've become very grand. Especially [Del Monaco], who has been very unpleasant to me. ... If I ever have the opportunity to block him when something important comes along, I'll do it gladly, even though I'm not the type who derives pleasure from that sort of thing" [June 8].

To put Callas's evaluation of her abilities and talent in context, it is important to note that the colleagues disparaged in her letters to Meneghini, including Fedora Barbieri (1920–2003), Mario Del Monaco (1915–1982), Cesare Siepi (1923–2010), and Nicolai Rossi-Lemeni (1920–1991), constituted the crème de la crème of the post-war Italian operatic establishment. At the time of the 1949 South American tour, all of them were much better known than Callas, having already sung at such prominent opera houses as La Scala and London's Covent Garden, and all of them went on to have prolonged and illustrious careers. In another letter from Buenos Aires later than month, Callas gloats about having her revenge on her "poor colleagues."

June 17, 1949 [After first performance of Norma]
While I was still on stage, director Grassi-Diaz came up and embraced and kissed me, saying, "I was so overcome I had to

tell you: today I wept." . . . My poor colleagues! God, who is good and great, has allowed me to have my revenge. And this is certainly because I have never tried to harm anyone, and because I have worked so hard.[28]

It is Maria's perception that a just God protects her from the slings and arrows of the hostile world. Maria's God understands her innocence, appreciates her hard work, and is well aware that she had never meant anyone wrong. Clearly, in Callas's opinion, God is not perturbed by her desire for revenge since, for example, the wish to block the career of another singer such as Del Monaco is allegedly devoid of any pleasure for her.

Callas believes in the superiority of her talent over that of the other singers, even insinuating that the Buenos Aires audience showed greater appreciation for her singing than for that of Claudia Muzio (1889–1936). Given Muzio's legendary status among sopranos of the first half of the twentieth century, this is a bold statement indeed—especially coming from a twenty-five-year-old singer at the beginning of her career! Callas also derives comfort and solace from the knowledge that, once back in Italy, she is going to be embraced in the loving arms of her Battista. It is easy to see how Maria's tendency to dichotomize the world into a good self and bad others fueled her sense of dependence. Given her blameless self, she surely deserved protection from someone like Meneghini, a protection that was essential as a buffer against a hostile, envious, and threatening world.

Callas's adversarial relationships with other singers, with few exceptions including lifelong friendships with Giulietta Simionato and Tito Gobbi (1913–1984), are now legendary. The same Mario del Monaco whose career Callas threatened to block in Buenos Aires refused to sing with her after she allegedly kicked him in the shin so that she could take a solo bow following a performance of *Norma* at La Scala. Similarly, after he needed to physically restrain her from appearing on the stage to take a solo bow, the Bulgarian bass Boris Christoff (1914–1993) refused to sing with her again. Such behavior was frowned upon in Italian opera houses of the 1950s, where it was expected for all the lead singers to appear on the stage together. At the Met, Callas insisted on having the Italian tenor Enzo Sordello fired after he held a high note longer than she did. In another, much publicized incident, Callas was photographed at New York's Idlewild Airport refusing to shake Sordello's hand as he extended it to her in reconciliation. Perhaps the most noteworthy confrontation occurred between Callas and Renata Tebaldi, a highly acclaimed soprano who was queen of Milan's La Scala before being dethroned by Callas. In a famous quote, Callas compared herself to champagne and Tebaldi to cognac, only to change cognac to Coca-Cola after realizing that the original juxtaposition of the two beverages might not work in her favor. In another exchange, she accused Tebaldi of having no backbone—to which Tebaldi retorted that at least she had a heart.

According to the Italian-American soprano Lina Pagliughi, Callas's tendency to reward friendliness with sharpness meant that, while admired by many, she was loved by none. "She rewarded friendliness with sharpness, and so finished up imprisoned in her expensive Paris apartment. In one respect she was lucky not to experience old age, because she was also so sarcastic and bitter while at the height of fame," wrote Pagliughi. "What is life if one is not surrounded with human warmth?" she asked.[29]

It is true that Maria's rigidity and tendency to perceive others in dichotomous black-or-white terms had a negative effect on her ability to relate with people. After all, friendships require tolerance of imperfections in others, an ability that is based on the willingness to inject shades of gray or doubt into how one evaluates others' behavior. Pagliughi is correct in her claim that Callas's adversarial relationships with others condemned her to solitude and to a lack of warm relations, features that gained particular prominence at the end of her life. Her polarized and unforgiving view of the world had an even more devastating effect when applied by her in self-judgment. In considering this aspect of her personality, it is important, however, to place Callas's behavior in the context of her unprecedented rise to fame and her popularity that exceeded that of past operatic divas and those who followed.

Notes

1. Volf, T. (2016). *Maria by Callas: In her own words*. New York: Assouline, p. 32.
2. The two quotes this paragraph come from Meneghini, G. B. (1982). *My wife Maria Callas*. New York: Farrar Straus Giroux, p. 15 and Stassinopoulos, *Maria Callas*, p. 67.
3. Meneghini, *My wife Maria Callas*, pp. 46–47.
4. All quotes in this paragraph come from Meneghini, *My wife Maria Callas*, pp. 47–49.
5. Callas, *Sisters*, p. 123.
6. Scott, M. (1991). *Maria Meneghini Callas*. Boston, MA: Northeastern University Press, p. 48.

7. All quotes from Meneghini, *My wife Maria Callas*, pp. 83–99, with the exception of quote from May 14, which comes from Allegri, R. & R. (1997). *Callas by Callas: The secret writings of "la Maria."* New York: Universe, p. 68.

8. All quotes from Meneghini, *My wife Maria Callas*, pp. 83–99 and Allegri, *Callas by Callas*, pp. 56–59.

9. Meneghini, *My wife Maria Callas*, p. 94.

10. Allegri, *Callas by Callas*, p. 72.

11. Meneghini, P. Seven years with Maria. In Tosi (Ed.), *The young Maria Callas*, p. 108

12. Ibid., p. 122.

13. Meneghini, *My wife Maria Callas*, p. 215.

14. Callas, *Sisters*, p. 172.

15. Stasinopoulos, *Maria*, p. 148.

16. Scott, *Maria Meneghini Callas*, p. 181.

17. Ibid., p. 222.

18. Meneghini, *My wife Maria Callas*, p. 48.

19. Meneghini, P., Seven years with Maria In Tosi, *The young Maria* Callas, p. 108.

20. Meneghini, *My wife Maria Callas*, p. 273.

21. Pensotti, Maria Callas. In Tosi, *The young Maria Callas*, p. 96.

22. Koestenbaum, *The queen's throat*, p. 145.

23. Galatopoulos, *Maria Callas: Sacred monster*, p. 418.

24. Ibid., pp. 90–91.

25. Dizikes, J. (1995). *Opera in America: A cultural history*. New Haven: Yale University Press, p. 560.

26. Bing, R. (1972). *5000 nights at the opera*. New York: Doubleday and Company, p. 238.

27. Information contained in this paragraph is based on my interview with Giovanna Lomazzi, Milan, November 2015.

28. All quotes from letters dated June 1–20 come from Meneghini, *My wife Maria Callas*, pp. 95–98.

29. Rasponi, L. (1984). *The last prima donnas*. New York: Alfred A. Knopf, pp. 168–169.

7 | I GAVE YOU EVERYTHING

"With the appearance of Maria Callas, lovers of musical drama ceased to underrate Italian opera of the early nineteenth century," notes Rodolfo Celletti, a foremost Italian author and musicologist. Regarding Callas's legacy on the world of opera, he offered high praise, indeed: "spurious vocal traditions generated by more than fifty years of Verism were discarded; standard theatrical repertoire was given a healthy jolt; the concept of actress-singer changed radically; and a new attitude toward singing for female voices was accompanied by a new conception of virtuosity on the part of the public and press." In other words, according to Celletti, "Maria Callas pioneered a revolution"[1] that continues to resonate today. To understand this revolutionary impact, we need to consider the qualities of her voice, her acting skills, and psychological factors, including a single-minded focus on her career and the unprecedented ability to merge with operatic roles she performed on stage and with her audience.

The Voice

Fedele D'Amico, chair of the famous 1969 Callas Debate among six Italian music experts, cites a seventeenth-century French

Prima Donna. Paul Wink, Oxford University Press (2021). © Oxford University Press.
DOI: 10.1093/oso/9780190857738.003.0007

musicologist to argue that, from the beginnings of opera, voices have been divided into beautiful ones and good ones. Good voices, like that of Callas, do not wallow in their own beauty but express what a performance requires. In principle, there is nothing to prevent a beautiful voice from also being a "good one." In practice, however, it is difficult for a soprano endowed with an immaculate creamy voice not to be smitten by its beauty. *Bel canto* operas, with their sharp distinction between recitatives and arias and an emphasis on embellishment and ornamentation, tempt singers to focus on famous, much beloved showpieces to the detriment of anything else. Adelina Patti, a soprano with a voice like a nightingale, offers a perfect illustration of the temptation to forsake musical substance in favor of beautiful sound. "Unhappily, I was not present at the soiree during which Patti was heard at Rossini's for the first time," recalled French composer Camille Saint-Saens. "It is known that when she had performed the aria from *Il Barbiere*, he [Rossini] said to her, after many compliments: 'By whom is this aria that you just have let us hear?' I saw him a few days later: he still had not calmed down." Saint-Saens continued, "I know perfectly well," he told me, "that my arias must be embroidered; they were made for that. But not to leave a note of what I composed, even in the recitatives—really, that is too much."[2]

Another reason why beautiful voices work against emotional truth lies in the fact that opera singers are expected to combine vocal prowess with good acting. While it is hard to imagine an opera superstar whose acting overshadows her vocal qualities—Mary Garden provides perhaps a notable exception—the history of opera is replete with prima donnas whose vocal talent outstripped their acting. Nellie Melba, Renata Tebaldi, and, more recently, Joan Sutherland, are good examples of famous sopranos with beautiful voices whose ability to convey the emotional truth of their roles was curtailed by a stilted stage presence. Vocal weaknesses, however, can prompt a soprano to experiment and compensate through exceptional acting. D'Amico points out that "the limitations of the vocal mechanism have always constituted throughout musical history a powerful stimulus toward invention." And he maintains that had Callas "been born with an immaculate, velvety, perfect voice, she would have simply wallowed in it as if in a bathtub."[3]

Callas's rather dark, moody, and penetrating voice is very different from the light, agile, and lyric voices of coloratura sopranos such as Louisa Tetrazzini or Amelita Galli-Curci (1882–1995).[4] Yet it is these lighter voices that dominated *bel canto* roles during the first half of the twentieth century due to an evolution in singing practices. *Bel canto* was "never meant to be just beautiful singing," as Callas pointed out. "Above all, *bel canto* is an expression. A beautiful sound alone is not enough."[5] Her assessment reminds us that the operas of Bellini and Donizetti were composed at the height of the Romantic era, with its emphasis on strong emotions and passion. Beginning with the late 1840s, *bel canto*'s popularity was gradually overshadowed by the musical dramas of Verdi and Wagner and, subsequently, by the realism of Puccini's operas and verismo in general. Consequently, many *bel canto* staples fell out of favor, and those that remained in the repertoire, such as *Il Barbiere* or *Lucia*, became the domain of sopranos with lighter voices. As a result, the emphasis shifted from a focus on emotional truth to the beauty of the voice—a reflection of Victorian sensibilities emphasizing restraint and decorum. Callas's voice represents a singing tradition very different from the one that dominated the world of opera in the 1940s and '50s. No wonder, then, that many who became Callas devotees were initially disturbed upon hearing her voice for the first time; indeed, Callas herself was even disturbed when she first heard it.

Rossini, Donizetti, and Bellini composed their operas without distinguishing between various types of soprano voices. During Callas's time, for example, Bellini's *La Sonnambula* was the domain of a lighter coloratura soprano, and *Norma* was sung by a heavier dramatic one. Yet both operas were originally composed for the same singer, Giuditta Pasta. Both Pasta and Maria Malibran, who premiered Donizetti's *Maria Stuarda,* were soprano *sfogatos* (vented), or unlimited sopranos, whose voices spanned the contralto with what is now called the coloratura range. Callas, too, was a *sfogato*. The extended vocal range of these singers not only allowed them to sing a wide repertoire of roles but also added a more human quality to their performances. This was achieved by the soprano *sfogato*'s ability to alter the quality of her voice to reflect the changing emotional demands of a single role— for example, the varied moods of Norma as a proud priestess; as a humbled, vengeful, and forgiving lover; and as a leader ready to sacrifice her life for the Druids. It allowed these singers to inject the high notes of a coloratura soprano with vigor and dramatic expressivity and to soften the histrionics that frequently crept into the singing of their dramatic counterparts. A *sfogato* combines the beauty of virtue, represented by the soprano voice of the aggrieved heroine, with the spice of vice, associated with the contralto of the "other woman." The wide-ranging voice of a *sfogato* soprano— Callas's voice, for example, spanned nearly three octaves—came at the price of vocal problems, however, including frequently a lack of voice smoothness and difficulty in keeping notes in tune.

Callas's vocal problems are similar to those of Pauline Viardot (1821–1910), the younger sister of Maria Malibran and a celebrated soprano in her own right. "Her voice was tremendously powerful, prodigious in its range, and it overcame all the difficulties in the art of singing," according to Saint-Saens. "But this marvelous voice did not please everyone, for it was by no means smooth and velvety. Indeed, it was a little harsh and was likened to the taste of a bitter orange. But it was just the voice for a tragedy or an epic, for it was superhuman rather than human."[6] Similarly, Celletti described Maria's voice as lacking natural beauty and possessing an essentially ugly timbre during the Callas Debate. Although it lacked the natural velvet and varnish, dampening the admiration of some listeners, it also made Callas's voice easily recognizable— an important asset for an opera singer. The natural flaws of her voice, which included rough transitions between her chest, middle, and head voices, and difficulty in holding high notes without a wobble, were amply compensated by her phenomenal technique, the result of countless hours of disciplined practice and those basic habits instilled by de Hidalgo during her Athenian years.

Callas described her technique, *bel canto*, as "a method of singing, a sort of straitjacket you must put on. You learn how to approach a note, how to attack it, how to form a *legato* [a smooth sound without break between notes], how to create a mood, how to breathe so that there is a feeling of only a beginning and ending," she explained. "In between, it must seem as if you have taken only one big breath, though in actuality there will be many phrases with many little breaths."[7] Similarly, when asked about

Wilhelmine Schroeder-Devrient, a great soprano of his times, Richard Wagner emphasized the importance of breathing control: "no she had no voice; but she knew so well how to handle her breathing and thereby to create, with so marvelous a musicianship, the true soul of a woman, that one thought no longer of singing nor of voice."[8] Despite weaknesses, both Shroeder-Devrient and Callas possessed magnificent voices, but their voices accounted for only one aspect of their strength as performers. Callas combined her vocal magic with exceptional musicianship. She was an excellent pianist, possessed perfect pitch, and, as noted earlier, had an almost photographic memory; she could learn the entire score of an opera in just a few days.

Callas the Performer

Callas's magic was the product not only of her voice and her musicianship, but also of her acting ability, her enormous capacity to render emotional truth. "Callas belongs to that rare species of actors—rare even in the straight theatre—who manage to appear physically different according to the character they are playing," notes musicologist Eugenio Gara, yet another participant in the Callas Debate. "Some actors contrive to make you believe that they are tall or short, as the case may be. Callas is one of them."[9] Those who saw Callas during her prime comment on the captivating minimalism of her movements, gestures, and eye expressions. In the words of the Met's General Manager, Rudolph Bing, "just the line of her arm when she struck the gong in *Norma*—what volumes it spoke. A few motions of her hand did more to establish a character and an emotion than whole act of earnest acting by other singers."[10] Callas's acting was rivaled only by Feodor Chaliapin, a Russian bass whose unprecedented acting skill revolutionized opera performance in the early part of the twentieth century.

Franco Zeffirelli contends that Callas possessed the same magical stage presence as Rudolph Nureyev and Sir Lawrence Olivier. She could "switch from nothing to everything, from earth to heaven," he declares. Zeffirelli was in awe: "What is it this woman has? I don't know, but when the miracle happens, she is a new soul, a new entity."[11] Others variously explain the Callas phenomenon in terms of an ability to transform black-and-white notes into color (Scott) and as having "an instantaneous hypnotic effect upon the soul of the spectator."[12] John Ardoin describes her portrayal of Leonora in Verdi's *Il Trovatore* "as if an old, romantic painting, beloved but dim, had been cleaned to its original tints."[13] The prominent Greek director Alex Minotis, who worked with her on three separate productions of Cherubini's *Medea*, recalls a moment of unprecedented dramatic truth: Watching Callas die at the end of *La Traviata* "you could see the light go out of her still open eyes."[14] Comparing Callas to Claudia Muzio, Andre Tubeuf suggests that both singers were able to "transform the weakness of their voices into confessions of the soul."[15] Given such acclaim, unfortunately, no film recordings of these Callas performances exist. The few available Callas video recordings from the late 1950s and early 1960s were made when she was no longer at her best; nonetheless, they offer a taste of her magnetic, bewitching stage presence and artistry. Perhaps the best evidence of Callas's magic as a performer is provided in Volf's documentary film *Maria by Callas*.

Callas's vision of opera as combining singing and acting in the joint pursuit of emotional truth meant an emphasis on the cohesion and integrity of the entire performance. Unlike many singers of the past, she did not mark her time, waiting to pull out all the stops for a famous aria. Every single bar of music, every recitative, aria, and even the final curtain call bow, were meticulously rehearsed and became vital components of each performance. Therein lay the power and magic of Callas's stage appearance and therein was the crux of the disagreement between her admirers and detractors. In the words of Gara: "It is only in the total picture of the role, in the grand tragic breath of the character, that the vocal blemishes disappear which her enemies never tire of enumerating."[16] Whether one loved or hated Callas depended, then, on the competing visions of opera as either a vehicle for famous arias sung with vocal purity or as a cohesive whole conveyed by a singer who was not afraid to inject ugliness into her voice when required by the events unfolding on the stage.

Single-Mindedness

Callas's single-minded focus on her art was instrumental to her success. During the height of her career, between 1949 and 1959, while she and Meneghini maintained an uneventful lifestyle, she lived and breathed singing and music. "Callas was driven, insatiable, omnivorous, grand, possessed," recalled Will Crutchfield. "She wanted the roles in which she could dominate, astonish, bewitch; her voice would do almost anything, and what few things it would not do she forced it to approximate."[17] As Honore de Balzac had noted regarding the young in one of his novellas, "when their will-power matches the ambitious size of the angle which they make, the world is theirs."[18] Callas possessed both will-power and ambition. She internalized her mother's determination and need for glory, blending it with her own love of singing, a passion that allowed her to escape her insecurities. Her hunger for acclaim and notoriety knew few bounds.

Most great opera stars tend to focus only on roles that portray their voice at its pinnacle. Adelina Patti specialized in the roles of Rosina, Lucia, and Traviata, for example, while Melba's repertoire was concentrated on a handful of roles in French (Faust, Romeo and Juliette) and Italian (Rigoletto, Lucia di Lammermoor, and La Traviata) opera. Callas performed or recorded a staggering forty-seven different roles during the brief ten years (or so) of her international career. Her eclectic reach included roles ranging from Gluck's Alceste to Kundry in Wagner's *Parsifal* and Giordano's Fedora. She was not hesitant to invest energy in preparing a role that she would sing for only one season, as she did for Verdi's *Macbeth*, Spontini's *La Vestale*, and Donizetti's *Poliuto*. So vast was her range that Callas single-handedly changed the opera landscape by reviving long-forgotten *bel canto* operas such as Bellini's *Il Pirata*, Donizetti's *Anna Bolena*, and Rossini's *Armida*. She also reintroduced Gluck's *Alceste* and *Ifigenia in Tauride*.

Many critics argued that certain roles could be potentially damaging to the voice when sung too early in a soprano's career. Callas was not shy about taking on vocally demanding roles such as those of Aida and Turandot, roles she approached with utter dedication. She took rehearsals seriously and, to the frustration of other singers, insisted on singing in full voice at the dress rehearsal. She had little interest in the historical background of the characters in preparing a role; instead, she dedicated her energies to assiduously studying the score and the libretto. She also relied on her impeccable musical intuitions. When asked by the conductor Nicola Rescigno why she portrayed the character of Anna Bolena in a particular way, Callas simply answered "because she is a queen."[19]

There is perhaps no better example of Callas's single-minded dedication to her art than her devotion to losing weight and maintaining it afterward. Opera heroines are typically young women emaciated by illness or by disappointment over lost love, so to enhance the credibility of her portrayal, Maria dropped weight. In December 1951, she weighed around 210 pounds; by the end of 1953, she was down to 144, according to Meneghini. Within two more years, she would be down to 117 pounds. She had attained her personal ideal—resembling the petite Audrey Hepburn. Most Callas biographers concentrate on determining her method for losing close to seventy pounds in less than two years. They variously attribute it to the ingestion of a tapeworm that Callas allegedly swallowed with a glass of champagne or to experimental hormonal treatments performed by a Swiss doctor. Callas herself never deviated from claiming that she lost weight simply through dieting.

Missing from this debate is the fact that Callas's ability to maintain her low weight is of much greater psychological importance than how she achieved it. Given that her weight dropped below her set point (a biologically determined optimal weight that an organism tries to maintain), it must have taken enormous willpower for her not to regain some of the lost pounds. During the first couple of years spent in Italy, Callas's typical dinner included soup, pasta, fish, meat, desert, and fruit. In subsequent years, her diet changed to rare-cooked steaks and salad, complemented by her habit of picking food from other diners' plates. Her sparse diet meant that she had to daily confront intense feelings of hunger. In a 1963 interview published in *Ici-Paris*, Callas justifies putting on a few pounds by saying "the fact is that I am always starving. I am ravenous and it wears me out."[20]

Although Callas's weight stabilized in the mid-1950s at around 120 pounds it was, in fact, borderline anorexic for a woman almost 5'9" tall. Her precipitous decline in weight suggests anorexia nervosa, as did her knowledge about how to induce vomiting by tickling her throat. Given that Callas did not have the severely distorted body image nor the incessant desire to shed more weight characteristic of the disorder, formal diagnosis is unwarranted. Regardless, Callas's weight loss demonstrates the enormous will-power and determination that she exercised with equal skill in controlling her body and in pursuing her opera career. According to Hilde Bruch, the need to control one's weight characterizes those who, in response to an intrusive and unpredictable child-hood environment, become convinced that their bodies are the only aspects of their life that they can control. Callas is a good example of Bruch's theory. Raised by the authoritarian Litsa, Callas relinquished responsibility for many aspects of her personal life, only to compensate for it by controlling her body weight and all aspects of her stage performances.

Performance as Quest for the Self

Like any good actor, Callas found it easy to identify with her roles. The fact that she personally shared with her wronged heroines a gamut of emotions including hatred, despair, and contempt made the task that much simpler. She had a special empathy for wronged, unhappy women, and, according to Ardoin, she "added the disquieting element of loathing."[21] Yet mere identification is not enough to explain the psychological power of Callas's stage presence. As we listen to the "sadness and terrible nostalgia of aggression and desperation in Callas's voice," suggests critic Teodoro Celli, we realize that it not only perfectly suits the musical drama but that it "contains a drama within itself, that it is an indication of an unquiet troubled spiritual state expressing and purifying itself in sounds."[22] This perceptive assessment points to much more than simple identification with an opera role. Callas needs to infiltrate her roles and merge with her characters as a way of compensating for her own personal conflicts and deficits. By losing herself in fictional others, she invests tremendous energy in the vain hope of finding her true self. Here again we witness Callas's dependence on others (self-objects), be they the men in her life or opera characters; all are necessary props for her psychological equilibrium.

Judy Garland, another performer with a magical stage presence who died young and in despair, was quite similar in her dependence on others. Christopher Finch, a Garland biographer, describes the relationship she formed with her art.

We find ourselves returning again and again to that statement: "I am Judy Garland [a stage name for Frances Gumm]." She had to prove to the world, and to herself, that she was somebody—without being sure who that somebody was. Only onstage, or in front of a camera, could she escape the dilemma. Her identity was inexorably bound to her ability to perform. This does not make her gifts any the less remarkable.[23]

Like Garland, Callas's transformation into her roles had much deeper roots than the routine role identification found among many accomplished artists. It provided both singers with an externally supported identity that temporarily healed an inner void. Yet a psychological lack can rarely be healed by external sources unless they are integrated or transmuted into an internally driven, stable self-image. Neither Callas nor Garland achieved this feat.

Callas's single-minded focus on opera during the height of her career differentiates her from other famous prima donnas. While singers such as Adelina Patti and Nellie Melba were undoubtedly dedicated to their art, both had interests outside of their singing career. At the height of her career, for example, Patti divided her energy between the stage and acting the role of the "Queen of Hearts" at her sprawling property in Wales: The property included a castle with cannons that announced her arrival with a salvo. Although a consummate professional, Patti was not averse to sending her brother to rehearsals to convey her instructions regarding her performance. This habit could be justified somewhat by the fact that she rarely changed her interpretation of the few roles in her repertoire. Yet her practice of not showing up for a rehearsal would have been unthinkable to Callas who not only valued rehearsals but also continuously worked on perfecting the ways in which she portrayed her roles. Like Patti, Melba, too, was often distracted by her non-opera interests; for example, she routinely hobnobbed with British aristocracy and Australian expatriates during her Covent Garden career. And both these prima donnas, were strongly interested in the income generated by their singing, further unlike Callas. At the height of their performance careers, both Patti and Melba balanced their opera with other interests. This provided them with a buffer against life's vagaries. In contrast, Callas displayed a single-minded devotion to her singing at the height of her career. She lived and breathed her roles to an unprecedented degree.

Callas's performance subverted the established order, "importing truth into opera, an art of the false." Once we accept the peculiarity of characters addressing each other in song rather than words, it is an easy next step to suspend belief when it comes to physical appearance (sound typically reverberates better in bigger bodies) and to expect that, even when close to death, the protagonists will use the opportunity to glorify their voice and sing with full vocal power. This is particularly true of operas' endings, which frequently contain some of the finest singing parts penned for the dying or bereaved heroines. This not only invites the soprano to show off her voice but also allows her to display stamina in retaining vocal power late into a performance. Part of Callas's magic consisted in challenging the long-standing premise of opera as the art of make-believe. She did not hesitate to adjust her voice, synchronizing it with the drama transpiring on the stage. In doing so, she was not cowed by the possibility that her actions would lead the audience and critics to think that "Madame Callas" got tired toward the end of the performance. In the case of *La Traviata*'s last act, for example, she injected frailness into her voice when depicting a heroine dying of consumption. Regarding the role of Medea, Callas famously asked how "could one say 'serpenti venite a me' with a velvety voice?'"[24] The phrase translates "serpents come to me," after all. There is no doubt that part of Callas's magic had to do with her willingness to defy some of opera's sacred conventions.

Callas's realism went even further, however. She drew the audience directly into the opera itself, making them part of the performance. In *Anna Bolena* (1958), as we saw in Chapter 2, she used the opera's libretto to dare the audience to judge her, and, a year later, she did so again in Bellini's *Il Pirata,* also at La Scala (1958). During that performance, she used the double meaning of the Italian phrase "*palco funesto*" (the Italian word "*palco*" signifying both the scaffold and the [opera] box) to pour scorn on the General Manager Antonio Ghiringhelli, who had barred her from future performances at La Scala and was therefore complicit in her "execution." Callas's total merger with her stage characters resurfaces in her 1961 performance of *Medea* at La Scala that, again like Bolena, elicited some jeers from the gallery. Realizing that she was not in good voice, Callas directed the second utterance of "crudel [cruel]," meant for Jason her onstage unfaithful lover, at her audience instead, followed by "*ho dato tuto a te*" [I gave you everything], once more redirecting to the audience a phrase meant for Jason. This was a cry of defiance and despair, and testimony to Callas's commitment to her audiences, her dedication to her art. This was no longer just realism; it was enactment of the opera with the audience drawn into the here-and-now of the action. Callas's clear intent is to say to her audience: "The operatic and mythical character of Jason may be cruel but so are you. I, as Medea, gave my everything to Jason, and, as the singer, I did the same to you my ungrateful listeners ready to betray me at a sign of weakness." Singers addressing their audiences directly is not unknown in opera. I, for example, witnessed the Hungarian soprano Eva

Marton admonishing the audience for sneering during a particularly far-fetched scene from *La Gioconda*. This outburst, which did not involve using the words of the libretto in addressing the audience, resulted, however, in breaking the opera's spell. Callas's outburst, by contrast, heightened the performance's magic.

Callas's energy when performing in front of an audience is palpable in many of the pirated recordings of her stage performance. It is this energy that explains why her live performances are more satisfying, more artistically persuasive than her studio recordings. Of course, any psychological explanation of Callas's magic cannot supplant the impact created by the sheer power of her vocal and acting brilliance and the certain *je ne sais quoi* of great performers. Yet the fact that the drama acted out on stage mirrored her own personal traumas surely influenced Callas's artistry and its emotional impact on her audiences.

Callas's use of her roles and her audiences for her own psychological gratification is a narcissistic act. It intensifies her artistic strength and charisma, but it also foreshadows her later psychological problems absent the opera stage. After watching Callas's 1954 Chicago debut in the role of *Norma*, Mary Garden admitted there had "not been anything like this since I was up there," referring to her own performances with the Chicago opera. "You know, she is a great actress, she is a great singer, but she acts on impulse. That's very dangerous."[25] Garden's reference to Callas's impulsivity reflects precisely the blurring of boundaries between Callas as singer and the character of Norma, a role she played more than ninety times. Psychoanalyst D. W. Winnicott offers a similar warning when reflecting on the relationship between creativity and the self.

The self is not really to be found in what is made out of products of body or mind, however valuable these constructs may be in terms of beauty, skill, and impact. If the artist (in whatever medium) is searching for the self, then it can be said in all probability there is already some failure for that artist in the field of general creative living [i.e., vitality and purpose in life]. The finished creation never heals the underlying lack of sense of self.[26]

Callas's stage presence did not heal her damaged self. It did not do so because, as I discuss in Chapter 9, she lacked the psychological strength to gain insight from her experiences. But it added emotional drama to the characters she portrayed on stage especially because so many of those characters are themselves troubled individuals grappling with issues of self-definition.

A Brief History of a Short but Impactful Career

Callas's 1947 Italian debut at Verona's Arena elicited only a lukewarm reception. Amilcare Ponchielli's *La Gioconda*, famous for its dance of the hours, was far from an ideal choice for showcasing Callas's talent. Written in 1875, many years after death of Rossini, Donizetti, and Bellini, the opera, a precursor to *verismo*, did not provide Callas with an opportunity to showcase her *bel canto* singing skills. It did not help that Maria sprained her ankle during a rehearsal when she fell through a trap door, which impeded her movement on stage. More importantly, it was the first time that Veronese audiences were exposed to Callas's voice, one that, as noted, differed markedly from the voices of other sopranos of the era, including Rena Tebaldi's creamy tones. In fact, Tebaldi was also present in Verona during the 1947 season, singing the title role in *Aida*. As Teodoro Celli describes it, "Callas was a star wandering into a planetary system not its own."[27] Not surprisingly it took time for audiences and critics to understand the nature of her talent. It is unlikely that Callas realized the perturbation caused by her unusual singing and acting style and its adverse effect on the launching of her career. Yet it was her distinct style that helped revolutionize the post-World War II opera landscape both in terms of artistic expression and repertoire.

It is not surprising that, after her mixed debut in Verona, Callas gained national attention only when given the opportunity to display her unlimited soprano range. This happened serendipitously. In January 1948, she was scheduled to perform at Venice's La Fenice, singing the role of Brunhilde in Wagner's *La Walchiria* (in the postwar years, Italian opera houses continued the tradition of having Wagner operas sung in Italian). When the soprano scheduled to sing the lead part in Bellini's *I Puritani* got sick, Callas was asked by conductor Tulio Serafin to perform the role. This meant she would alternate between singing the role of Brunhilde, a heavier, vocally dynamic soprano role, with that of *I Puritani*'s Elvira, composed for a lighter coloratura voice. The two roles would have to be sung within just a few days of each other. Callas learned the role in ten days, despite having never previously performed Elvira. Her performance was stunning and created inordinate excitement among La Fenice audiences. The feat of singing both a Wagnerian and a *bel canto* role had not been duplicated since Lilli Lehmann's (1848–1929) era. Using a sport analogy, what Callas achieved with her two Venice performances is equivalent to an athlete being a starter in both the National Football League and the National Baseball League in the same season—not impossible but an exceedingly rare accomplishment.

Following the triumph at La Fenice, Callas's career took off dramatically. Several of her memorable early live performances are available on record, including the roles of Abigaille in *Nabucco* (at Teatro San Carlo, Naples in 1949), Kundry in *Parsifal* (RAI, Rome, 1950), and Elena in *I Vespri Siciliani* (Teatro Comunale, Florence, 1951). That year, 1949, also saw her first studio recordings of Bellini and Wagner arias for the Italian label Cetra. Of these Cetra recordings, her rendition of the aria "Qui la voce" from *I Puritani* has achieved legendary status and provides a wonderful example of young Callas's voice. Starting in 1950, Callas spent three consecutive summers performing with a cast of mostly Italian singers at the Palacio de Bellas Artes in Mexico City. For many of her devotees, the pirated recordings of these performances are a treasure trove of Callas singing at her vocal best. The voice is powerful and clear, and the high notes sustained. There is little of the affectation that would creep into her singing toward the end of her career as she tried to nurse her deteriorating voice. Callas's live recordings from Mexico of *Il Trovatore* (1950), *La Traviato* (1950), and *Lucia di Lammermoor* (1952) brim with excitement, even as they may lack refinement and subtlety. We hear in them Maria's fierce competitiveness as she spars, still in her twenties, with lead tenors and clamors unashamedly for the audience's applause.

A good illustration of the occasionally wild and unrestrained atmosphere of the Mexican performances is provided by an incident that occurred during the 1950 premier of *Aida*, where Callas sang the title role opposite Kurt Baum's Radames. Before the performance, Caraza-Campos, the opera's director, encouraged Callas to interpolate a high note (E-flat) at the end of the Triumphal Scene. Although the note did not exist in Verdi's score, Caraza-Campos knew that the audience would go wild hearing it. Callas demurred but changed her mind after Baum's insistence on holding his high notes in a way that infuriated not only Maria but also the other singers. Predictably, as Callas's voice soared to the E-flat at the end of the Triumphal Scene, the audience enthusiastically responded with rapturous and sustained applause. Afterward, Baum swore he would never perform with Callas again (the "never," in opera terms, meant a hiatus of two years). In typical fashion, Maria offered the following assessment of the performance in her letter to Meneghini: "Aida went marvelously well the other night. The audience was ecstatic, at least over Simionato [the mezzo-soprano singing Amneris] and myself. The others had a stroke when they saw who were the favorites of the public."[28]

Despite these triumphs, the doors to Milan's La Scala remained closed to Callas until the end of 1951 because of antipathy by its General Manager, Antonio Ghiringhelli. It is hard to know the exact reason for his resistance. It might have had something to do with Callas's non-Italian background. Although foreign singers had a history of singing at La Scala, Callas's behavior and manner marked her as a clear cultural outsider. While Callas was dignified when on stage, she otherwise was indifferent to her self-presentation. In 1951, Wally Toscanini (the daughter of the legendary conductor Arturo) offered the following portrait of Maria: "she's fat, ugly, and half-blind but with a remarkable voice and stage presence."[29] And, after watching Callas perform in Florence that same year, Rudolph Bing thought her to be "monstrously fat and awkward." He felt that while she had remarkable potential, she still had a lot to learn before she could become a star at the Met. Although publicly Callas appeared unaffected by this distasteful criticism from respected figures within opera, it must have hurt not only by demeaning her as a person but by also highlighting her "*autre*" or outsider's status. It is comments like these that fueled her competitive spirit and her resolve to lose weight and metamorphose from "an ugly duckling into a beautiful white swan."

Ghiringhelli's hesitance to offer Callas a contract may have been driven by his concern over the potential rivalry between Callas and Tebaldi and their respective followers. At the time, Tebaldi was the well-entrenched darling of the Milanese audiences. She was a protégé of Arturo Toscanini who, having conducted the premiers of Puccini's *La Boheme* (1896) and Leoncavallo's *Pagliacci* (1892), was La Scala's living legend and whose imprimatur of a singer was considered sacred. Ghiringhelli would have thought twice before displacing Toscanini's protégé. Tension between Callas and Tebaldi spilled over after a concert performance in Rio de Janeiro in September 1951, when Maria accused Renata of violating their mutual agreement not to sing encores during a concert performance. Ghiringhelli finally capitulated after Callas's huge triumph at the Teatro Comunale in Florence, in May of 1951. She performed the role of Elena in Verdi's *I Vespri Siciliani,* conducted, with a stellar cast, by the highly esteemed Erich Kleiber. Though anxious to sing at La Scala, Callas was not to be overwhelmed by the opportunity when Ghiringhelli finally offered her the chance to open the opera's 1951–1952 season. Just a year earlier, when asked by reporters how it felt to sing as a substitute for Tebaldi at the legendary venue, Maria coyly proclaimed "La Scala, magnificent theater. Yes, I am thrilled, of course, I am thrilled. Great theater. But I am nearsighted, you see. For me all theaters are alike. Am I excited? La Scala is La Scala, but I am nearsighted: ecco tutto [that's all]."[30] Now, when finally offered a permanent contract, Callas not only made demands about fees, but also extracted from Ghirnghelli the highly unusual promise that she would be able to sing in *La Traviata*, Tebaldi's signature role. Although Ghirnghelli never intended to fulfill this promise, Callas made sure that he did, resulting in spectacular Traviatas staged by Visconti and conducted by Carlo Maria Giulini.

With La Scala as the new stage for Callas's exceptional performances, Tebaldi stopped singing there not long after her arrival and found a new home at New York's Metropolitan Opera. Nonetheless, throughout Callas's reign as La Scala's queen (1952–1959), the Milanese audiences continued to be deeply divided between Tebaldists and Callasites, resulting in several disruptive incidents during Maria's performances. In one such incident, she was showered with radishes at the end of her performance in Rossini's *Il Barbiere di Siviglia* (La Scala 1956), though the short-sighted Maria initially mistook them for flowers. Callas once famously declared, "when my enemies stop hissing I shall know I'm slipping."[31] She remained unperturbed by such occurrences throughout her time at La Scala and received enormous acclaim, not only for opening La Scala's winter season in 1952 with Verdi's *Macbeth*, but also for her performance in Verdi's *La Traviata* in 1954 and Bellini's *Norma* in 1955. Her seven-year reign at La

Scala included appearances in twenty-one different roles more than 157 performances—an unprecedented number for any soprano, then and now. During this same period, she performed in all the major opera houses of Europe, as well as in Chicago's Lyric Opera (1952–1953) and at the Met, where she made her debut in 1956. Callas's live performances in *Macbeth* (Milan, 1952), *La Traviata* (Milan, 1955), *Lucia di Lammermoor* (Berlin, 1955), *Norma* (Milan, 1955), *La Sonnambula* (Cologne, 1957), and *Medea* (Dallas, 1958) are legendary. Equally acclaimed were her La Scala performances of *Medea* (1953) and *La Sonnambula* (1955), conducted by the young Leonard Bernstein. Additionally, among her studio recordings, *Tosca* (1953), *Un Ballo in Maschera* (1956), and *Norma* (1960) offer particularly fine examples of her artistry. Even though Tebaldi maintained a successful career at the Met and recorded a number of highly acclaimed and popular operas with Mario del Monaco for the Decca/London label, there was no doubt that, in the mid to late 1950s, it was Callas who was opera's undisputed star.

Callas had a short career. If we discount her Athenian sojourn, it lasted just over ten years, from 1948 to 1959, demarcated by her first triumph at La Fenice (January 1948), where she alternated singing the roles of Brunhilde and Elvira, and her performance of *Lucia* in Dallas (in November 1959). Though the Dallas performance was met with acclaim, Callas was keenly aware of the vocal flaws increasingly interfering with her singing ability, and, after 1959, her opera performances were sporadic. At the height of her career she averaged fifty performances a year. In contrast, between 1959 and the start of her disastrous farewell concert tour in 1973, she made only a total of twenty-eight appearances, the majority of which were confined to performances in *Tosca* and *Norma* in 1964–1965.

Callas's voice was never perfect. "Maria Callas is a most unusual singer," declared a music critic for *Roma*, commenting on her 1949 performance in *Turandot*. "In softer passages her voice is beautiful and insinuating, yet her high notes are metallic and piercing. She has a nightmarish upper extension—awesome, sinister, inexorable."[32] A similar mixed assessment of Callas's voice is expressed by the music critic of the *Excelsior* following the Mexico City performance of *Aida*, also in 1950: "she played her role with such authority, such refinement, such feeling, such musicality, that whatever objections certain critics have made about her middle register disappear before her more important merits."[33] This comment reinforces the contention that, even at the height of her career, Callas's power as a singer resided in the totality of her performance rather than in the sheer beauty or perfection of her voice.

Critics' concerns intensified by the mid-1950s. In assessing her role of Norma during her 1956 debut at the Met, Howard Taubman, the *New York Times* music critic, called hers a "puzzling voice" that occasionally "gives the impression of having been formed out of sheer will power rather than natural endowments. The quality is different in the upper, middle, and lower registers, as if three different persons were involved. In high fortissimos, Miss Callas is downright shrill. She also has a tendency to sing off pitch when she has not time to brace herself for a high note."[34] A contributor to *Time* magazine, commenting on the same performance, also used the word "shrill" to describe Callas's notes "in the upper register." "But in the low and middle registers she sang with flutelike purity, tender and yet sharply disciplined, and in the upper reaches—shrill or not—she flashed a sword-like power that is already legend."[35] Evaluating Callas's performance in La Scala's 1958 *Anna Bolena*, Peter Dragadze of *Musical America* asserts "her performance was excellent, and although she did not have the physical strength and power behind her voice as in the past, her supreme mastery of the art of singing made it a joy to listen to her."[36] Callas managed, at times, to hide vocal blemishes with her supreme artistry. But there was a limit to the extent to which the totality of a performance could compensate for escalating problems in sustaining high notes and wobble.

"Maria Callas sounds to be in big vocal trouble," announced the music critic of the *Chicago American*, commenting on her 1958 concert performance at the Lyric Opera. How serious the trouble "only she is equipped to measure. But last night, heard for the first time in 12 months, her voice was recurrently strident, unsteady and out-of-tune. It seems to have aged 10 years in one."[37] Summarizing her 1959 performance of Lucia in Dallas—the very performance that led Callas to comment to a friend that her career may be coming to an end—the *Dallas Morning News* offered a scathing attack.

Madame Callas made the fourteen-minute episode [the "Mad Scene"] theatrical, telling, rather pitiable and certainly full of meaning. When singing in mezza voce and in the middle of her voice she produced superlative sound. The screeched high notes had to go with it and also some badly aimed attacks which she barely covered by roulades downward into the more comfortable register. . . . No doubt there will be many to say: "I have heard Callas as Lucia and must

get her out of both my eyes and my ears before I can accept
another."[38]

Callas's vocal problems were well-known by the late 1950s. As
Irving Kolodin of the *Saturday Review* argued in his review of her
1958 performance of *La Traviata* at the Met, the disparagement
of Callas's ugly sound is "on par with the discovery that the Venus
de Milo has no arms."[39] In other words, Callas's vocal problems
were long evident, and, by the late 1950s, the criticism grew more
intense

There is no doubt that as early as 1955 her voice had begun
to deteriorate, followed by a much more precipitous decline
during the next three years. There are various explanations for
its decline: the loss of power following her severe weight loss;
the long-term effect of technical deficiencies, combined with
attempts to sing unduly taxing roles early in her career, including
Turandot and Aida; the voice's natural flaws; and her tendency
to overintellectualize performances that then compounded her
emergent vocal problems. And, of course, her psychological insecurities may have played a role as well. Irrespective of the causes,
Callas's declining voice placed her in a difficult situation. Her
reluctance to pursue adjustments that would make it easier to
cope with the increasing unpredictability of her voice only made
matters worse, but, as Zeffirelli noted, "Maria is a stupid woman,
so professional that if she cannot cope with all the notes written or expected, she will not do the piece."[40] Zeffirelli called this
attitude a crime, arguing that she could have easily extended her
career if she relaxed her standards, something she could never
agree to do.

Callas's perfectionism—such an asset in her youth and at the beginning of her career—now became a detriment. She struggled to adjust to declining vocal powers, and in this regard she differed widely from Adelina Patti, who showed considerable willingness to make gradual adjustments to her singing: An extra breath here and there, the transposition of notes down, the judicious use of a fan when approaching a difficult passage. In 1905, when Patti heard the first-ever recording of her then sixty-two-year-old voice, she exclaimed: "Ah! My Lord! Now I understand why I am Patti! Oh, yes! What a voice! What an artist! I understand all!"[41] Few who listened to this recording of an aged and seriously compromised voice concurred with Patti's self-assessment, yet her expansive attitude no doubt made her life easier. Callas was bereft of such an attitude. Her perfectionism and intransigence, assets in her prime, would seriously compromise her ability to deal with her declining vocal powers.

Perfectionism's Pluses and Minuses

In the Greek myth, Icarus fails to heed the warning of his father, Daedalus, and flies too close to the sun during their daring escape from the clutches of King Minos of Crete. The sun's heat melts the wax holding together Icarus's wings, thus plunging him to his death. Icarus's tale portrays the dangers of illusion inherent in narcissistic grandiosity, both the content of beliefs (i.e., I am great) and the steadfast attitude held toward these beliefs (i.e., nothing will change my mind about this point of view). Stephen Mitchell has written that "[a]ll of us probably experience" the feelings and thoughts associated with grandiose narcissism, but the "problem of narcissism concerns issues of character structure, not mental content." Referring to problems caused by narcissism, Mitchell argues, "it is not so much what you can do and think as your attitude toward what you do and think, how seriously you take yourself."[42] In other words, the tragedy of narcissism lies not only in its grandiosity, but in the rigidity with which the distorted views of the self and others are held. "In some narcissistic disturbances, illusions are actively and consciously maintained," Mitchell writes. "[R]eality is sacrificed in order to perpetuate an addictive devotion to self-ennobling, idealizing, or symbiotic fictions."[43]

Mitchell's thoughts on the destructive aspects of narcissistic illusions capture Callas's predicament upon encountering the decline of her stage career. Her vocal difficulties presented a genuine dilemma, not only because of the speed of the decline, but also because of its timing. All singers know that their careers are time-limited, but for the decline to occur so early—as it did for Callas, still only in her mid-thirties and so soon after reaching the peak of her triumphs—seems unjust. To cope with such unexpected disruption would require personal flexibility, self-confidence, and a range of other interests, all things Callas lacked. She was narrow-mindedly devoted to her career, a fanatical perfectionist. This is not a favorable constellation of characteristics for a prematurely fading superstar. It left her with the conviction that there was nothing else for her to be.

In a 1958 EMI recording session of the Sleepwalking Scene from Verdi's *Macbeth*, Callas told artistic director Walter Legge, whose perfectionism equaled her own, "That was, I think, some good singing." Legge replied "Oh, extraordinary. But you will hear it and you will understand that you have to redo it." Maria felt "proud when [she] stepped down to listen to the playback," for she "was in quite good voice that day," so Legge's response caused considerable shock. But she listened again, only to acknowledge that Legge was right—the "main idea of the Sleepwalker scene was not underlined." As soon as Callas finished listening to the playback, she said, "Well, you are right, now I understand, and I went back and performed it."[44] The resulting retake did full justice to the complexity of the aria in which Lady Macbeth experiences emotions ranging from awe, disgust, and shame to defiance and contempt as she meditates on her and Macbeth's role in the murders of Duncan and Banco. According to Ardoin, the recording is "one of the most descriptive moments of singing ever captured on record; it is a summary of Callas's unparalleled power to give words shape and dimensions through vocal colorations."[45]

Callas's perfectionism drove her dynamic success, particularly early in her career. It was evident already during her teenage years in Athens. Trivella, Maria's first mentor, describes her as fanatical, uncompromising, and dedicated to her studies heart and soul.[46] This opinion was echoed by de Hidalgo, who felt Callas practiced so hard and so intensively that, at times, it was almost a folly. Maria's pursuit of perfection continued into adulthood and characterized her entire opera career. "I want the best in everything. I want the man in my life to be the best of all. I want my art to be the most perfect. I want, in short, to have the best of everything" a then twenty-four-year-old Callas confided in Meneghini, writing from Rome in 1948. "I know that all this is not possible, and it torments me."[47] Commenting on her perfect diction, color, inflection, and above all her feeling as a singer, Tito

Gobbi, the Italian baritone who famously played Scarpia opposite Callas's Tosca, extols her total dedication to her art. Similarly, Robert Sunderland, the pianist who accompanied Callas during her 1973–1974 farewell concert tour with di Stefano, was left with the impression that she spent her entire career searching for perfectionism. But there were both positive and negative aspects to her relentless pursuit of perfection. She was conscientious in her desire to do better, as evident in the serious and professional manner in which she approached rehearsals and her total absorption in her performances. This pursuit nurtured her independence of judgment and her imperviousness to the opinions of others as she imposed her own standards of excellence on her acting and singing. For Callas, the integrity of her performance superseded any other consideration. This integrity and intransigence came, however, at a high personal price.

Despite its occasional positive consequences, perfectionism can also undermine personal relationships and the person's own self-confidence and self-esteem. A key element of perfectionism is criticism directed toward the self, others, or both simultaneously. The specific target and source of the criticism depends largely on the type of perfectionism. Anxiety-driven, neurotic perfectionism results in a sense of guilt over not meeting expectations and letting oneself or another person down. In narcissism, perfectionism expresses the belief that the behavior must meet one's own self-imposed expectations. The "shoulds" torment those with narcissistic perfectionism, according to Sorotzkin.

The tyranny of the shoulds of the narcissistic perfectionist focuses on the self (I should be perfect). The failure to live up to the dictates of the shoulds evokes thoughts of "I am worthless," "I am a nobody" (shame). In contrast, the focal point of the neurotic individuals' should is action to be done or not done (I should never get angry). The failure to live up this expectation evokes thoughts of "I am bad: (guilt).... The shame-prone individual would be obsessed with the question "How could *I* have done that?" whereas the guilt-ridden person is more likely to wonder "How could I have *done that*?"[48]

Narcissistic perfectionism resulting from grandiose narcissism is associated more strongly with criticism of others and feelings of rage (how dare they do this to me), whereas vulnerable narcissism tends to lead to self-focused criticism and shame and feeling of disintegration. Maria exemplified both of these traits: She never suffered fools and was not averse to criticizing others. "Is that the way you do it?" Maria declared after canceling her 1954 performance of *Aida* in Verona following a disagreement with the conductor Fausto Cleva. "Well, that is not the way I do it."[49] Callas's perfectionism, tinged with an imperial insistence on having things done her way, also prompted the renowned Austrian-born conductor Karl Bohm to quit during a rehearsal in 1956. After an argument with her, he complained, "I am a conductor and not an accompanist."[50] Although encounters such as this add to Callas's legend as a capricious diva, they inevitably reflected her unwillingness to compromise rigidly held high professional and personal standards.

Though critical of others, Callas reserved the harshest criticism for herself. In a 1965 interview with Banzet, she confided "I know my character very well and I also see my faults. If I criticize others, you can believe that I start by criticizing myself."[51] And criticize herself she did. According to Pia Meneghini, Maria always found fault with her voice; never satisfied with her achievements, she seemed always wanting more. In fact, as argued by Huffington, Maria was her own worst critic. She tormented herself with doubts and fears, studied every note, left nothing to chance, and scrutinized every failure. A slight vocal misstep singing Gilda in *Rigoletto* (Mexico City, 1952) was enough to ruin the entire season for her despite receiving enthusiastic reviews and thunderous applause. While readily susceptible to flattery when it came to her personal life, Callas the artist had her own high standards of performance that were impervious to others' opinions. She alone knew whether her performance was good or not and, to the surprise of Meneghini, was not interested in reading newspaper reviews following a performance. More frequently than not, the verdict was negative. Callas lived with a constant desire to improve; as she stated flatly, she had never been "capable of enjoying what I do well."[52]

A particularly devastating aspect of narcissistic perfectionism is that a self-perceived shortcoming or failure in one domain spills over to impact the person's entire self-concept. This again exemplifies the narcissistic propensity to view things in an all-or-nothing manner (i.e., I am all good or I am all bad) as well as the lack of differentiation of the narcissistic individual from the objects used to prop up their fragile self. In Callas's case, fusion with her opera roles (as narcissistic props) meant that a less than perfect stage performance threatened the disintegration of her entire personhood. "You see, dear, I am such a pessimist and everything afflicts and disturbs me," Maria wrote to Battista in November 1948, while in Rome preparing for her performance of Norma in Florence. "I am convinced that I do everything badly. Then I undermine my confidence even more. At times I reach the point where I wish that death would release me from the torment."[53] Callas's perfectionism-driven pessimism persisted throughout her life. In 1973, she reiterated the fear and negative self-appraisal voiced twenty-five years earlier.

> My biggest problem is that I am a terrible pessimist. I often think I am incapable of doing well, so I always try to do better. But there is the danger of trying too hard and ruining something beautiful by losing control or exaggerating. But a good hard, sensible look at your work is still the best teacher an artist can have.[54]

In this comment, Callas reiterates the positive role played by perfectionism and high standards on her career while, at the same time, highlighting its corrosive effect on self-esteem and general outlook on life.

Dan McAdams isolates two distinct patterns in adult life narratives.[55] Many individuals depict their lives using a *redemptive script*, where bad personal events lead eventually to good outcomes (a prototypically American motif, according to McAdams). Contrasting narratives are characterized by a *contamination script*, where good things end up turning bad. Not surprisingly, this narrative is associated with low levels of well-being and indifference to the welfare of others. As conveyed by her deeply ingrained pessimism and her psychological vulnerabilities, Callas's self-narrative had a contaminative rather than redemptive quality. In 1968, looking back on her life following her break-up with Onassis, she concluded, "in life, before you do something, you must realize that there will be consequences. And if you're honest, you pay a big price, though it should be normal, honesty should be a part of you."[56] "Just like life—there's nothing without a thorn," Callas said on another occasion, in 1970, after being pricked by a thorn from flowers she was arranging with Robert Sutherland: "Just when you think everything is going ok there's trouble somewhere in the background—somebody waiting to stab you in the back."[57]

It is easy to see how Callas's self-criticism and perfectionism did not equip her well to deal with her escalating vocal problems. Her perfectionism prevented her from singing once she could no longer perform according to her own high standards (a view expressed by Onassis's sister Artemis). As it turned out, the threat of disintegration attendant on her inability to perform and fuse with her opera roles was to be abated by yet another older man, Aristotle Onassis.

Notes

1. Celletti, R. (unknown). Liner notes from *Maria Callas: Arie celebri*. Fontit Cetra CDs.
2. Cone, *Adelina Patti*, p. 56.
3. *The Callas debate*. In *Opera*, 1970, 21(9), p. 816.
4. A stark contrast between the singing style of a prototypic coloratura soprano and Callas is evident by comparing Callas's version of the "Mad Scene" from *Lucia di Lammermoor* with its rendition by Lily Pons, Met's darling soprano during Callas's childhood in New York City (recording available on *Lily Pons – Coloratura Assoluta,* Sony, Masterworks Heritage.)

5. Ardoin, J. (1998). *Callas at Juilliard: The master classes.* Portland, OR: Amadeus Press, p. 3.

6. Saint Saens, C., http://deeprootsmag.org/2015/10/11/the-superhuman-voice-of-pauline-viardot/

7. Ardoin, *Callas at Juilliard*, p. 3.

8. *The Callas debate*, p. 815.

9. Ibid., p. 819.

10. Bing, *5000 nights at the opera*, p. 246.

11. Ardoin, *Callas: The art and the life*, p. 25.

12. Stassinopoulos, *Maria*, p. 77.

13. Ardoin, *Callas: The art and the life*, p. 16.

14. Gage, *Greek fire*, p. 240.

15. Tubeuf, in Lowe, *Callas as they saw her*, p. 164.

16. *The Callas debate,* p. 815.

17. Crutchfield, *The story of a voice*, p. 100.

18. Balzac, H. De. (1834/1977). A tragedy by the sea. In *Selected short stories.* New York: Penguin Classics, p. 197.

19. Ardoin, *Callas: The art and the life*, p. 13.

20. Remy, *Maria Callas: A tribute*, p. 159.

21. Ardoin, *Callas: The art and the life*, p. 8.

22. Ibid., p. 9.

23. Finch, C. (1975). *Rainbow: The stormy life of Judy Garland.* New York: Ballantine Books, p. 390.

24. Segalini, S. Singing rediscovered. In Lowe, *Callas as they saw her*, p. 177.

25. Turnbull, M. T. R. B. (1997). *Mary Garden.* Portland, OR: Amadeus Press, p. 198.

26. Winnicott, D. W. (1971). *Playing and reality.* New York: Tavistock Publications, pp. 54–55.

27. Ardoin, *Callas: The art and the life,* p. 7.

28. Menghini, *My wife: Maria Callas*, p. 129.

29. Scott, *Maria Meneghini Callas*, p. 66.

30. Stassinopoulos, *Maria Callas*, p. 84.

31. Ibid., p. 270.

32. Lowe, *Callas as they saw her*, p. 21.
33. Ibid., p. 26.
34. Taubman, H. (1956). *The New York Times,* October 31.
35. *Time,* 1956, November 26.
36. Dragadze, P. (1958). *Musical America,* April 7.
37. Dettmer, R. (1958). *Chicago American*, March.
38. Rosnefield, J. (1959). *Dallas Morning News,* November 7.
39. Kolodin, I. (1958). *Saturday Review,* February 14.
40. Ardoin, *Callas: The art and the life*, p. 22.
41. Cone, *Adelina Patti*, p. 243.
42. Mitchell, S. A. (1988). *Relational concepts in psychoanalysis: An integration*. Cambridge, MA: Harvard University Press, p. 194.
43. Ibid., p. 200.
44. Ardoin, *Callas: The art and the life*, pp. 17–18.
45. Ardoin, J. (1995). *The Callas legacy: The complete guide to her recordings on compact disc* (4th ed.). Portland, OR: Amadeus Press, p. 137.
46. Petsalis-Diomidis, *The unknown Callas*, p. 98.
47. Meneghini, *My wife: Maria Callas*, p. 62.
48. Sorotzkin, B. (1985). The quest for perfection: Avoiding guilt or avoiding shame. *Psychotherapy*, *22*, 564–571.
49. Scott, *Maria Meneghini Callas*, p. 131.
50. Ibid., p. 181.
51. Banzet, M. (1965). *Trois jours avec Maria Callas*. RTE, Paris, February 8.
52. Harris, K. (1970). *The Observer*, February 8 and 15.
53. Meneghini, *My wife Maria Callas*, p. 61.
54. Ardoin, *Callas at Juilliard*, p. 10.
55. McAdams, D. P. (2013). *The redemptive self: Stories Americans live by – Revised and expanded edition*. New York: Oxford University Press.
56. Ardoin, *Callas: The art and the life*, p. 42.
57. Sutherland, *Maria Callas: Diaries*, pp. 15–16.

8 | A MATTER OF THE HEART

Maxim's was brilliantly lit, its tables glistening with soft white candlelight. The elegant posh restaurant, located in the heart of Paris on the rue Royale in the Eighth Arrondissement, was regarded as one of the best in the world. Caviar, saddle of lamb a la Callas, and asparagus tips were served for the couple's adoring guests. It was April 21, 1959. Maria and Battista were celebrating their tenth wedding anniversary, and, as the meal ended, the couple cut into an almond cake while a violinist played *Happy Birthday to You*. "I could not sing without him present," Maria announced, using the occasion to reiterate her commitment to Titta. "If I am the voice, he is the soul."[1]

After Maxim's, the Meneghinis and friends continued their celebrations at Le Lido, a nightclub located on the Champs-Elysees and renowned for its burlesque show. A slew of famous singers had performed there, including Edit Piaf, Marlene Dietrich, Maurice Chevalier, and Josephine Baker. To the eyes of the public, these festivities suggested a perfect marriage. Throughout the twelve years they spent together, Maria did not give any reason for gossip regarding her relations with other men, and she publicly proclaimed her devotion to Titta on several occasions. "If Battista had wanted, I would have abandoned my career without regret, because in a woman's life, love is more important than artistic

Prima Donna. Paul Wink, Oxford University Press (2021). © Oxford University Press.
DOI: 10.1093/oso/9780190857738.003.0008

triumphs," she asserted in one interview. "I would give my life for him, immediately and joyfully."[2]

Only three months later, on July 22, Maria and Battista boarded Aristotle Onassis's yacht *Christina* for a three-week Mediterranean cruise that would take them from Monte Carlo to Italy, mainland Greece, the Greek Islands, and Turkey. They would travel in the company of Sir Winston Churchill and his entourage. Nonie Montague, the wife of Churchill's private secretary, described the Meneghinis on first meeting them as "turtle-doves" with "all sort of cooing and whistling to each other, kiss, kiss blowing."[3] Although Nonie's somewhat derisive tone reflects the antipathy felt toward Callas by the Churchill group, it confirms the close relationship between Maria and Battista, even if the affection of their relationship is a bit intensified by the novelty of the situation. It must have been quite a shock for Battista when, two weeks into the voyage, Maria informed him that their marriage was over. On August 6, while the *Christina* was docked in Istanbul, Onassis invited the spiritual leader of the Eastern Orthodox church, Patriarch Athenagoras, for lunch on board of the yacht. Maria and Aristo knelt in front of the patriarch who, though perhaps confused about their marital status, nevertheless blessed them as though in a marriage ceremony. That night the two most famous Greeks in the world consummated their affair. Maria told Battista their marriage was over the following morning.

The cruise ended in Monte Carlo on August 13. Though Maria and Battista took the train together back to Milan, Maria stayed behind and suggested Titta go on his own to the couple's summer home in Sirmione on the shores of Lake Garda, about a two-hour's drive from Milan. On August 26, after several meetings and consultations with Onassis, she requested Battista send the clothes she left behind back to Milan. Battista finally confronted Maria. He claimed she was committing an unspeakable sin by breaking their marriage vows. He told her she had ruined his life. Callas retorted, "you can be grateful to be in such good health at your age.[4] You have lived your life and should be prepared to stand aside. I've been with you for twelve years. Enough is enough. I have the right to change things."[5] Following a series of tense encounters, the couple would see each other face-to-face only one more time, on November 14, 1959, during separation proceedings held in a Brescia courtroom (divorce was not yet legal in Italy).

Slow Start to an Affair

Callas and Onassis knew each other before that fateful cruise on the *Christina*, having first met at a party given in Maria's honor on September 3, 1957, at socialite Elsa Maxwell's home. It was the same party that precipitated Callas's refusal to take part in the unscheduled performance of *Lucia di Lammermoor* in Edinburgh. Maxwell introduced Callas and Onassis to each other as the two most famous living Greeks in the world. The day after the party, Onassis made his motorboat available to the Meneghinis; they spent several hours with Onassis and his wife, Tina. But there is no evidence to suggest that either Maria or Aristo felt particularly drawn to each other. Their next meeting occurred more than a year later, on December 9, 1958, during Callas's gala performance at the Paris Opera House. This well-publicized charity event for the benefit of the Legion d'Honneur drew a star-studded audience, including the Duke and Duchess of Windsor, the Rothschilds, the Aga Khan, and numerous representatives of the art world such as Brigit Bardot, Juliet Greco, Francoise Sagan, and Charlie Chaplin. Although Onassis was not an opera fan, he could not have failed to be impressed by Callas's fame and glamour. She wore a champagne-colored satin dress and a million dollars worth of diamonds loaned to her by Van Cleef & Arpels.[6]

During their next meeting, at a party given by Wally Toscanini[7] in the spring of 1959, Onassis invited the Meneghinis to join him and Tina for a summer cruise on the *Christina*. His interest was piqued. Callas doubted whether she could fit the trip into her busy schedule, but Onassis swung into full action. He not only attended Callas's June 17, 1959, Covent Garden performance of *Medea*; he also bought thirty-three highly coveted tickets to the event, secured on the black market, for a distinguished set of guests including Gary Cooper, Douglas Fairbanks, and Lord Harewood. Onassis threw a party for Maria at the Dorchester Hotel after the performance. The reception room was decorated with pink roses to match the free-flowing pink champagne. With Callas still vacillating about the cruise, Onassis called the Meneghinis on July 15 and finally managed to get Tina to persuade the reluctant couple. They accepted the offer. A week later, Maria and Battista flew to Monte Carlo, where they boarded the *Christina*.

What psychological sense are we to make of Callas's sudden pivot away from Meneghini and toward Onassis? In some respects, what happened on the *Christina* should not have come as a big surprise. Tensions simmered under the smooth façade of the Meneghini marriage. Maria increasingly found herself engaging with the world of the glitterati, and, with her increased fame, Battista lost much of his luster. His role gradually shifted from beloved husband to manager of Maria's career and emotional needs, and her mounting vocal problems only added to the tension. Maria wanted to curtail her singing engagements, increasingly tortured by the unpredictability of her voice, but Battista resisted this desire, seeing in Maria valuable merchandise. He justified his objection by insinuating that Maria could not retire because of lack of money. This claim was partly true—he had siphoned off some of her earnings into his private account, behavior he justified as compensation for his loss of income owing to switching from being a businessman to becoming her manager. His insistence that she continue singing revived Maria's dormant suspicions about being used for her talent, suspicions that lingered from her childhood experiences with Litsa. In an unusual move, just before the cruise on the *Christina*, Callas requested that the proceedings from her concert in Amsterdam not be deposited into the couple's joint account but rather be forwarded directly to her. Despite public pronouncements to the contrary, by the late 1950s, Callas was no longer in love with Battista. It is highly unlikely that she would have left him, however, had she not been "swept off her feet" by Onassis.

Maria was not good at initiating action. As described in the preceding chapter, she was quick to respond to someone else's behavior in her professional life, especially if it was interpreted as a slight, and she swiftly protected her rights as a diva. But otherwise her personal life was marked by passivity, intermittently disrupted by tantrums. The passivity had its origin, as we saw, in being stripped of agency by the domineering Litsa. She was bound to Battista by a sense of gratitude for his help in the early stages of her career, and she relished the routine of their daily lives that left her free to concentrate on singing. Callas was also quite moralistic and took a very dim view of divorce. She never forgave her parents for their divorce, and she disowned her father after he remarried.[8] Her traditional view of marriage included her publicly expressed belief that a wife should be subservient to her husband. This attitude accounts for her pronouncements that she would do anything that Meneghini asked of her.

Callas created a distorted narrative to rationalize the end of her marriage to Battista, a distortion of events that helps compensate for the dissonance between Callas's emphasis on the sanctity of marriage and her own infidelity. Maria became convinced that Battista had left her, allegedly because he took exception with Maria's desire to handle her own business affairs. "Battista himself said that our marriage would have been pointless unless he could have complete authority over me," she stated. "I think that was the only thing he wanted. I didn't want to marry an impresario."[9] While there is some truth to this, there is absolutely no evidence that Battista ever thought of divorcing Maria. In fact, to him the breakup of their relationship came as a complete shock; he reluctantly agreed to the separation. Perhaps Callas's ambivalence about her actions also helps explain the brutal way in which she confronted Meneghini with her decision to end the marriage, a callousness reminiscent of how she broke off her relationship with her mother, and how, earlier, Litsa separated from her mother.

While the changing nature of their marital relationship and her rapidly increasing vocal problems pushed Callas away from Meneghini, Onassis's personal charm pulled her forcefully into the shipping magnate's orbit. Short in stature and not particularly handsome, Onassis exuded personal magnetism and was known as a great lover. Power is the ultimate aphrodisiac (as Henry Kissinger once quipped), and Onassis possessed plenty of it. The owner of numerous tankers and of Olympic Airways, he was one of the richest men in the world. In 1946, Onassis married Athina (Tina) Livanos, the daughter of a well-established shipping magnate. She was seventeen years old. He was forty-two. Onassis had two children with Tina, Christina and Alexander, and he was a devoted father, especially to Alexander. Onassis did not feel any compunction to remain faithful to Tina, nor did he see his numerous affairs as posing a threat to their marriage. Tina had her own affair with Reinaldo Herrera, the playboy son of an Argentinean millionaire. There is no reason to believe Onassis intended to divorce Tina after he started his affair with Callas, but he underestimated the passion that engulfed their relationship. Tina filed for a divorce, and Onassis's first marriage came to an end in 1960.[10]

The Lighting Strikes

In Francis Ford Coppola's film *The Godfather*, Part 1, Michael Corleone meets Apolloni Vitelli while hiding in Sicily and, according to his bodyguards, falls immediately and passionately in love with her, as though he was struck by a thunderbolt. The same can be said of Callas and Onassis's time on the *Christina*, except, in this case, the thunderbolt seized both lovers simultaneously. For Maria, the relationship with Onassis offered a first chance to enact her passion in real life rather than fulfilling it in operatic roles of Violetta, Tosca, Lucia, or Norma. Maria's passion for Onassis had a strong sexual component. According to Maria, who was never shy in discussing body issues, she experienced her first orgasm with him. While the binding power of their sexual attraction should not be underestimated, the Callas–Onassis relationship had additional depth: The two of them were united not only by their Greek roots but also by a common history of hardship and deprivation.

It seems improbable, but Onassis, born in Smyrna (Ismir today), the son of a wealthy merchant family specializing in the import-export of cotton and tobacco, was actually a self-made individual. And, just like Maria Callas, Onassis shared her history of war-related trauma. In 1922, at age sixteen, he watched as the Turkish army massacred the city's Greek inhabitants. Following the end of World War I, the Greek army invaded Asia Minor to recapture territory previously lost to Turkey, but the campaign ultimately ended in defeat. In the ensuing reprisal, several of Aristotle's close relatives were murdered, including a favorite uncle. Given the horrors experienced by Aristo in Smyrna—he witnessed thousands of massacred bodies; panicked men, women, and children drowning in the city's harbor; and eventually the fire that engulfed the city—it is likely he would have been diagnosed with posttraumatic stress disorder in today's era. This syndrome is associated with emotional blunting, which may account for some of Onassis's callousness and cruelty. Seeing the mayhem as he himself fought to stay alive might at least partially justify his difficulty in committing to close interpersonal relationships. It is likely that, to him, closeness was associated with the threat of loss. One mechanism of coping with being subjected to trauma is to turn the passive experience inflicted onto the self into an active one inflicted on others. It is done in the hope of managing the trauma through the process of acting it out in a way that is now under the original victim's own control. This mechanism may account for the cruelty and control that was to creep into Onassis's relationship with Callas once the first throes of passion wore off.

Aristo not only managed to survive the ordeal of Smyrna; he also cunningly helped his father escape from a Turkish prison by bribing Turkish officials. After the ordeal, the Onassis family lived in Athens. Disappointed by a lack of business opportunities, Aristotle emigrated to Argentina, in defiance of his father, who wanted him to become an architect. Once in Buenos Aires, Onassis began work as a telephone technician, but, within the span of five years, he rose to own a cigarette company, manufacturing his own brand of cigarettes, "Claudia Muzios," named after the famous opera singer. He made his own fortune and subsequently purchased a fleet of tankers. Onassis was a self-made individual—just like Callas.

Onassis was one of the richest men in the world, but Callas was more famous. It was she who drew crowds of onlookers wherever they went. Onassis's previous love affairs with celebrities such as Eva Peron, Gloria Swanson, Greta Garbo, and Ava Gardner were fleeting. Maria and Onassis had plenty of shared experiences to talk about, given their Greek cultural backgrounds, but they were also united by a sense of marginality in their respective social circles. Like Maria, Aristo had little formal education. Despite a propensity to flaunt his wealth, he felt most at ease living a simple life, drinking ouzo with Greek fishermen. Both possessed few intellectual interests. Maria's favorite pastime was *Reader's*

Digest and cheap Italian romance novels or watching Westerns on television. Onassis and Callas must have felt a shared comfort in being able to interact with each other without the pretense of the jet-set surrounding them. Now, for the first time in his life, he was smitten with a woman promising him an equal partnership, a combination of physical passion and a meeting of minds, a merging of heart and soul. In talking with her friend, a physiotherapist, Callas claimed that the mutual respect between her and Onassis would always be there, even if their paths were to divide, because of their common roots: "We are Greeks—the same stubborn race. We started from zero and reached the top only thanks to our own will and our own abilities. *We do not reflect others' light; we radiate our own.*"[11] The last sentence here is particularly important to understanding the strong attraction between Maria and Aristo during the first phase of their relationship. What a wonderful image of two independent, yet presumably intertwined, sources of light—an image conveying mutuality, respect, equality, and self-sufficiency.

A relationship based on respect and mutual understanding was not only novel to Maria; it was also unknown to Aristo. Tina was a beautiful woman, a cosmopolitan socialite, and a charming hostess. But she did not share Aristo's "Greekness," nor had she experienced poverty, as he had in Argentina before acquiring wealth. Tina was raised in a traditional and highly affluent Greek family living in the United States; she did not share Onassis's rags-to-riches story nor was she interested in the world of fierce business competition among Greek ship oligarchs that her husband inhabited. Callas's relationship with Meneghini was also unequal: it started with Battista as the powerful benefactor and ended up with Maria as the domineering diva. It must have been refreshing, therefore, for both Maria and Aristo to discuss their private and public affairs as equals with a sense of mutual understanding. Looked at from the perspective of psychological growth, it is unfortunate that the relationship could not last.

The early stages of Maria and Aristo's relationship were infused by passionate love on both sides. Onassis could be a very attentive and considerate partner. He showered Maria with expensive jewelry (which he bestowed on Jackie Kennedy after Callas left the pieces behind). Flying back from Dallas in 1959, where she had made an appearance in *Lucia*, Callas found the first-class seat next to hers filled with roses from Aristo. In the early 1960s, he owned a stake in the world-renowned Monte Carlo Casino, along with other property in the principality. Before the breakup of their relationships, he was on friendly terms with Prince Rainier and his wife Princess Grace (formerly Grace Kelly). Maria and Aristo would frequently descend on Monte Carlo in their private helicopter, launched from a pad on the *Christina's* deck, and party with their rich and famous friends late into the night. Maria, who did not smoke and who did not like to drink, learned to tolerate these nightly escapades, although dancing was far from her favorite activity—unless it was with Aristo. How could Maria have been anything but impressed by the unimaginable opulence that Aristo offered her, on both land and sea? The *Christina*, a converted navy frigate, was a stately pleasure craft with a swimming pool, a helicopter landing pad, golden fixtures in the bathrooms, and bedrooms decorated with frescos. Onassis took pride in a set of bar stools covered with the foreskin of whales and was particularly gleeful when women sat on them. But he could also be considerate: When the couple stayed in the penthouse apartment in his Monte Carlo office, Onassis ordered employees to take off their shoes so that Maria would not be disturbed from her afternoon nap. With Onassis, Callas experienced the heights of physical and spiritual passion.

For the first time in her life, Maria felt that her love was reciprocated. She was desired and fully appreciated as a woman, not merely as a performer, as she made clear to Onassis's sister Artemis: "Everyone in my life has used me. Aristo is the only person I have ever met who does not take something from me. Instead, he offers me everything. Everything I could ever want."[12] In response to Zeffirelli's early warning about Onassis's trustworthiness, Callas retorted, "Can't you see? He adores me, he can't live without me."[13] This conviction said more about Maria's state of mind than it did Aristo's; nonetheless, the new experience visibly transformed Callas's behavior. Some changes were positive. People who knew Callas in the early stages of her relationship with Onassis found her to be a kinder and more considerate person, and an added layer of emotional complexity now crept into her singing. In his review of the 1960 studio recording of Bellini's *Norma*, John Ardoin notes how Callas's portrayal had become more multifaceted: The new Norma was "more giving, more complex and drawn in finer lines."[14] Ardoin elaborates, explaining that while Callas's singing remains fearsome, her voice is also more transcendent. Callas's newfound love for Onassis likely facilitated her identification with the role of a woman who, in revenge for her lover's betrayal, is prepared to sacrifice their own two sons.

Trouble in Paradise

There were also changes in Callas's behavior that were less positive. According to the French weekly celebrity news magazine *France-Dimanche*, Callas's relationship with Onassis brought forth a new image of a meek and mild young woman in love: "She does everything he wants, talks if he wants to talk, keeps quiet if he does, smiles when he is in a good mood. . . . She has given him the ultimate proof of submission by virtually abandoning her career for him." "You would not recognize Callas," Paul-Jean Remy, a French intellectual and Callas's biographer, was told upon arriving in Milan; "she is as meek as a kitten. It is Onassis who has performed this miracle."[15] These descriptions are belied by the ways in which Callas resisted Onassis's bossiness. They also distort the true reason behind Maria's curtailed singing career. But they do accurately reflect the difficulty she encountered in balancing submission with assertion in responding to a man she loved madly. For a novitiate in the art of love like Maria, this task was made doubly difficult by Onassis's domineering and forceful personality. His life was infused with a highly competitive spirit. In his relations with men, this manifested in fierce competition, especially among other Greek shipping magnates, for contracts and for women.

Aristotle had a complex personality capable of extremes, much like Maria's. He was a shrewd and ruthless businessman with no compunction about using any possible means to get what he wanted, including signing checks with fading ink. He was known for his volatile temper and angry outbursts that he quickly forgot. He did not hesitate to exploit women sexually, discarding them at a whim, as did many men of his generation. Aristotle's treatment of women was rather typical among Europe's wealthy elite in the 1950s and '60s. His was a social scene reminiscent of Paris in the 1920s, as depicted in Hemingway's *A Moveable Feast*, an artistic world where women and men lived lives uninhibited by petite bourgeois conventionality. In his relationships with women, Onassis's dominance manifested in cruelty, a suffocating control, and a demeaning attitude. These attitudes were mixed with generosity, tenderness, and sexual fulfillment, a confusing mixture for sure. Maria entered dangerous territory by committing herself to a relationship with Aristo. As clinical psychologists well know, the past is the best predictor of the future, and Onassis's personal history when it came to intimacy was far from consoling. His domineering cruelty became increasingly prominent as his relationship with Maria began to unravel.

There "was something in treating Onassis like a sultan or god that brought out the despot in him," writes Arianna Huffington in her psychologically perceptive account of Maria's relationship with Aristo. "Or, perhaps, she exacerbated these tendencies in him."[16] Maria, who called Aristo "my Pasha," treated him with both the tenderness of a loving wife who cares for her husband and the affection of a doting mother who spoils her child. On the *Christina*, where Aristo typically paraded dressed only in shorts, Maria would run to fetch his shirt or sweater at the sign of a rising sea breeze. Frequently, she would send *Christina*'s cook to bed and prepare their midnight snacks herself. When the couple entertained guests, like a dutiful Greek wife, Callas was happy to obey Onassis's commands and get "so and so" more champagne. According to Korinna Spandiou, the couple's physical therapist,

Callas never tired of listening to Aristo's life stories, spun on board of *Christina*.[17] Maria adopted Aristo's friends and acquired his interests. An acquaintance who met her in London was struck by Maria talking incessantly of politics, tourism, and the future of air travel, the latter reflecting Onassis's ownership of Olympic Airways. When Onassis was with his two children, Maria did not mind walking behind the threesome. Alexander and Christina, who were united in their hatred of Callas, responded by calling her "the ugly one," "the singer," or "Kolou"—a twist on the name Callas meaning "big ass."[18] If Maria waited for Aristo to come to her defense, she was sadly disappointed. It never came.

Maria's love of Onassis certainly changed her, but there is little evidence of a change in Onassis. Onassis never attempted to block or curtail Callas's singing career, contrary to popular belief and despite his lack of enthusiasm for the opera. But while proud of her status as a famous singer, he diminished the importance of her achievements. Onassis ostentatiously missed Maria's 1961 performance of *Medea* at the open-air theatre in Epidaurus, an event attended by the Prime Minster of Greece, the elite of Athenian society, and many international glitterati. On another occasion, he turned to Callas in front of guests and asked her, rhetorically, "Who are you?" Onassis answered his own question. "You are nobody. You are a woman with a whistle in her throat that doesn't work anymore."[19] During failed negotiations over a contract to film *Tosca*, he dismissed Maria with "Shut up! Don't interfere, you know nothing about these things. You are nothing but a nightclub singer."[20] When Callas declined to consider the opportunity to star in the film *The Guns of Navarone*, "I get up every day of my life to win!" an infuriated Onassis shouted. "I don't know why you bother to get up at all."[21] Onassis impatience was likely driven, in this case, by the prospect of basking in the glory of Callas's new-found notoriety as a film star. In these exchanges, he showed, however, gross insensitivity to Maria's insecurity over how her face and body would come across on the silver screen.

While undoubtedly hurtful, Onassis's attacks on Callas's abilities as a singer paled in significance to his demeaning attitude. He seemed to get a thrill from attacking Callas's anxiety over her body and her appeal as a woman, and, according to Kiki Moustsatsos, his long-term private secretary, he took total control over her appearance. Since eye shadow, lipstick, and rouge displeased him, Maria wore little if any makeup. He forbade Callas from wearing glasses, claiming they made her look ugly, and he forced her to wear contact lenses, against her will. Maria cut her hair short and bought several black dresses to please him, as he liked her in that color. During her fittings, Onassis would call the dressmaker Biki with instructions. If, when she sat down to dinner, Aristo indicated that he did not like what she was wearing, Maria would get up and change. Her massive weight loss made her appear more attractive on stage, but it did not fully assuage her body image concerns. Callas harbored a "pervasive and persistent conviction that she was ugly." Maria felt "that the beautiful woman the world responded to was a mask, a disguise, almost a trick," writes Huffington. "She remained convinced to the end of her life that it was the package of clothes, hairdos, jewelry, figure and furs that was admired and never Maria herself."[22]

There was also public humiliation. On one occasion, at a formal dinner, when Maria asked him what he thought of her new hat, Onassis responded: "either you cut your nose off to match the hat, or you get a bigger hat to match your nose."[23] On another occasion, Aristo suggested that Maria loan one of her dresses to a mutual acquaintance. "Maria," he said, "Look at her bust. Look how beautifully her bust fills out that dress of yours." On yet another occasion, he humiliated her at dinner. Aristo and Maria were dining out with Larry Kelly, a Dallas opera impresario. "As soon as they settled in the restaurant, Maria propped one of her legs on a vacant chair," explains John Ardoin, a friend of Kelly's. Maria "did this whenever she could to relieve her poor circulation." During dinner, Larry Kelly recounts how his hair loss began when he was very young, that his vanity led him to seek a "horribly painful and costly transplant." Onassis, who was "stroking [Maria's] leg under the tablecloth," turns to Larry and said, "Poor Larry, you paid so much money to put hair on your head and Maria pays so much money to take it off her legs. Right now, she feels like a plucked chicken."[24]

Perhaps the greater humiliation was living with Onassis as his mistress. Maria had terminated her friendship with Ingrid Bergman because she divorced her husband and started cohabiting with Rossellini. Now she found herself in the same situation. To highlight her inferiority, Onassis would remind Maria of her status as a guest on the *Christina*. When Winston Churchill accepted an invitation to vacation on the boat in June 1963, Onassis unceremoniously ordered Maria off the *Christina*, citing her mistress status as the excuse. Conveniently, her absence on the trip allowed Aristo to begin an affair with Lee Radziwill, Jackie Kennedy's younger sister. Maria was similarly banished a few months later when both Lee and Jackie joined Onassis for a Mediterranean cruise on the *Christina*, a trip Onassis organized to console Jackie over the loss of her son Patrick, who recently had died shortly after birth.

In 1966, Callas renounced her American citizenship in a highly publicized event. The precipitating reason was a 1946 Greek law that rendered illegal the marriages of Greek citizens not conducted in the Orthodox church. By switching from American to Greek citizenship, Maria's marriage to Meneghini became null and void everywhere except in Italy. The press headlines forecasted an incipient exchange of marital vows between Callas and Onassis, seemingly confirmed by Maria's coy public denials that such an event was to take place. But wedding bells never rang. Instead, Onassis played a cruel joke on Maria when, in 1967, he falsely told the press they had missed the marriage ceremony; he and Callas were wed fifteen days earlier. Onassis not only refused to marry Callas, but he denied her aspiration to be a mother. Although Meneghini has claimed Callas was not capable of becoming pregnant, it seems that in 1966 she accidentally conceived a child with Onassis and, following his insistence, underwent an abortion. "I don't want a baby by you!" Callas recalled Onassis declaring after she told him of her pregnancy. "What would I do with another child? I already have two."[25] Callas obeyed, even though she had moral reservations about abortion and also deeply desired to marry Aristo and have children with him.

Maria did not take Onassis's abusive behavior calmly, although some of its negative impact was probably mitigated by the memory of Litsa's abusive attitude toward George. In private, the relationship proved to be more turbulent and volatile than suggested by the *France-Dimanche* article. Callas would flee a room in tears after being confronted with Onassis's slights. At times, the couple engaged in physical fights, with Maria well-equipped to stand her ground—she was significantly bigger than Aristo. On many occasions, the *Christina* crew witnessed Callas's fits of jealousy over Aristo's affairs with other women. Tears mixed with threats to leave frequently preceded his business trips. Faced with a newspaper photo of Onassis dining with Lee Radziwill, Maria threatened suicide, claiming she would jump overboard. Onassis was known for expunging his guilt with handsome gifts—though he would never admit wrongdoing—and, given his tendency to quickly forget his angry outbursts, there was ample opportunity for reconciliation. At the same time, several people who knew Callas well during the years she spent with Onassis described her as emotionally childish and easily placated.

One afternoon the couple was relaxing on the beach on Onassis's privately owned island of Scorpios when Maria spotted several waterskiers. She yelled to Onassis to "get them away," according to Kiki Moutsatsos. Aristotle was amused. "Oh Maria," he answered her laughing, "let the young lady do her waterskiing. She is so pretty and thin. It is nice to look at her." Maria was furious. She began to "storm away from him," but Onassis firmly grabbed her arm, pulling her back to his side: "But you know I prefer women who are tall and a little bit fat like you, my darling," he said. Moutsatsos notes that he delivered this message "lovingly," and it only took Maria "a few minutes to smile again and continue to enjoy herself."[26] This incident illustrates the confusing double-bind or mixed message in Onassis's comments about Callas' physical appearance. On the surface, the reference to the pretty waterskier is meant as a put down, yet the subsequent comment regarding his preference for women who are "tall and a little fat" sends a message affirming Callas's physique. It must have felt, therefore, consoling for Maria to feel that she was accepted by someone who was not blind to her own body concerns that she felt were justified. In this way, some of Onassis's derogatory comments appear to reaffirm Callas's belief that he was the only one to go beyond her false persona and truly accept her. It is also clear that, as the relationship progressed, Callas fused her identity with Onassis; she became convinced that she could not live without him, and she allowed him to define her as a woman. Callas's relationship with Aristo satisfied her longing to end her isolation and merge herself with another human being, as Huffington has noted. Maria's initial pronouncement—that she and Onassis were two independent beacons radiating their own light—is indicative of this desire for partnership, but it no longer held true.

The Outsider

Being with Aristo ushered in a radical change in Maria's lifestyle. The self-absorbed artist who led the life of a "vestal virgin focused on home-theatre-home,"[27] according to Nicola Rescigno, Callas's favorite conductor of the late 1950s, was now thrown into Onassis's socially demanding orbit. And that orbit included royalty, various gradations of nobility, and other celebrity figures.

Maria never possessed the social skills expected of a rich and prominent man's partner. On one occasion, when she was married to Battista, he kicked her leg beneath a table to bring her attention to a blunder. Callas turned to him and asked, "Titta why are you kicking me under the table?"[28] And during her time with Onassis,

Callas played a distant second role when it came to socializing. Maria was a forthright person who spoke her mind freely. Her forthright attitude was accompanied by a rather poor, almost nonexistent sense of humor, so she frequently appeared gauche in Onassis's world. Socially isolated as a child, she never developed the playfulness or prankishness that comes with attending a boarding school and, more generally, spending free time with kids of her own age. Maria was always a bit reserved and distant, and this aspect of her personality presented a side of Maria which was not at all Greek. Her limited cultural and intellectual knowledge also failed to impress the Onassis crowd. When she was shown photos of frescos from Pompeii by a friend in Athens, Maria expressed her admiration, but then said, "What a great artist this Pompeii was. When did she live?"[29] As Prince Michael of Greece recounted, "When the conversation was on her art, she was the epitome of the self-assured professional. When it was general, she turned into a hesitant, middle-class Greek discussing curtains, carpeting and little dogs."[30] Though reserved and distant with others, the main reason for her low profile among Onassis's circle of acquaintances was her utter lack of interest in anyone other than her lover.

Maria could spend an entire day standing on the deck of the ship gazing into the distance, like the wife of a fisherman out at sea, waiting for Aristo's return from a trip.

When asked to have dinner by Lord Harewood, one of the few people she knew well, Maria refused, saying that she expected Aristo to return the following day and that she therefore needed to go to bed early to look her best for his arrival. Her single-minded focus on Onassis meant that she lacked the social support provided by a network of friends to whom one could turn in times of adversity. Her disdainful attitude toward others prevented her from currying favor with those who might have helped strengthen her relationship with Onassis. Take Artemis, Onassis's formidable sister who had a lot of influence over him. She opposed their liaison, ostensibly because the two were too much alike, though she also likely was put off by Maria's manner that jarred her upper-class Greek sensibility. "Maria did not seem that interested," according to Kiki Moutsatsos, who at first "thought she might be afraid of Artemis." But Moutsatsos soon realized that Maria "was not that concerned with anyone . . . except for her lover."[31] Callas found it hard to compliment anyone, whether the ship's crew or opera colleagues. She made no effort to engage Artemis, nor did she attempt to show a side of herself that might assuage her reservations.

Maria's isolation was compounded by her continuing estrangement from her family, relationships which could have provided her with a source of support. She refused to have any contact with Litsa, saw Jackie only sporadically, and severed communication with her father in 1964, when George finally married his long-term companion Alexandra Papajohn. It was Onassis's own initiative to retain contact with Maria's family. However, according to Kiki Moutsatsos, Callas told him that "she would much rather have him be kind to her dogs, which she loved, than cater to the relatives she disliked."[32] Callas, alienated from her family, could not profit from any advice they may have offered her on how to handle her relationship with Onassis. Maria met with her sister Jackie in 1964, near the time of her performance of *Medea* in Epidaurus, their first meeting in almost seventeen years. Jackie barely recognized her sister, who had changed from an overweight and insecure young woman to a suave and poised diva. Over one of two lunches they had together, Maria overheard another diner refer to Jackie's lovely voice. Her response was swift: "Doctor," said Maria coldly, "the donkeys bray and think they have a voice." In response to Jackie's assertion that she once did have a voice but threw it away because of her love for her long-term partner Milton Embiricos, her sister yelled "You, a voice? Do you want me to start breaking dishes?"[33] A couple of days later, as Jackie left the *Christina*, Maria told her to take a bus home even though a Mercedes with a bored chauffeur was parked by the jetty. In dealing with her immediate family, Callas showed little insight that the dismissive and contemptuous attitude she showed toward them could easily spill over into her relationship with Onassis, with contempt breeding contempt.

Love Is Blind—Or Is It?

Why did Callas stay with Onassis? Why did she tolerate so much humiliation and abuse with so little resistance? Why did she let Aristo define her identity as a woman and control the most minute and intimate aspects of her life? These questions penetrate to the core of Callas's personality, and they defy easy answers. Any explanation of her behavior is complicated by the interplay between her psychological needs and the gender role expectations of the 1950s and '60s.

Most straightforwardly, Callas's relationship with Onassis provided her with a convenient escape from her psychologically taxing operatic career, one that had become increasingly so with the decline in her voice. Onassis did not block her career, but their relationship did coincide with her precipitous withdrawal from the world of opera. Before she began living with Onassis, in 1959, following their first cruise on the *Christina*, she would give an average of sixty performances a year; by 1969, her total number of performances for the *entire decade* was sixty. The decline in performances is striking: In 1958, Callas gave twenty-eight performances of seven operas, whereas in 1960, she gave seven performances of two operas. Stripped of her career, self-isolated from her family, and lacking friends, it could be argued that Maria had little choice but to become dependent on Onassis for emotional and practical support. Nicholas Gage favors this interpretation: "by the beginning of 1963 there was nothing left in Maria's life but her relationship with Aristo."[34] His interpretation evokes traditional gender roles—Callas's behavior fits the image of a woman who feels inadequate to negotiate the vicissitudes of life on her own and who, therefore, subjugates her needs to those of her partner—but Gage's interpretation must be treated with caution.

Callas's stage career and the brisk sale of her opera recordings made her an independently wealthy woman. Following her death, an estate worth several millions of dollars was divided between Meneghini and her mother and sister. Maria had no financial worries, though as an unmarried partner, she was not entitled to financial compensation should she and Aristo split. Although her performances during the 1960s generated their share of negative evaluations by music critics—many of whom were put off by vocal flaws that had become more prominent in her singing—she continued to be adored by legions of admirers who met her sporadic concert and operatic appearances in the 1960s with thunderous applause, particularly her performance in *Tosca*. In anticipation of her two performances of *Tosca* in New York, the queue for the tickets formed a week in advance. Her Paris *Norma*s in 1964 and 1965 met with the same excitement, although the last performance ended in disaster when she collapsed on stage as a result of a drop in her blood pressure. There is thus little substance to the claim that Callas's decision to tolerate Onassis's abusive behavior was dictated by material dependence or a lack of artistic opportunities. It is also atypical for the world of opera. As was the case with Renata Tebaldi and Rosa Ponselle, many divas managed to craft a fulfilling life and a successful career without a partner, as did Nellie Melba and Louise Tetrazzini before them. The rough and tumble of a diva's life required and reinforced independence and emotional hardiness, traits that Callas, however, appeared to lack.

Zeffirelli offers another explanation of Callas's attraction to Onassis: her "stupid ambition of becoming a great lady of café society,"[35] which Zeffirelli attributes to her difficult childhood. While Maria might have suffered humiliation in private, to the larger public she continued to be a mega-star whose fame as an opera singer was only enhanced by her romance with one of the richest men in the world. This newfound status, despite its emotional cost, provided Callas with a worthy substitute for the adoration and admiration of her opera audiences. While having merit, Zeffirelli's claim offers only a partial explanation of Callas's behavior as, given her own celebrity status, she could have maintained a high societal profile without Onassis.

Maria's relationship with Onassis ironically fulfilled her mother's own fantasies of wining and dining with the rich and famous. Litsa turned a humble Chinese meal into a sumptuous banquet—as will be recalled from Chapter 4—and transformed the wooden floor of their New York apartment into a palace ballroom to captivate the young imaginations of her daughters with the glamour of wealth. Now, in Aristo's company, Maria realized this dream by dining with real royalty in real palaces. Though she had severed physical ties to her mother, Litsa's dreams and aspirations were indelibly enshrined in Maria's psyche. Such introjection of her mother's desires was unlikely to have happened consciously. Rather, Callas unconsciously acquired her desire for fulfillment as a woman and as a mother by spending her childhood and adolescence in the company of Litsa and Jackie, both of whom valorized traditional gender roles and expectations. Such learning, akin to what psychologists call *implicit* or *nondeclarative knowledge*, functions outside of a person's awareness and manifests itself in a visceral sense of what seems right or what gives one satisfaction. Although Callas's pronouncement that she would gladly relinquish opera stardom to be a wife and mother may have sounded insincere at the time, it has some merit.

Callas's attachment to Onassis had deeper psychological roots, a narcissistic component that went beyond the adulation she received from being his partner or enacting the role of a subservient Greek wife. "I was very impressed by his charm, but above all, I was impressed by his powerful personality and the way he held everyone's attention," Maria told Stelios Galatopoulos several years after the breakup. Callas "began to feel strangely relaxed."[36] As Huffington has argued, "Maria's fear of losing Onassis was compounded by her fear of losing the spontaneity, joy, and passion that he had brought into her life."[37] When Zeffirelli asked her, "Why didn't you leave him?" Callas responded "How can I? By now I am at the mercy of this man. He was everything to me."[38] Once again, just as in her earlier relationships, it is evident that Maria's love for Aristo had a narcissistic—self-serving—component.

Callas's merger with Onassis's idealized persona provided her with a powerful way of regulating her own emotions, and it also injected vitality into her life. A relationship rooted in idealization is based on the attitude "you are great, but I am part of you," and for Maria, a slew of older men fulfilled this role of idealized object, including Meneghini, Serafin, and Visconti. Describing Callas's relationship with Visconti, Michael Scott argues that she was "always prepared to sit like Paul at the feet of Gamaliel [Visconti] as she had done before in front of Serafin and Toscanini."[39] She did so despite Visconti's vulgarity, his aristocratic disdain for petite bourgeois values, and the fact that his openly gay lifestyle irked the highly moralistic Callas. The same dependence characterized her relationship with Tulio Serafin, a renowned conductor. From practically the beginning of Callas's Italian career, Serafin offered Maria practical and emotional support, as well as guidance on the intricacies of *bel canto* singing. Time and again, Callas's psychological health and vitality were dependent on merger with a powerful external figure who provided her with security, cohesion, and personal meaning. This worked to her advantage early on in life, during the height of her operatic career, but ended badly in the case of Onassis.

Women who are "in a particular relation of dependent subservience to one man," one "whom they consider great and admirable and without whom they cannot live,"[40] are typically overcritical of themselves, according to Annie Reich, whose research focuses on love choices. These women are "willing to bear anything and masochistically to make all kinds of sacrifices," thus they weave a pattern of idealization that functions to redress feelings of inferiority through the process of merging one's identity with a strong other person. The result is "a feeling of oneness, of being one body with the grandiose sex partner, a feeling which is the complete opposite of the over strong feeling of ugliness and inferiority that predominates when [they] evaluate their personality. It is obvious that a separation from such a partner is intolerable." Reich's description captures aspects of Callas's relationship with Onassis; it explains the strength of her attachment to him and her identification with his interests, passions, and way of being.

Maria's craving to merge with the idealized Onassis reflects her lack of an independent or mature self. She was unable to function unless buttressed by an external power source, either through having her needs mirrored by others or by her identification with an idealized figure. She had also attempted to idealize Meneghini in the early phase of their relationship. But the gauche, provincial, and ultimately dull Battista proved hard to keep on a pedestal once the initial bloom of love wore off. At the height of her career, Maria did not need a strong source of vitality and well-being from an intimate relationship—most of her narcissistic needs were being met by adoring opera fans—but things changed radically when she met Onassis. He not only totally captured her imagination and fulfilled her sexually, thus strengthening their bond and their merged unity, but he also filled the void caused by her diminished number of opera performances by a mirroring that was no longer accessible.

Reich's thoughts also explain Callas's willingness to tolerate Onassis's assault on her physical appearance. On a superficial level, she accepted his abuse because this was a price she was willing to pay for staying with him. On a deeper level, however, as argued by Nadia Stancioff, Callas "was actually attracted by Aristo's evasive, domineering traits. It made her feel feminine."[41] In other words, a degree of masochism crept into Maria's relationship with Onassis and it functioned to consolidate her (aspiring) identity as a traditional wife or partner. As she once told John Ardoin, "Greece looks European, but believe me, it is totally Eastern. The man is the Pasha."[42] Indeed, two of Callas's European biographers describe her as a slave to Onassis. Of course, Onassis's disparagement of her physical appearance struck a raw nerve as it reinforced Callas's long-present doubts about her body. But given her perfectionism and penchant for self-criticism, she was likely to accept the criticism as justified on some level. Onassis's infidelities, in fact, threatened her more than his derogatory comments. Callas's willingness to tolerate the demeaning comments about her appearance probably only strengthened Onassis's attacks; paradoxically, his taunts were most likely driven by his discomfort with his own unimposing physique.

The claim that Callas's attraction to Onassis had a masochistic component is bound to be contentious. But it fits with narcissism. It also fits with emerging views on nonbinary and fluid sexualities that validate consensual sadomasochistic relationships. These nontraditional views of sexuality refuse to privilege romantic relationships based on equal power-sharing between partners. In this view, irrespective of whether a relationship is based on equality or a consensually negotiated power imbalance, it can yield personal and sexual gratification. Of course, an alternative explanation is that Onassis's dominance over Maria lacked her consent and instead reflected her belief that it was the price she had to pay for being with the man she loved deeply—an attitude reinforced by her traditional view of gender roles. These varying explanations are not mutually exclusive.

Irrespective of the explanation, there is little doubt that Maria loved Onassis with the intensity and passion she typically reserved for her operatic roles. This proud woman was prepared to abort a child and sacrifice her dignity for him. "How softly and gently he smiles, how sweetly his eyes open—can you see, my friends, do you not see it? How he glows ever brighter raising himself high amidst the stars? Do you not see it?"[43] These words of ecstasy uttered by Isolde upon seeing Tristan's dead body could easily have been uttered by Callas about Onassis, who surely was the love of her life. The fact that her love for him had a self-referential and self-serving component should not detract from an appreciation of the depth of her feelings. Indeed, one could argue that truly passionate love cannot exist without the fusion of psychological give-and-take. Their relationship allowed her to become less self-absorbed and to open herself up to another human being—a precious gift, especially given the many ways in which her personality and her early family experiences blocked her ability to be open to others. Callas never stopped loving Onassis, even after his marriage to Jackie Kennedy. She lost her own desire to live following his death and died just over two years later. The tragedy of their relationship is that, just as Maria played Isolde to Aristo's Tristan, it was only once he abandoned her that Onassis realized that Callas, and only Callas, was his true Isolde.

Enter Jackie

Another way to contextualize Maria's relationship with Aristo is to compare it with Onassis's relationship with Jackie Kennedy, whom he married in 1968. After their first meeting in 1963, on the cruise with her sister Lee Radziwill, they met again later that year when Onassis flew to Washington to console Jackie following the assassination of Jack Kennedy. The first sign of Jackie and Aristo's romantic involvement was in the summer of 1967, when Gianni Agnelli, the owner of the Fiat corporation, spotted Jackie on Scorpios. They were married in a private ceremony a year later, in October 1968, the marriage delayed only to avoid negatively impacting Bobby Kennedy's presidential campaign.

Jackie's marriage to Onassis caused an outcry in the United States. She was the revered, heroic widow of an assassinated president, an American icon, yet now she was perceived as selling herself to a rapacious, ill-mannered oil tycoon who was not only a foreigner but also twenty-three years older. The motives behind the marriage were complicated. There was certainly a financial element. Fond of spending money, Jackie felt constrained by the $175,000 (roughly $1.4 million in 2019 dollars) annual allowance that the Kennedy family provided. She also sought a refuge for herself and her children as she continued to be traumatized by the death of her husband and of Bobby Kennedy, the man whom she allegedly loved more than his older brother. Nevertheless, wealth and a private Aegean island provided some escape from her personal trauma as well as from the turbulence in America during the late 1960s. In turn, Onassis's attraction was fueled by Jackie's status as the most glamorous woman of her generation. "I really had only one thing against him [Onassis]," Callas noted in her conversation with Galatopoulos, quite perceptively, in fact. "It was impossible for me to come to terms with his insatiable thirst for conquering everything."[44] And to Aristo, Jackie Kennedy seemed like the greatest conquest of them all—plus, by marrying Jackie, Onassis had hoped he might advance some of his American business ventures, including a plan to build an oil refinery in New Hampshire. In contrast to the passion that engulfed Maria and Aristo in the early stages of their liaison, Jackie's marriage to Onassis was based, on both sides, on more practical considerations.

Jackie's relationship with Ari, as he was nicknamed by the Kennedy clan, flourished during their first two years of marriage. Onassis was enamored with Jackie's beauty and took great pride in his world-renowned bride. Jackie's status as the widow of an American president buffered against Aristotle's domineering condescension. She took pleasure in redecorating the Pink House on Scorpios and, to the chagrin of the gardeners, altered the landscape to reflect her own taste. She also relished learning Greek and familiarizing herself with Greek history. The marital bond was further strengthened by a fulfilling and imaginative sex life. Both Ari and Jackie received from the marriage what they desired: glamour and prestige for Onassis, financial stability and a feeling of safety for Jackie.

The marriage deteriorated for a number of reasons. Jackie frequently traveled to Europe, as well as to New York City, where her children Caroline and John Jr. were attending school, and Onassis gradually became upset by the increased time the couple spent apart. Aristotle also became dismayed by Jackie's spending habits. An inveterate shopper, she found his $30,000 monthly shopping allowance inadequate, though the figure represents approximately $200,000 in today's dollars. In the first year of their marriage, she spent an additional $1 million on clothing, and Jackie even used to resell many unworn pieces to a second-hand clothing shop to secure additional income (a practice not uncommon among wives of rich men).

Beyond Jackie's own behavior, Onassis also blamed a series of devastating personal losses and setbacks on a curse that he associated with his marriage to Jackie. His beloved son Alexander died in a 1973 airplane crash. The following year, his mother died, followed shortly thereafter by his first wife, Tina. There were also financial setbacks, including the need to sell the verging-on-bankruptcy Olympic Airways to the Greek government and the collapse of his plans to build oil refineries because of local community opposition to the project. Adding to the strain, Aristo was diagnosed with myasthenia gravis, a degenerative condition which resulted in his death in a Paris hospital in 1975. Because all of these events occurred within five years of their marriage, Onassis and his family, including his powerful sister Artemis, began to think of them as "Jackie's jinx."

Predictably, as their relationship deteriorated, Onassis's cruel and demeaning behaviors resurfaced. He threw tantrums and humiliated Jackie in front of others. On a Caribbean cruise, he forbade her and her sister Lee from going ashore, a prohibition Jackie violated by getting into her bathing suit and swimming.

When Jackie asked a Greek professor whether he thought Socrates really existed, Ari dismissed her intellectual interests by sniping "What a stupid question. Have you ever noticed the statue of the man with the mustache that is in the center of Athens?" he asked. "Are you too stupid to know that is a statue of Socrates?"[45] On another occasion, when Onassis discovered a photographer taking the couple's pictures surreptitiously, he got Jackie to stand up. Lifting her skirt, he challenged the photographer: "Is this what you are after?" Kiki Moutsatsos argues that whereas Maria responded to Aristo's bad behavior by "screaming, yelling, and carrying on like a crazy woman," Jackie's approach was much more refined and effective.

> Jackie was always so clever when she talked to Aristo, playing with him as if she were a cat stalking a mouse, complimenting him when she wanted something, and making it seem as if her request was his idea. Mr. O was a shrewd businessman and prided himself on knowing how to get anything he wanted from his opponents in a business struggle. Yet with Mrs. J, I felt he was often outmaneuvered. She knew his moods so well. And when he was not in the mood to give her something, she never wasted her time asking. If he was in a bad mood, she accepted his crankiness stoically, never providing him with any reason to be angry at her.[46]

Although a contemporary sensibility might favor Callas's more forthright approach, it was Jackie who mastered the rules of "the feminine game" played in the 1960s. Additionally, unlike Callas who was estranged from her family and virtually friendless, Jackie surrounded herself with a swath of acquaintances, admirers, and family who were frequent visitors on the *Christina*. Many of them, such as her sister Lee, her mother-in-law Rose Kennedy, and Ted Kennedy were welcomed by Onassis, but some he barely tolerated, such as Rudolph Nureyev, whose gayness jarred him. Jackie's network of rich friends clearly buffered her against a toxic marital environment. Furthermore, and again unlike Maria, Jackie had broad artistic and intellectual interests; she was an avid reader and photographer and liked to discuss art and philosophy with prominent Greek scholars.

In sum, Jackie possessed a sense of agency and personhood that Maria lacked. This did not necessarily make Jackie's marriage to Onassis psychologically healthier than Maria's. It simply made the affair safer because she was buffered from its adverse consequences. In addition to their overt marital conflict, Onassis spent the last year of his life scheming how to divorce Jackie and leave her as little money as possible. But her strong social network, a plethora of interests, and skill in manipulating domineering and emotionally abusive men provided her with psychological options Maria lacked. Callas's assertion that she and Onassis constituted two independent sources of light appears to better fit Jackie's than Maria's relationship with him. Nonetheless, for Jackie and Ari, the two light beams never really intersected, thus rendering the relationship emotionally safe but psychologically barren. In contrast, although Maria's light beam collapsed into Onassis's, their liaison exuded passion and commitment. It gave Maria an unexpected though ultimately tragic gift.

Notes

1. Remy, *Maria Callas: A tribute*, p. 139.
2. Gage, *Greek fire*, p. 42.
3. Gage, *Greek fire*, p. 68.
4. At the time of the voyage on *Christina*, Meneghini was sixty-three, Onassis fifty-three, and Callas thirty-six years of age.
5. Allegri, *Callas by Callas*, p. 132.
6. Callas's performance of the aria "Casta Diva" is available on YouTube by typing: "Callas – Casta diva Paris." The entire Paris concert is also available on an EMI Classics DVD titled "La Callas . . . Toujours."
7. Wally Toscanini, named after the heroine of Catallani's opera *La Wally*, was the daughter of the arguably greatest conductor of the twentieth century. Wally and Maria had a stormy relationship, with Toscanini's daughter not impressed that Maria refused to see Toscanini's corpse lying in repose. With her usual bluntness Maria indicated that she was tired after a trip and that while she was alive, Toscanini was dead.
8. In fact, she refused to attend her father's funeral, citing the need to continue with a recording session as her justification.
9. Allegri, *Callas by Callas*, p. 137.
10. Following the divorce, Tina married Stavros Niarchos, another Greek shipping magnate and Onassis bitter rival. The choice of her marital partner was unusual in so far as Niarchos's first wife was Tina's sister who died under suspicious circumstances. Tina herself died in her forties as a result of alcohol and drug abuse.
11. Gage, *Greek fire*, p. 15.
12. Ibid., p. 225.
13. Allegri, *Callas by Callas*, p. 140.
14. Ardoin, *The Callas legacy,* p. 156.
15. Both quotes come from Remy, *Maria Callas: A tribute*, p. 149.
16. Stassinopoulos, *Maria Callas*, p. 272.
17. Gage, *Greek fire*, p. 245.
18. Ibid., p. 227.

19. Stassinopoulos, *Maria Callas*, p. 272.

20. Ibid., p. 274.

21. Gage, *Greek fire*, p. 230.

22. Stassinopoulos, *Maria Callas*, p. 142.

23. This and the following quote come from Stancioff, *Maria Callas remembered*, pp. 163 and 156.

24. Ibid., p. 163.

25. Ibid., p. 161.

26. Moutsatsos, N. F. (1998). *The Onassis women*. New York: G. P Putnam's Sons, p. 84.

27. Ardoin, *Callas: The art and the life*, p. 38.

28. Pensotti, Maria Callas. In Tosi, *The young Maria Callas*, p. 98.

29. Petsalis-Diomidis, *The unknown Callas*, p. 553.

30. Stancioff, *Maria Callas remembered*, p. 143.

31. Moutsatsos, *The Onassis women*, p. 81

32. Ibid., p. 84.

33. Callas, *Sisters*, p. 163.

34. Gage, *Greek fire*, p. 233.

35. Ardoin, *Callas: The art and the life*, p. 37.

36. Gage, *Greek fire*, p. 71.

37. Stassinopoulos, *Maria Callas*, p. 210.

38. Allegri, *Callas by Callas*, p. 140.

39. Scott, *Maria Meneghini Callas*, p. 146.

40. Reich, A. (1953). Narcissistic object choice in women. *Journal of the American Psychoanalytic Association*, 1, 22–44.

41. Stancioff, *Maria Callas remembered*, p. 144.

42. Ibid., p. 144.

43. The quote is taken from the EMI Classics recording of Wagner's *Tristan and Isolde,* conducted by Wilhelm Furtwangler, p. 251.

44. Galatopoulos, *Maria Callas: Sacred monster*, p. 411.

45. Moutsatsos, *The Onassis women*, p. 240.

46. Ibid., p. 166.

9 | NOTHING LEFT TO GIVE

Callas was forty-four when Onassis forced their separation, placing her in a difficult situation. She was publicly humiliated, with the news that she had been jilted in favor of the glamorous Jackie Kennedy splashed across newspapers and tabloids the world over. And the wound was likely rubbed by the fact that Jackie Kennedy shared the same first name as Maria's envied sister. Not only did Maria lose the love of her life—the one to whom she had given her all—but she also had to face this adversity without emotional support from family or close friends. She was also unlikely to resume her career, given her severely damaged voice. Yet diminished physical capabilities, although premature in the case of Callas, is the fate of individuals as they age. So are personal losses, including the loss of loved ones, and coping can be a challenge that requires considerable resources. Maria lacked those resources.

Successful aging is premised on two conditions, according to Erik Erikson, the foremost theorist of adult development. The first is *generativity*, an ability to mentor younger generations, derive meaning from the experience, and enjoy pleasure in their achievements. The second is *ego integrity*, a willingness to accept the idea that one's past life is the only life one could have lived, which allows aging adults to celebrate their accomplishments

Prima Donna. Paul Wink, Oxford University Press (2021). © Oxford University Press.
DOI: 10.1093/oso/9780190857738.003.0009

without regrets of what might have been.[1] Never a quitter, Callas showed resolve in dealing with her setbacks, but, in the end, she was unable to negotiate these two interrelated tasks. She spent the last decade of her life battling feelings of emptiness, envy, and despair. Four pivotal moments during her post-Onassis years shed light on her psychological functioning: her "flight" immediately after the breakup with Onassis, the filming of *Medea*, master classes at Juilliard, and a farewell concert tour with Giuseppe Di Stefano.

The Flight (August–October 1968)

By the beginning of 1968, the romance between Jackie and Onassis had intensified though their liaison remained secret. In May, Jackie spent a few days cruising the Caribbean with Ari. He managed to dispatch Maria on the pretext that she would be bored while *Christina* made the seventeen-day Atlantic crossing back home to Skorpios. Jackie had already consented to marry Ari, but she held off the announcement until after the November US elections so that she would not jeopardize Bobby's presidential candidacy (as noted earlier). Of course, this consideration lost relevance after Bobby's assassination on June 5, 1968, a tragedy that strengthened Jackie's resolve to leave the United States and distance herself from the seemingly doomed Kennedy clan.

Aristo persuaded Maria to leave the *Christina* and return to Paris that August—a preposterous request given that no one in their social circle dared to be seen in Paris at the peak of the summer holiday season—but, by then, Callas had come to realize that she was being displaced by Jackie. Her nine-year relationship with Onassis was over. A couple of weeks after she left the *Christina*, the news of her being admitted to the American Hospital in Paris made the headlines of major French newspapers. Despite rumors of a failed suicide attempt, Callas maintained that the reason for the hospitalization was an accidental overdose of sleeping pills.

Soon after being discharged, she arrived in New York City at the suggestion of Larry Kelly, then Director of the Dallas Opera. Over the next six weeks her "flight" would take her on what can be described as an aimless journey whose itinerary included Kansas City, Colorado Springs, Santa Fe, Las Vegas, Los Angeles, San Francisco, Pebble Beach, and Cuernavaca, Mexico. The trip ended in Dallas, where Callas recuperated after a fall in Mexico. On her journey, she was accompanied by an entourage of acquaintances, including the socialite Mary Carter, as well as their friends. During this frantic trip, Maria fluctuated between despair and denial of reality. She displayed little patience for others, paced hotel rooms with a boom box blaring jazz, and watched Westerns on television. Always close to the phone, she waited impatiently for the hoped-for phone call from Aristo, a call that never came. Callas met with John Ardoin for the first time after the breakup in Dallas; she went so far as to tell him that the flowers in her room were from Aristo, though they had in fact come from Costa Gratsos, a mutual friend of hers and Onassis's who lived in New York City. More problematic in terms of psychological functioning was the fact that her long-standing problems falling asleep had by now made her reliant on Mandrax (methaqualone-diphenhydramine compound), a highly addictive sedative drug used in the 1960s for insomnia. And she was incapable of being alone. When Mary

Carter, exhausted by Callas's neediness, informed her that she had to take her daughter from Dallas to her school on the East Coast, Maria responded, "Of course you do. When do we leave?" "I can't bear watching her pain," Carter's young daughter revealed. "I hope I never, never care so much about anyone."[2] Although evident all her life, her increasing dependency became a psychological concern—and it foreshadowed the rapid deterioration she would experience, alone, in the two years prior to her death.

Callas damaged her rib cartilage when she slipped and fell on the marble floor of the house at which she was staying in Cuernavaca. While recuperating from her injuries in Dallas, she gave a revealing interview to John Aroin that provides insight into her mental state during "the flight." When the official portion of the interview ended, she allowed Ardoin to continue taping her personal reflections on the breakup with Onassis. Much of what Callas said was no-holds-barred, an emotional outpouring of understandable rage and grief over her abandonment by Onassis that should be interpreted cautiously. Nonetheless, the published excerpts of the transcript include three salient themes that go beyond mere transient anguish over her abandonment; these themes deepen our understanding of the more stable aspects of her personality and the way she interpreted reality.

The first conveys Maria's tendency to associate being a woman with weakness and a need for protection. "I am a woman. I'm undefended. I've been undefended all my life," Callas bemoaned. She complains that, as a woman she cannot walk alone outdoors during sleepless nights. "What does a woman do? A woman with all her weaknesses," she laments.[3] Coming from the mouth of a diva dubbed "the Tigress," these convictions appear strange indeed, but, as I have argued throughout the book, Callas's dependence and lack of agency had deep psychological roots that reflect a fragile self, irrespective of gender. Callas unquestioningly accepted traditional gender role expectations, and she construed her weakness as a "natural" consequence of being a woman. Such attitudes may have been prevalent among some women before Betty Friedan's *The Feminine Mystique* and the Women's Movement mobilized their questioning. Callas's conventional attitude is surprising nonetheless, given her public image as an assertive and strong-willed prima donna accustomed to moving in the international jet set. Few of the women in her social circles, even those who were financially dependent on their husbands, would have described themselves as weak or unprotected. Their methods of goal attainment may have differed from those of men, but this was not synonymous with a lack of agency or a self-perception of weakness.

Callas's distorted view of reality is a second theme highlighted throughout the interview. Maria convinced herself that once she ceased being a reliable source of income, Meneghini instigated the dissolution of their marriage (i.e., that the true reason was not her affair with Onassis). She refers to her ex-husband as a pimp, indicating her belief that Meneghini forced her to prostitute her voice for money, just as Litsa had made her do in Athens (allegedly). Callas also convinced herself that because of his domineering manner, she had abandoned Onassis (rather than the other way around). Further evidence of her tendency to reconfigure events is in the accusations she hurled against her mother and sister for failing to be proud of her accomplishments and leaving her alone during the spring of 1968 student riots in Paris. Her resentment palpable, Callas voiced: "I've never had support from the people

I care for the most." She even complained that it was her mother and sister who should have been at her bedside during a recent hospitalization, rather than her loyal maid Bruna; this is surprising, to say the least, since Maria had once suggested to her mother that she commit suicide and publicly compared her sister's voice to that of a braying donkey.

Maria ultimately shunned contact with both Litsa and Jackie, yet she blamed them for failing to support her in times of need. These distortions of reality are evident in other interviews as well, not just in her monologue taped by Ardoin. In a 1970 interview with David Frost, for example, she vehemently denied having ever quarreled with the conductor Tulio Serafin. Yet Maria disowned him for two years after he *dared* to record *La Traviata* for EMI with another soprano in the title role—even though it was *her* contractual obligations with the Cetra label that barred her from recording this role with another label for several years. Callas's distorted view of her personal relationships, along with her insistent acceptance of stereotypical gender roles, prevented her from gaining insight into the sources of her own problematic behavior: her passivity, self-centeredness, and vulnerability.

Blaming others for her own shortcomings buffered Callas against the full brunt of negative feelings. By renouncing responsibility for her own behavior, Maria assuaged the fear she felt for her future, her sadness, and her remorse, but this denial came at a price: It was a veil that ensured she would never shed her myopic view of the world. Callas simply did not have the psychological strength to do so. In her view, she was always the victim, and the other party always the aggressor. There was no nuance in how she made sense of her negative feelings and experiences, no shades of gray. Maria was unable to translate her experience of adversity and trauma into personal growth, largely because she construed the world in black-or-white terms, a tendency that impeded any ability to consider how her own behavior may have contributed to the ruptured relationships of her past. Black-or-white thinking is a typical mechanism used by the narcissistic split-self to separate the grandiose from the vulnerable aspects of the individual's personality. Consequently, Callas was unable to profit from these negative experiences, nor was she able to moderate some of the stress they caused. She could not synthesize her imperial artistic persona with the inadequacies she felt in her personal life; as a result, she was left psychologically fractured and depleted. Even though the inadequate Maria was entangled in the imperious Callas, and vice versa, this did not help her integrate her self's two opposing and extreme aspects.

A third theme revealed in Callas's cathartic interview with Ardoin is her fatalism and anger at living in an unjust world. In life, she asserts, she has met several dishonest and weak individuals who tried to pull her down. Her reference to weak people is directed at Rudolph Bing, the Met's General Manager who fired her in 1958. In recounting the firing, Callas attributes Bing's actions to his own anger, ostensibly at other singers who had enraged him more than even she had. She conveniently forgets the intransigence that she and Battista displayed while negotiating her contract, a stubbornness that resulted in her discharge from the Met. Similarly, she came to construe the negative publicity garnered in Rome over her mid-performance cancellation of *Norma* as instead owing to hatred by others. Feeling misunderstood by a public who failed to acknowledge her vocal difficulties, she expresses the wish to spit in the face of her enemies and make them crawl in front of her on their knees. Even in the depth of her despair, the tigress in Callas is clearly present. But behind the veneer of anger lurked more deeply felt depression. Reflecting her grief and anguish over the break up with Onassis, she ends the interview asserting: "There are people born to be happy and people born to be unhappy. I am just not lucky."

Filming of Medea (June 1969–December 1969) and the Aftermath

During her nine years with Onassis, Callas considered starring in several different movie projects aimed at filming an opera. None bore fruit. She was hesitant due to concerns regarding the propriety of putting opera on film (a concern shared by Visconti), a growing doubt over the state of her voice (she resisted the idea of dubbing any film's soundtrack with a recording of one of her prior performances), and insecurity about how she might appear on film (as will be recalled, she declined to consider a role in *Guns of Navarone* because of concerns over her appearance).[4] Now, with little else in her life, her interest was piqued by an offer to star in the cinematic version of *Medea* from accomplished Italian producer Franco Rossellini and film director Pier Paolo Pasolini. Callas was drawn to the project because of her success in performing Cherubini's *Medea* on stage. And, in her current frame of mind, the idea of a scorned woman taking ultimate revenge on her unfaithful lover by murdering their children was likely also enticing. The main drawbacks to the project were Pasolini's communist political views and his homosexuality, neither of which she approved. She had walked out of a screening of *Teorema,* Pasolini's most recent, award-winning film because she was revolted by the idea of a stranger having sex with an entire bourgeois family, including mother, father, daughter, son, and maid. The defense that the mysterious stranger symbolized either god or the devil struck her as blasphemous. Yet, in June 1969, she arrived on *Medea*'s film set, undaunted by its location in the remote village of Goreme, situated in Turkey's heartland. She was accompanied by Nadia Stancioff, her newfound companion and private secretary; her maid Bruna Lupoli; her chauffeur cum butler Ferruccio Mezzadri; and two poodles, Djedda and Pixie.

Callas's relationship with the much younger Stancioff, the daughter of a Bulgarian ambassador now living in Italy, is another example of a friendship based on *twinship.* The initial meeting between the two got off to a bad start, with Callas expecting a secretary, based on her film contract, and with Stancioff assuming that she was hired as a public relations person. After venting her anger about the misunderstanding at Franco Rossellini, *Medea*'s producer, Maria offered Nadia employment, confiding that she needed a friend more than a secretary. Just as in the case of Giovanna Lomazzi, Callas became dependent on Stancioff for company, comfort, and understanding. They became inseparable during the shooting of *Medea.* Subsequently, Callas visited Stancioff in Rome, and the two spent two summer holidays on the private Greek island of Tragonissi. Nadia found Maria a very enjoyable companion, much as did Lomazzi. The two playfully chased each other around Villa Borghese carrying balloons, swam, and went to movies. They drove around Rome in Stancioff's Fiat Cinquecento and were entertained by Nadia's young friends. Callas's joie de vivre in such situations is exemplified by a photo in the La Scala museum depicting her slurping spaghetti good humoredly in the company of two other women. Stancioff's only complaint was Callas's reluctance, during the filming of *Medea*, to let go of her at night; subsequently, when the two lived apart, sporadic but seemingly interminable late-night phone calls became cumbersome.

Callas acted with consummate professionalism during the filming of *Medea*. She woke up early and withstood the hardship of filming in Goreme's hot and humid conditions while dressed in heavy, dark robes and decorated with weighty necklaces. Whenever possible, she insisted on doing the scenes by herself without the use of a double or a stunt person. Her main concern was the desire to act well and not disappoint the film's crew. When she fainted from exhaustion, she begged forgiveness for incurring cost and wasting time. Her professionalism is not surprising as it was a continuation of the behavior that characterized her stage career. And her commitment to the film was heightened by her falling in love with Pasolini.

Pasolini was a film-maker, an intellectual, and a celebrity, much like Visconti, but he was introverted and sensitive, unlike his aristocratic counterpart, and he had disdain for vulgar language. He and Callas were attracted to each other by shared insecurities and vulnerabilities. Pasolini was interested in the archaic and primordial origins of the modern psyche, and in Callas he found a mysterious and magical woman with inner conflicts that straddled between the ancient and the modern. He did not hide his sexual attraction to men—his long-term lover Ninetto Davoli was present on the film's set—yet, unlike Visconti, he never flaunted his gay lifestyle. Yet according to Nadia Stancioff, despite her myopia, Callas could not fail to notice the adolescent boys emerging from caves counting money, with Pasolini trailing them. In one instance, she took off her glasses not to witness his fascination with a thirteen-year-old boy who was serving at their dinner table. Encouraged by Pasolini telling her that she was the only woman he had ever loved other than his mother and that if he could desire a woman it would be her, she developed the conviction that she could save him from "self-destruction." The ancient ring he gave her at the end of filming *Medea* also fueled her romantic fantasies. Although it was meant as a token of appreciation and friendship, Maria interpreted it as a sign of an incipient engagement. Her fantasy was further strengthened when Pasolini's lover Ninetto abandoned him to marry a woman, which ignited hope that she could change Pier Paolo's own sexual orientation. Even though their relationship never became physical, they remained friends after the filming of *Medea* was over. They travelled together for a showing of *Medea* at the Mar del Plata film festival in Argentina and vacationed in Mali and Yemen, accompanied by a pair of Italian writers, Alberto Moravia and his long-term partner, Dacia Maraini.

The fruit of Callas and Pasolini's relationship was a series of poems he wrote about her. One such poem, *La Presenza* (Presence), includes the dictum *"esse est percipi"* (to be perceived is to exist), from Bishop Berkeley, the eighteenth-century British philosopher. The allusion suggests how Callas's psychological existence was inextricably dependent on being mirrored by the admiring gaze of the other. Pasolini ends his poem with the following lines:

> And yet she, that little girl,
> neglect her for only a moment
> and she'll feel lost forever –
> ah, the wind blows not over motionless islands,
> but over the terror of non-being,
> the divine wind
> that does not heal, but indeed makes one sicker and sicker;
> and there's never a day, an hour, a moment
> when the effort might cease;
> you grab onto anything you can
> and it makes one want to kiss you.[5]

Pasolini eloquently captures Callas's girlish innocence, her dependence, her need for affirmation, and her heroic, ceaseless effort to overcome the terror of non-being or personal disintegration. We see these traits in the way she came to life in her romantic relationships with Meneghini and Onassis and in her professional involvement with Serafin, Visconti, and Glotz, a record producer, in Paris. This need to be seen is at the essence of her being; it counterbalanced the experience of not being "seen" in childhood.

Medea was acclaimed as a *succes d'estime* (critical success) upon its release, meaning that, in reality, it was a commercial flop. *Medea* was simply a bad film, as the audiences' reaction suggests, with deep philosophical underpinnings that jar against comic book-like action sequences. The minimalism that worked well in the contemporary urban setting of *Teorema* fails to convince—in my opinion—in the epic recreation of the myth of Jason and the Golden Fleece. Throughout the film, Callas remains largely silent other than speaking sporadic dialogue. She looks old and stilted, lacking the spontaneity, grace, and freedom of her opera performances, and she sings just one short lullaby before stabbing her children. Catherine Clement, the French feminist philosopher and critic, is among the very few who defend the film. She lauds Pasolini for rendering Callas mute, a deliberate ploy, Clement argues, to liberate Maria from the shackles of oppression imposed by her greedy and exploitative mother and by the men in her life.[6] Her thesis is challenged, however, by the fact that long scenes without any spoken words were already present in Pasolini's *Teorema*, shot two years before *Medea*. In other words, Pasolini's silencing of actors was a cinematic ploy he adopted independently of Callas's role as Medea. In any event, Callas's decision to make her film debut in *Medea* was a bad move as the fiasco further undermined her confidence and added to personal and professional disarray. Unwilling to expose herself to another setback, Callas foreclosed any prospects of a future film performances.

Back to Onassis

Given Callas's deeply felt love for Onassis and her abject despair over her abandonment, what are we to make of her infatuation with Pasolini and her fantasy of marrying him less than a year after the breakup with Onassis? The most straightforward explanation is that, by the time of *Medea*'s shooting, she had lost her romantic interest in Aristo. Such a change of heart would have been fully justified by Onassis's cruel and demeaning behavior toward her and his inveterate philandering. Though plausible, this scenario does not fit the facts.

Just two weeks after his marriage to Jackie, Onassis knocked on the door of Callas's Paris apartment, on the fashionable Avenue Georges Mandel, begging to be admitted. The idea of having a wife and a mistress was not new to him as he aspired for a similar arrangement with his first wife, Tina, after he began his affair with Callas. Her pride wounded, Maria was initially reluctant to see him and refused to let him in. Onassis, however, managed to change her mind by threatening to create a commotion outside her apartment. With their relationship rekindled, they talked frequently over the phone and met occasionally in person, almost to the time of Onassis's death; in fact, his office staff took care of Callas's passport, credit cards, and travel arrangements right up to his death. Although they saw each other privately on numerous occasions between 1969 and 1974, Callas insisted to her friends that she would not have sex with Aristo unless he divorced Jackie and married her. These assertions may not provide the full story, however. In the early 1970s, Maria visited Nadia Stancioff in Rome, concerned she might have to abort Onassis's child. (The suspected pregnancy, however, proved to be a false alarm.)

Onassis's relationship with Jackie began to deteriorate by 1970, within two years of their marriage, precipitated by the publication in an American newspaper of love letters Jackie wrote to Roswell Gilpatric (US Deputy Secretary of Defense in the Kennedy administration). Some of these letters were penned after she married Ari. Marital tensions escalated in the next three years because Jackie was spending a good deal of time in New York City with her children, as noted earlier, and also because Ari encountered a series of personal catastrophes that he attributed to a "Jackie jinx." He spent the last three years of his life scheming how to divorce her while losing as little money as possible. Onassis came to believe that Maria, and only Maria, was the love of his life; he grew obsessed with the idea of marrying her, while Maria publicly referred to Aristo in derogatory terms, calling him a "pig" and a "dirty little Greek." Yet she could not hide the continued emotional power he held over her. It is no accident that her physical and mental health declined precipitously after his death in 1975, nor that she died just over two years afterward.

Maria and Jackie had quite different approaches to relationships, as evidenced in their behavior following the publication of Jackie's letters to Gilpatric. Onassis's marriage to Jackie was a folly, and, given the strength of Callas's attachment to him, his continuous courting provided an opportunity for Maria to win him back. Maria's wounded pride and her passivity undermined this possibility, as did her desperate need to have someone's company in the present moment. Angered and hurt by Jackie's letters, Onassis turned to Callas and made sure that the photograph of their having a tête-à-tête dinner at Maxim's was splashed across the world press. Jackie flew immediately from New York City to Paris so that the two could be photographed having dinner at the same Maxim's table. After this maneuver, Maria was hospitalized again, due to a purported overdose. Jackie's agency, her willingness to fight for what she deemed hers, is showcased in this incident, despite her waning interest in Onassis's company. In another instance, during a Caribbean cruise in 1970, Jackie appeared on *Christina*'s deck. Sensing Ari's anger at her, she "demurely" announced, "I went upstairs, darling, and I put perfume wherever Mr. Lanvin [name of the perfume maker] told me to put it, and you never came up. I put perfume *everywhere*."[7] The incident leaves little doubt that, in erotic game-playing, Onassis had met his match. Maria herself was not averse to sexual play. On one occasion when she and Aristo stayed in Monte Carlo, Maria's personal masseuse found her lying in bed bejeweled but otherwise completely nude. "Aristo likes me this way,"[8] she responded to the masseuse's quizzical look. The contrast between Jackie's active, if contrived, and Maria's passive, if sincere, approaches to romance could not be starker. "It was Callas's inability to believe in the seriousness of Onassis's resolve and repentance that transformed their relationship into the status of a Greek tragedy," Mary Carter recalled. Although Onassis, who was by now serious about divorcing Jackie, implored her time and again to marry him, Callas demurred. "She was not a woman who forgot or forgave easily."[9]

Given the emotional intensity of Callas's relationship with Onassis, it is tempting to interpret her infatuation with Pasolini as a rebound, a reaction driven by her desire to show Onassis she no longer needed him. Her pride wounded, she must have relished how those glamorous press photos with Pasolini might have wounded Aristo. Her relationship with Pier Paolo was more complicated than this, however. She needed tangible, day-to-day involvement with a significant other in order to maintain a modicum of emotional stability. Her partly real, partly fantasized romance with Pasolini met this need; it was much more than a contrived attempt to teach Onassis a lesson and incite jealousy. The intensification of their relationship was beyond Maria's conscious control, for she lacked the capacity to be on her own. Of course, the whole gist of this book is that our lives are governed not by external events but by how we interpret them. This does not diminish the power of Callas's emotional entanglements with the significant people in her life, but it does underscore the importance of probing those psychological factors behind the emotion.

Master Classes at Juilliard (October 11, 1971– March 16, 1972)

Following the *Medea* fiasco, Callas was given another professional opportunity, this time in the United States. In February 1971, she was invited to give a series of master classes at the Curtis Institute of Music in Philadelphia. The invitation was not a surprise given Callas's enormous popularity in America, both as a stage performer and a recording artists. Her opera recordings, marketed in the United States on the Angel label, continued to sell briskly. She was engaged by the Curtis Institute to teach a two-week course, but she terminated the commitment after two or three days, thus severing the lifeline she was offered. Larry Kelly suggests she did so because the role did not present an opportunity to act as a *prima donna assoluta*.[10] A more benign interpretation is that the eighteen students selected for the master class were not equipped to meet Callas's high standards. The Philadelphia master classes may have been a failure, but it set the stage for a similar opportunity at the Juilliard School of Music in New York City, beginning in October that same year. This time around, Callas was given the authority to select the program's twenty-six participants from a pool of more than three-hundred applicants, each of whom she personally auditioned that spring.

The Juilliard stage was bare, other than for the accompanist's piano, Callas's high stool, and a table filled with scores. During each master class Maria worked individually with three or four students, frequently devoting forty to fifty minutes to a single aria. The class met twice a week in the evening; there were two separate six-week sessions, with twenty-three meetings devoted to the study of key operatic works. The repertoire ranged from Mozart to Massenet, and included the works of Rossini, Bellini, Donizetti, Verdi, and Puccini. The event was open to the public, and, as the word got around, tickets became a hot commodity. Juilliard's 1,000-seat auditorium was typically filled to capacity with the crème de la crème of the music world auditing her class, including opera singers Tito Gobbi, Bidu Sayao, Placido Domingo, and Elisabeth Schwarzkopf; past and current Met impresarios Rudolph Bing and Goeran Gentele; conductors Thomas Schippers and Michael Tilson Thomas; and the stage director Franco Zeffirelli. Reflecting her professionalism, Callas forbade the audience from clapping during the class.

The recorded excerpts from the master classes show that Callas was a serious, passionate, dedicated, and highly focused teacher.[11] She tried to convey the same approach to singing that had made her an extraordinary star. She emphasized fidelity to the score and to the intent of the composer. She emphasized cleanness and simplicity in ornamentation. She did not hesitate to suggest practical changes, such as altering a word of the libretto if it would capture the emotional truth of the sung phrase. And she even developed the habit of singing along with the students to illustrate a point or show how the aria should sound. At times Maria would sing the entire aria, thereby breaking the self-imposed exile that had kept her away from the opera stage for more than five years. The informal setting of the class permitted Callas the freedom to escape her inhibitions, and the audience was rewarded with a vivid reminder of the magic in her singing, its raw emotional power. Robert Clark captures his experience of the master classes with an analogy to Rembrandt in his article for *Stereo Review*. Rembrandt had "made his clients look more serious. He made them seem to have important and sometimes complex things on their minds. Maria Callas' gift," Clark argued, was her ability "to endow the Italian operatic heroine with a similar kind of depth and significance." And her performing was all the more remarkable because she achieved it *in spite of* the limited raw material afforded an Italian operatic heroine, material "not often among the most compelling products of the Western dramatic imagination."[12] Clark's comment illustrates the enormous impact of Callas's stage presence on Juilliard's audiences that, in many ways, transcended her power as a teacher. Despite her brilliant gifts, Maria found it hard to communicate many of her insights and intuitions. Her effectiveness as a teacher was impeded by the unusual nature of her voice, which, while certainly part of her stage magnetism, was simply hard to teach others. She often resorted to singing the part herself, then encouraging the student to follow her example. Maria was "unable to tell them how to do it," explains John Ardoin. She "would demonstrate how *she* would have done it. Just do it *this* way, she'd say as if it were as simple as the ABC's [emphasis added]."[13] This strategy proved limiting. Perhaps both the strength and weakness of her approach to teaching is revealed in her response to a student who asked for the best way to interpret a certain piece of music: "Love it," she exhorted. Although fully committed to what she was doing, Callas was rarely complimentary of her students, though she never demeaned them. She presided "like a Delphic oracle before sold-out audiences of other students, fans, the musical press, and luminaries from the world of the performing arts,"[14] according to one music critic, which goes to the heart of the problem with the Juilliard classes and their value as a learning experience for the twenty-six students. It is hard to be a good teacher with so many diverse constituencies to please.

On the surface, Callas's involvement in Juilliard appeared to be truly generative. Here was a world-famous diva willing to teach a group of young, up-and-coming singers for twelve weeks free of charge. But matters were made more complicated, as always with Callas. Hesitant about staying in New York on her own, Callas suggested to Nadia Stancioff that she join her at the Plaza Hotel. She argued that surely there would be a place for her friend in the hotel suite as she was owed a favor by Juilliard for doing the classes for free. But, as Stancioff suggests, Maria failed to account for "a suite at the Plaza, a limousine waiting at the door, first-class travel arrangements, food, and fresh flowers in every room" as factoring toward her remuneration.[15] Others who knew her well also expressed doubt about the altruism of the Juilliard commitment. "Maria thought of it [the master classes] in term of herself and not in terms of the kids," suggested Larry Kelly, a friend and confidant who spent time with Callas in the aftermath of her breakup with Onassis. "As a human being she was extremely attractive, extremely careless and extremely selfish. The classes were really her way of presenting herself to an audience for the first time in six or seven years. She needed an audience's reaction, and with time the handful of people grew into a paying audience of a thousand."[16]

The setting of the master classes and her teaching role liberated Callas to test her vocal powers in front of a discerning crowd of critics and prominent members of the musical establishment. It must, however, have had a daunting effect on the students. Although she banned applause and appeared to be focused solely on her students, listening to the audio recording of the proceedings gives the distinct impression that part of Callas's teaching performance was aimed at the audience as well. This is exemplified by the audience's hearty laughter in response to Maria admonishing a student to wear a longer skirt because otherwise she might reveal to members of the public sitting lower than the stage more than she might intend to. It is also evident when, in the middle of working with a student, Callas turns to a music historian in the audience to validate her anecdote concerning Rossini's quip in response to Adelina Patti's mutilation of his aria. Even taking into consideration Callas's steel will, things could not have been otherwise once she agreed with Juilliard's decision to make the classes open to the public. Callas also embarked on a course of private study with Metropolitan Opera coach Alberta Maisiello during her time at Juilliard, in preparation for an anticipated return to the stage. This training, combined with her "performance" while teaching these classes, indicates that Kelly's claim has merit.

The Juilliard master classes serve as the basis for Terrence McNally's 1995 play, *The Master Class*, with Maria, its main character, modeled on Callas.[17] Though it offers a discourse on the origins and consequences of supremacy in art, the play intersperses the proceedings of the master class with several episodes from Callas's past. It ends with the main character quoting verbatim fragments of Maria's closing remarks to her Juilliard students. "Do not think singing is an easy career," Maria exhorts. "It is a lifetime's work; it does not stop here." She goes on: "Whether I continue singing or not doesn't matter. What matters is that you use whatever you have learned wisely. Think of the expression of the words, of good diction, and of your own deep feelings. The only thanks I ask is that you sing properly and honestly. If you do this, I will feel repaid." A fitting end to a play with its central character modeled on the world's most famous prima donna.

However, McNally's dialogue also includes words that were never uttered by Callas, either in her own farewell address or elsewhere, including the lines "I have to think that we have made this world a better place" and "The older I get, the less I know but I am certain that what we do matters."[18] These additions reflect McNally's conviction regarding the purposefulness of life and his understanding that it's psychologically healthy for artistic supremacy to actually generate concern for making the world a better place. Such sentiments, however, were not shared by Callas, who showed minimal concern for others and, indeed, had little confidence in the emerging generation of opera singers. She gave the following comments in an interview with the *International Herald Tribune* a couple of months before her arrival at Juilliard: "It will not exactly be teaching. I would like to try to pass on some of my experiences to others. Opera is in crisis. I have been saying that since 1954."[19] When I interviewed her, Lomazzi revealed that, after her breakup with Onassis, La Scala's General Manager asked Callas to teach at the opera house, but Maria did not want to mentor younger singers. Of course, part of the problem was Callas's unorthodox voice and unique singing and acting styles, which would have made it hard for her to pass on acquired knowledge and experience to students. Given her perfectionism, it is likely that these factors contributed to Callas's reluctance to embark on a teaching career.

Final Concert Tour (October 25 1973, Hamburg–November 11 1974, Sapporo)

Callas was lonely during her prolonged Juilliard stay in New York, despite a brief romance with Peter Mennin, then Juilliard's president. Though he was willing to leave his wife for Callas, he failed to win her heart. She was therefore happy when the tenor Giuseppe ("Pippo") Di Stefano reappeared in her life. She and Di Stefano (1921–2008) first met in 1951, in Sao Paolo, Brazil, where both had starred in *La Traviata*. They also appeared together in the famous studio recording of *Tosca* (1953) and the equally renowned 1955 performance of *Lucia* in Berlin, but their relationship became strained when Callas took a solo bow at the finale of La Scala's *La Traviata* on opening night in 1955. Disgusted, Di Stefano refused to sing with her in subsequently scheduled performances, but perhaps unsurprisingly (given the volatility of opera life), the two singers reconciled. They sung together again in La Scala's highly acclaimed 1957 production of Verdi's *Un Ballo in Maschera*, their last collaboration before meeting again in New York.

Di Stefano arrived at Maria's Plaza suite early in 1972, bearing a bouquet of roses and a proposal to resume their joint singing association. His career had declined as well during the mid-1960s; gross overuse and a hectic lifestyle of late-night drinking and socializing exacerbated his deteriorating voice. During a 1971 tour of Korea and Japan, he was enticed by the tour's promoters to return with a soprano: $4,000 for Anna Moffo, $6,000 for Renata Tebaldi, and $10,000 for Maria Callas. He turned to Callas after receiving negative response from Moffo or Tebaldi, whom he approached first assuming that they were more likely to accept his offer. Maria "was completely down in the dumps," according to Di Stefano. The Callas he encountered at the Plaza "kept on saying 'Every day that passes is a day less for me to live.' "[20] Nevertheless, tempted both by the offer and the prospect of his company, Maria agreed to perform.

Di Stefano began to instill in Callas a new confidence in singing through coaching and by praising the quality of her voice. The two became lovers. Maria needed Di Stefano for emotional support, whereas Di Stefano's motivation for their partnership was twofold: He found Maria physically attractive, and he was also in desperate need of money, both to support his lavish lifestyle and to afford treatment for his adolescent daughter Luisa, who had been diagnosed with brain cancer. Callas and Di Stefano spent the fall of 1972 in a London studio recording Verdi and Donizetti duets for Philips. She had spent the summer with him and his wife (also named Maria), along with their three children, in their San Remo apartment. Though the summer may have gone well, the recording sessions did not. The soundtrack was never released. "She [Callas] was against the recording from the start," claimed Antonio de Almeida. "She was artistically egotistical. She was using the recording as a warm-up for a farewell tour."[21] Both Callas and Di

Stefano struggled with their seriously compromised voices. It was during these recording sessions that Callas received a telegram from her sister. Her father had died, and Jackie asked if she would attend his funeral in Athens. Callas refused. She never forgave her father for remarrying. Besides, she did not like funerals and was busy in the recording studio. January 1973 also saw the death in a plane crash of Onassis's beloved son Alexander, a personal blow from which Aristo, with whom Maria was still in close contact, never fully recovered.

In the spring of 1973, Callas and Di Stefano travelled to Turin, where she produced *I Vespri Siciliani*, a performance marking the reopening of the Teatro Regio after it burned down in 1936. This project, too, proved calamitous, despite Callas's best efforts. Neither she nor Di Stefano had any previous experience in staging an opera and were unschooled in the details, such as where to position the singers or the chorus. According to Zeffirelli, Callas was always so involved with her own performances at the height of her career that she failed to notice what transpired around her. Severe myopia further impeded her awareness of what happened on stage, and she refused to wear contact lenses during performances. The Turin production of *I Vespri* received scathing reviews. According to one critic, Callas did little more than turn the lights on and off.

In May 1973, Di Stefano and Callas led a master class for winners of the *Madama Butterfly* singing competition, named after Puccini's opera, set in Japan. Their decision to embark on a world concert tour materialized during this trip. Beginning in Hamburg in October 1973, the tour consisted of close to fifty concerts given in Europe, the United States, Canada, and Korea, before ending in Sapporo in November 1974. The grueling schedule included successive concerts scheduled only a few days apart. For example, after opening night in Hamburg on October 25, there were concerts in Berlin on October 29; in Dusseldorf on November 2; and in Munich on November 6. In the United States, the April 18, 1974, concert in Cincinnati was succeeded by performances in Seattle on April 24 and Portland on April 27. According to the contract signed with impresario Sander Gorlinsky, Callas was to receive $20,000 for each concert, of which $5,000 was paid to Di Stefano. In today's dollars, the tour yielded Callas around $3 million plus expenses, with Di Stefano receiving roughly a million.

The concert tour was doomed to fail. Two artists with severely compromised voices accompanied by an octogenarian pianist (Ivor Newton) who no longer had the capacity to keep up with the singers were bound to be a disaster. Music critics praised Callas's presence and manner but were in unison in lamenting the state of her voice. They gave scant attention to Di Stefano. Callas's decision to tour with him was described as a folly and an act of despair. Andrew Porter, a renowned English music critic, wrote about Callas's November 1973 appearance at London's Royal Festival Hall: "An artist as great as she has been must not be insulted with less than the truth from an admirer. Her voice was a shadow of its former self. Perhaps it could be said that the voice has, at least, been in some sense 'tamed'—in that the interpretations were kept carefully within the bounds of what it can still do."[22] Porter's assessment was echoed in the *San Francisco Chronicle*'s review of Callas's May 1974 performance at the War Memorial Opera: "The will to perform and the emotional commitment that made her a unique diva came through. Yet it was inescapably sad to think that

Miss Callas so needs to relive the past glory and cherish the adulation that she will put herself through this experience."[23]

In retrospect, the farewell raises two questions. Why did Callas, the consummate perfectionist, expose herself to the ignominy by abandoning her high standards and performing with a severely tarnished voice? Even an uninitiated listener to the recording of the first London concert will likely agree with Porter's assessment that her voice was merely a shadow of what it was in her prime. Furthermore, why did someone with such high moral principles agree to conduct an affair with a married man in the presence of not only his wife, Maria Di Stefano, who frequently joined them on the tour, but also his dying daughter? "I know they're having an affair," Luisa told her mother, "but we need the money."[24]

Callas's decision is quite understandable, psychologically. The tour brought back the excitement of appearing in front of adulating fans in the company of a man who offered her artistic and emotional support. Callas needed adulating audiences to buttress her fragile self, and the tour accomplished this, according to Di Stefano.

> Callas came back to life with me. She came out of the tunnel of despair and rediscovered the certainties and joys of past times. She laughed and joked. She could also be capricious, as she was when we were at La Scala together. The atmosphere of concerts, the rustle of applause from her audience, which had never forgotten her, were like a miraculous medicine.

And there was "something more" to their passionate affair, according to Di Stefano. They felt an "infinite tenderness, artistic complicity of the highest level, the desire to win again, mature love."[25] Di Stefano's assessment is overly optimistic and self-serving, as we shall see, but there is truth in his image of an energized and rejuvenated Maria breaking free from the shackles of despair. Maria needed to recreate her glory days. In her prime, Callas was addicted to her audiences' applause. She experienced the thrill of being on stage as something else taking over, something that made audiences "just go wild,"[26] and now she needed to persuade herself that she could still do it, that she still had that same magic. This was necessary both for her psychological equilibrium and for her physical well-being. Callas gave her audience all she had during the height of her career, but the gratification derived from acclaim was short-lasting. She needed constant external stimulation to recharge the "internal dynamo" of her fragile self. As argued by John Ardoin "the only time she ever kidded herself artistically was during the last tour."[27] Time and again, Callas's inability to self-soothe without an external prop or stimulus becomes evident. The same consideration explains her need to cling to Di Stefano: She believed their relationship was based on mutual love for each other.

The tour did indeed fulfill some of Callas's needs and expectations. There was the comfort in being once again on the road in the company of a lover, just as with Meneghini in the early years; a trusted accompanist (Robert Sutherland replaced Ivor Newton midway through the European segment of the tour); and her butler and maid. Despite negative reviews, Callas and Di Stefano sang, at least during the European segment of the tour, in fully booked concert halls; they also enjoyed throngs of admirers at the end of each concert. In London alone, the ticket office received

30,000 requests for the 3,000 seats at the Royal Concert Hall. Although vocally flawed, Callas's performance at the first London concert met with thunderous applause. On December 2, 1972, the audience at London's second concert was moved when Di Stefano initiated singing "Happy Birthday" to Maria. He got the audience to sing along. "If 3000 people received us the way they did," Callas said after the tour's first stop in Hamburg, "why should we worry about the odd twenty."[28] The twenty dissenting voices were the music critics, however, and although Callas was nourished by the audience's affirmation, she was too much of a perfectionist to capably ignore their negative reviews. As suggested by Wayne Koestenbaum, during the farewell concert tour there was something of Norma Desmond, the deluded, tragic, aging star of *Sunset Boulevard*, in Maria.

Throughout the tour, Callas brimmed with confidence and maintained a dignified public persona. When asked during a press conference in New York City about the negative reviews of her European concerts, she responded that she was her hardest critic, that none of the performers of her era sing as well as in their olden days—a clear reference to her own glory days. Yet she also stated she would be happy to resume singing at the Met, notwithstanding her complaint about the growing power of producers and directors. In private, however, long indeed her own best self-critic, she had enough self-awareness to acknowledge the severe limitation of her voice. "They love me more than I deserve for today," Callas confided to Sutherland after the London concert feting her birthday. "They love what I was, not what I am."[29]

Callas did not abandon her formidable work ethic during the concert tour. This would have been impossible for someone who, since her early years in opera in Athens, creatively altered Descartes dictum "Cogito ergo sum," to "I work therefore I am." She worked on her voice incessantly, coached by Di Stefano, but he proved to be the wrong tutor for her. Di Stefano's mantra *"Aperta la gola* [keep your throat open], was of little help to Maria, whose singing required much greater finesse. As in her youth, Callas was an obedient pupil, but she soon became exasperated with Di Stefano's persistent injunction to keep her throat opened. Robert Sutherland recalls the affair.

> Suddenly Maria could take it no longer. She froze for a second, then exploded. In a rage she railed at him, spewing out invective with the voice of a navvy [laborer], her face distorted, teeth bared, huge black eyes flaring like a caged animal, her long fingers with their blood-red varnished nails curled like the talons of an eagle. The bright, sunlit room became grey and cold.[30]

Sutherland argued that Callas "spent her career searching for perfection," while Di Stefano "believed he was born with it."[31] This combination proved untenable.

The stress of the tour manifested in Callas's increasing reliance on sleeping tablets and injections. Administered before each concert by Luis Parrish, the tour's doctor, the injections consisted primarily of over-the-counter supplements, such as calcium gluconate and ascorbic acid. But occasionally they included something extra, most likely an amphetamine, which may account for Callas's incoherent tirade attacking the Met's administration at the end of her Carnegie Hall concert to benefit the Metropolitan Opera's Guild.

Her accusations included old grievances over having to perform at the Met, with its old sets and a changing cast of singers. She was found lying unconscious in her hotel room after taking too many sleeping tablets on two other occasions, one of which, in New York City, resulted in the cancellation of a scheduled concert performance. Following her Carnegie Hall rant, Callas asked Dr. Parrish for advice. In his Southern drawl, he told her to "Git a life an' staap watching Westerns."[32] Unfortunately, Callas could do neither.

Callas's behavior during the farewell tour challenges the assumption that her personality was neatly split between the supremely confident, entitled, and narcissistic Callas, the opera diva, and Maria, the vulnerable and inadequate woman. There was plenty of evidence of the imperial Callas during the tour. She made headlines with her frequent insistence on changing her hotel reservations. In Madrid, it was because the hotel room's ceilings were too low; in Munich it was because she didn't want to be overshadowed by Princess Margaret and the Dalai Lama, who had stayed in the same hotel. In Chicago, Di Stefano's reminder that their hotel's rules did not allow dogs led to her angry rejoinder: "Rules? Rules? What do you mean rules? Wherever I stay I make the rules. Let them talk to me about the rules and then we'll see what Callas is."[33] Throughout her career, Callas was plagued by insecurity, reflecting in part her perfectionism and in part the unpredictability of her voice. She did not possess the supreme confidence in her voice of an Adelina Patti, who was enthralled with the beauty of her singing right into old age, when her voice was a shadow of its former glorious self. Granted, Callas never possessed Patti's crystal-clear voice. Nonetheless, her increased reliance on mind-numbing medication during the farewell tour shows the extreme vulnerability lurking behind her confident artistic persona. She could neither face the humiliation of not living up to her high standards nor give up the thrill of being on stage in front of an adulating audience.

Visitors to the Nellie Melba museum, established at her home in Melbourne's distant suburb of Coldstream, can watch a short video of the aged singer returning to Australia (while they view her memorabilia and partake of scones with strawberries and cream). After disembarking from a ship, Melba is shown directing a seemingly puzzled cockatoo with great gusto. This short clip demonstrates the supreme self-confidence that characterized Melba's public and private persona, a joie-de-vivre that was in evidence right until the end of her life. She had her own vulnerabilities, despite her imperiousness, and she, too, feared being upstaged. Melba ruthlessly rid herself of potential rivals to her reign as Covent Garden's prima donna. She made sure that Luisa Tetrazzini, a rival soprano with an equally spectacular voice, ceased being invited to the Royal Opera House after her successful performances in Melba's absence. She also barred Titta Ruffo from performing, even though, as a baritone, he clearly was not a direct competitor; with his exceptionally fine voice, she feared his applause would detracted from hers. Extending the grandiosity into her private life, Melba, awarded jewel-encrusted pins to individuals whose behavior pleased her, mimicking the English King Edward VII, and she issued certificates of appointment to tradesmen. Unlike Callas, whose artistry was enhanced by her close immersion in the psychological conflicts central to the roles she performed, Melba's performances remained largely one-dimensional. Arguably, Melba's grandiosity made her an inferior singer to Callas, but while her largely unconflicted ego-centrism allowed her to retain a sense of well-being and purpose throughout her life, Callas did not have the psychological capacity to do likewise (as I have argued). Melba might have inflicted hurt on others but not on herself; her grandiosity buffered her from life's slings and arrows. This was not the case with Callas; her grandiosity was tinged, at every turn, with self-criticism and self-consciously experienced fragility.

Just as vulnerability infiltrated and undermined Callas's artistic persona, narcissistic grandiosity penetrated her everyday life. Callas's predicament was exacerbated by feelings of entitlement, a lack of esteem for others, and envy—all feelings associated with narcissistic grandiosity, a characteristic that kept Maria from gaining personal strength and solace from relations with others. The narcissistic features of her personal life were already evident in how she treated Litsa, Jackie, and Meneghini. And during the farewell tour, she was contemptuous of Di Stefano's wife: She had little sympathy for her attempts to salvage their marriage, she complained of having her around, and she accused her of being stupid or at best insensitive to the needs of artists. Maria insisted on one occasion, during the American leg of the tour, that Di Stefano's wife should move to a different floor of the hotel; on another occasion, she demanded Di Stefano send her home. Callas was also insensitive toward her trusted helpers. She made sure that Bruna, her devoted maid, and Ferruccio, her butler, flew first class with her, even if it meant displacing other passengers, but she did not hesitate in getting Ferruccio to lift her heavy luggage despite his bad back. When Bruna was delayed in joining her on the American portion of the farewell tour because she was taking care of her dying mother, exasperated Maria kept asking, "Why doesn't the old woman just die?"[34] There is added complexity to this seemingly one-dimensional picture of her self-centeredness, however. During the tour, she joined Di Stefano in Milan for a benefit concert for his daughter Luisa. This was a generative act in view of Luisa's overt hostility toward her.

The concert tour provides additional evidence of how Maria's mean-spiritedness is entangled in her fragility. It was Elizabeth Taylor who helped Callas prepare for her film role of Medea, along with Richard Burton, and Taylor happened to be in Hamburg when Callas was getting ready for the first concert of the farewell tour. When asked whether Taylor should be sent complimentary tickets, Callas responded: "Well, I think not. Why should I let her cash in on my publicity?"[35] In Cincinnati, the violinist Isaac Stern invited her to an after-concert dinner, an invitation she spurned. "He's another social climber," she said. "He only wants to use me so that all the rich people will come to his party."[36] She used a similar claim in declining an invitation to a gala dinner following the Chicago concert from Dan Walker, Governor of Illinois. Callas's behavior toward Taylor, Stern, and Walker is reminiscent of her childhood pleading with Litsa not to give Alexandra Papajohn the thread and needle she needed to fix her skirt. Maria did not feel enough goodness in her life to afford generosity, just as when she was a child. The farewell tour shows how Callas was unable to fully benefit from the affirmation of her audiences because their adulation was undermined by her own self-criticism. Nor could she gain fulfillment from her personal relationships as they tended to be marred by her envy and her suspiciousness of their sincerity.

The End

"Dear Louis," Callas wrote to Dr. Parrish in January 1975, "I fin-ished the tour very well but arriving in Paris I collapsed—and I'm not joking. They couldn't wake me up (and I had taken no pills)."[37] Maria recovered physically from the collapse, but she never recov-ered emotionally, and there were several reasons for her inability to respond. Her personal collapse coincides with the deaths of several important people in her life. In September 1974, just before the end of the tour, Larry Kelly died of cancer, and although he had mixed opinions about her, Maria said that Kelly's death affected her more than that of her own father. Not long after, in November 1975, Pasolini was brutally murdered by a young man he solicited outside of Rome. Four months later, in March 1976, Visconti died follow-ing a stroke. Although Callas was no longer in close contact with these three men, their deaths exacerbated her pessimism and her dis-enchantment, both with the state of the world and with her own life.

Onassis died in March 1975. Aristo spent the last weeks of his life at the American Hospital in Paris, but Maria was not able to visit him—she was barred from visiting by his daughter Christina, who continued to blame Maria for breaking up her parent's mar-riage. Neither Callas nor Jackie Onassis were in Paris when Aristo died. Jackie shuttled to and fro between New York and Paris during his illness, but she decided to return to New York shortly before he died, even though the medical staff informed her that his days were numbered. Maria, in contrast, fled from Paris to Palm Beach, Florida, unable to bear the anguish of his imminent demise. Again, we see a telling contrast in how Jackie and Maria construed their relationship with Onassis.

Talking to Stancioff, who called her from Rome shortly after his death, "Nothing matters much anymore because nothing will ever be the same again," Maria said, "without him."[38] Onassis "was the whole meaning in her life," according to Ardoin, "and after his death she felt there was no point in going on—because everything she had done after they separated was to prove to him that she still meant something."[39] Callas had her own reasons for undertaking the farewell tour and engaging emotionally with Pasolini and Di Stefano, independent of Onassis's looming emotional presence. Nonetheless, Ardoin's claim captures the strength of her bond with Onassis. Maria talked with Aristo almost daily over the phone during their farewell tour, illustrating their continued emotional entanglement.

Onassis strongly discouraged the tour because of his misgivings about Di Stefano. On the phone, they discussed business issues, but Maria was afraid to tell him about her troubles with Di Stefano lest he insist she cancel the tour. Onassis continued to hold power over Maria, but he also provided her with the emotional stability lacking in her volatile relationship with Di Stefano. Aware of Di Stefano's propensity to cancel, or threaten to cancel, performances, Onassis reassured Callas that "if he doesn't turn up to sing, just give me a call and I'll come over and appear with you. The audience will be just as pleased."[40] Although tinged with bravado, this is the kind of caring gesture that Maria yearned for her entire life. Initially, she placed her hopes that these sorts of words or actions would come from Meneghini, but they never did. It was her relationship with Onassis that provided her with the personal affirmation she so badly wanted and needed, even as it was also interspersed with his cruelty and demeaning behavior.

What makes Maria a tragic and yet heroic figure is that she gave her all, both in her professional life and in her relationship with Onassis. And only with Onassis. The fact that she gave everything to her singing career and to her audiences made her the great artist that she was (recall her phrase "*ho dato tutto a te*" uttered during the performance of *Il Pirata*). Callas also gave everything of herself to Onassis, which is precisely why his abandonment was such a harrowing disappointment. And similarly, because she gave everything to her voice, she could not cope with its decline. That she was unable to deal with these setbacks is not surprising. It could not have been otherwise because giving everything to a cause or to a person leaves one depleted when confronted with loss and other adversity. In addition, Callas's early family life and socialization did not equip her with the necessary skills for independent living and for negotiating relationships with others, as we saw in earlier chapters. The irony is that Callas could not have achieved what she did without giving it her all, and yet she could not survive beyond having done so.

Predictably, Maria and Di Stefano's relationship ended after the farewell tour came to a close. She never really loved him, and he did not need her any more. With all the important men in her life gone, Callas spent her last two years secluded in her Paris apartment in the company of her two poodles and Bruna and Ferruccio. Her interactions with acquaintances made during her relationship with Onassis dwindled; Callas had a tendency to cancel or postpone meetings, and she did not bother to cultivate them. Instead, going against Dr. Parrish's advice, she spent her days watching television (Westerns remained her favorites) and playing cards with Bruna and Ferruccio. Both of them became such an important part of her life—they served as the last props of her enfeebled self—that she routinely begged them not to take their days off.

Although no longer appearing on stage, Callas drew satisfaction from listening to her past recordings. Loyal admirers mailed a steady stream of pirated recordings of her live performances. She listened to those recordings without being able to derive meaning and satisfaction, however; recordings of past accomplishments, reminiscent of her glory days, only intensified her despair. When she stopped singing, "she thought that everything was finished in that domain," asserts Placido Domingo. "She had drawn a line through her career and avoided discussing that period, and it was almost impossible to talk about music with her."[41] Domingo's telling remark demonstrates the destructive power of envy: It destroyed the things she could no longer possess. Even though Rosa Ponselle was her childhood idol, Maria never attempted to meet her in person. "I will not see that woman," she explained to Walter Legge. "She started out with better material than I did."[42] Callas disparages Ponselle for having a beautiful voice that she herself could never have, a perfect example of envy, which extracts its emotional toll through desire of the unattainable.

Callas's despair is evident in her last public interview, given to the French journalist Caloni, in which she decries the current state of opera. She criticized a recent staging by the Paris Opera of Gounod's *Faust* that transposes the plot to a New York City ghetto. She attributed opera's crisis to the diminished emphasis on quality and the absence of great conductors, even including Herbert Karajan in her criticism, though he had presided over her great triumph in Berlin's performance of *Lucia*. Asked directly by

Caloni whether she felt she had become useless, Callas replied, "I am completely useless. It's sad to say that's the way but it is."[43]

Bruna found Maria lying unconscious in the bathroom on the morning of September 16, 1977. She died later that day. The cause of her death was never established conclusively. She was cremated and buried on September 19, within three days of her death. The absence of an autopsy and the haste of the burial led some to speculate that she committed suicide. It is most likely, however, that her death was caused by her deteriorating physical health—she suffered from chronic low blood pressure—and her overreliance on both sleeping tablets and stimulants. She left neither a testament nor a suicide note. As can be clearly seen from the last existing photograph of Callas, by the time of her death she was physically only a shadow of her previous self.

Toward the end of her life, Maria resumed her relationship with her sister Jackie, whom she needed to send her supplies of Mandrax (this sleeping medication had been banned by then in France because of its highly addictive properties but was still sold legally in Greece). According to Renzo and Roberto Allegri, entries in her unpublished diary contain messages of terrible despair. "I know of no affection or esteem for me: I am infinitely alone," she wrote. "I have never depended on anyone in my life: Today I am the slave to a bottle of pills," she wrote in another. "I think that, for me, ending this life will be a joy: I have no happiness, no friends, only drugs."[44] Franco Zeffirelli, who met her in Paris less than six months before her death, was struck by her physical and emotional frailty.

I had noticed that her once beautiful hands now looked transparent; you could see the veins below the skin. Then, as I walked her back to her apartment after lunch, I was appalled to realize that she was actually afraid. She kept close to me, terrified that she would come into contact with passers-by. . . . She kept on talking about how dangerous the world had become, that terrorists were everywhere and she would never go back to Italy because of all the kidnappings.

Zeffirelli notes that her behavior "was beyond any normal distress at the present state of the world, it was paranoia."[45] It was clear that Maria had fallen into a deep despair that overshadowed any hope or faith in the meaning of life. Callas's funeral service, held in Paris' small Greek Orthodox Church, was packed with mourners, certainly many acquaintances, but no close friends. The official mourning party included Bruna; Ferruccio; Jackie, who flew in from Athens; Sandor Gorlinsky, the impresario who organized the farewell tour; Franco Rossellini, the producer of *Medea*; and Princess Grace of Monaco and her daughter Caroline. Also present was Devetzi Vasso, a woman who befriended Callas toward the end of her life and who subsequently would be accused of embezzling part of Maria's estate. Outside, the coffin was greeted with enthusiastic applause from six hundred or so of her admirers who resoundingly cried out "Brava Maria."

Notes

1. See Erikson, E. (1963). *Childhood and society*. New York: Norton.
2. Gage, *Greek fire*, p. 283.
3. All quotes in this section are taken from Ardoin, *Callas: The art and the life*, pp. 43–45.

4. This aspect of Callas perfectionism is movingly portrayed in Zeffirelli's film *Callas Forever*, offering a fictionalized account of the last years of her life in Paris.

5. Pasolini, P. P. (2014). *The selected poetry of Pier Paolo Pasolini*. Chicago: University of Chicago Press. Fabrizio Cigni alerted me to the existence of Pasolini's poetry about Maria Callas.

6. Clement, C. (1988). *Opera, or, the undoing of women*. Minneapolis: University of Minnesota Press.

7. Gage, *Greek fire*, p. 312.

8. Ibid., p. 245.

9. Ibid., p. 336.

10. Scott, *Maria Meneghini Callas*, p. 244.

11. See EMI Classics CD. (1987). *Maria Callas at Juilliard: The Masterclasses*.

12. Ardoin, J. (1987). *Learning from Callas*. EMI Classics CD, p. 9.

13. Stancioff, *Maria Callas remembered*, p. 209.

14. Ardoin, *Callas at Juilliard*, p. xvi.

15. Stancioff, *Maria Callas remembered*, p. 208.

16. Ibid., p. 209.

17. McNally, T. (1998). *Master class*. New York: Dramatists Play Services, Inc.

18. All quotes come from McNally, *Master class*, p. 50.

19. Stancioff, *Maria Callas remembered*, p. 208.

20. Allegri, *Callas by Callas*, p. 155.

21. Stancioff, *Maria Callas remembered*, p. 219.

22. Porter, A. (1973). *Financial Times,* November 27.

23. Commanday, R. (1974). *San Francisco Chronicle*, May 10.

24. Sutherland, *Maria Callas: Diaries*, p. 187.

25. Allegri, *Callas by Callas*, pp. 154 and 156.

26. Sutherland, *Maria Callas: Diaries*, p. 109.

27. Stancioff, *Maria Callas remembered*, p. 231.

28. Sutherland, *Maria Callas: Diaries*, p. 51.

29. Ibid., p. 89.

30. Ibid., p. 22.

31. Ibid., p. 22.

32. Ibid., p. 158.

33. Ibid., p. 152.

34. Ibid., p. 136.

35. Ibid., p. 41.

36. Ibid., p. 193.

37. Ibid., p. 266.

38. Stancioff, *Maria Callas remembered*, p. 233.

39. Gage, *Greek fire*, p. 367.

40. Sutherland, *Maria Callas: Diaries*, p. 146.

41. Domingo, P. Singing after Callas. In Lowe, *Callas as they saw her*, p. 189.

42. Legge, W. (1982). *La Divina*. In Schwarzkopf, E. (ed.), *On and off the record: A memoir of Walter Legge*. Boston, MA: Northeastern University Press, p. 201.

43. Caloni, P. (1976). *Hommage a Maria Callas* (radio interview). Radio-France Musique, Paris (https://www.youtube.com/watch?v=wCyVOGIMNVU).

44. Allegri, *Callas by Callas*, p. 158.

45. Zeffirelli, F. (1986). *An autobiography*. New York: Grove, p. 298.

EPILOGUE

For someone who injected reality into opera's make-believe world, it is befitting that Callas's life mimicked that which she enacted on the stage. There was an element of Tosca's haughty pride in her demeanor, a part of Violetta's fragility in her self-evaluation. But it is the fate of Bellini's Norma, a Druid princess who was abandoned for another woman, that bears an uncanny resemblance to Callas's life. Norma is immolated in the arms of Polione, a Roman Proconsul in Gaul. Her fickle lover realizes that it was she who had been the love of his life all along—but the epiphany comes too late. The parallels between *Norma*'s plot and the real-life triangle of Callas, Onassis, and Jackie Kennedy are obvious. Callas debuted the role of Norma in 1948 at Florence's Teatro Communale, and it proved to be one of her favorites. In fact, it was the role she performed most frequently during her career. The dramatic nature of Callas's life and the curious manner of her death undoubtedly add to her charisma and legend: Her life continues to fuel fascination even today, more than forty years after her passing. Given her prominent status in the Pantheon of operatic stars, it may seem jarring or perhaps even sacrilegious to subject her life to a psychological analysis that is bound to reveal feet of clay. Her legacy extends beyond opera, exercising a hold over our imaginations. Callas's rise and fall shows how human strength and weakness can interact, propelling a person to greatness before contributing to their downward spiral.

A character in Tess Hadley's novel *Late in the Day* proclaims that "he didn't think that [a friend] had the necessary cruelty that made an artist, or the incompleteness in himself." Callas, in contrast, possessed both. She could not have achieved stardom without cruelty, a trait which allowed her to sweep aside all obstacles blocking her way, including fellow artists and traditions. The cruelty mentioned by Hadley as a prerequisite for artistic success undoubtedly includes self-centeredness, arrogance, and a sense of destiny, necessary prerequisites for survival in the fiercely competitive world of the performing arts. These buffer musicians, dancers, and singers against the ever-present specter of a stage mishap, against the slings and arrows swiftly fired by a critical public. But "cruelty" on its own fails to accounts for Callas's psychological downfall or, for that matter, her phenomenal artistic success. Nellie Melba and Adelina Patti, the quintessential operatic divas, were known for arrogance and self-centeredness, like Callas, yet they did not seem to pay a psychological price for their haughty demeanor.

Incompleteness caused Callas's personal disintegration at midlife while at the same time elevating her to the highest echelons of operatic artistry, surpassing arguably the accomplishments of any other soprano of the recorded era. Callas's incompleteness manifested itself in the narcissistic split between *la Callas*, the successful and self-assured operatic diva, and the gauche and hesitant Maria of everyday life—a split evident by Maria's tendency to refer to her public persona in the third person. Each part felt lacking when separated from the other. Maria grew up in a psychologically troubled family trying to make a living in a new land at the height of the Great Depression, and she never received the psychological sustenance or affirmation necessary to develop a firm and cohesive sense of self. Instead, she desperately latched onto acclaim generated by her singing talent, an acclaim that never felt quite real. It covered up a private self that felt real but was never experienced as fully affirmed. Callas's outer diva's persona was lacking because it failed to be softened by her own, split off human and vulnerable side. Maria, the person, felt incomplete and depleted because she was cut off from the vitality and glory of Callas the singer. Once it developed, Callas found it impossible to bridge this split partly because of her own fragility and in part because of a cascading series of external events, including further deterioration in family interactions and hostility experienced from fellow singers during her adolescent years spent in Athens. Instead, she became a slave to public acclaim and, in her private life, to the need for merger with the idealized other for psychological equilibrium.

Callas's desire for completeness allowed her to merge in an unprecedented way with operatic roles enacted on stage, and, when combined with her exceptional voice, these qualities made Callas the extraordinary performer that she was. Her relentless pursuit of artistic perfection and acclaim bordered on the monomaniacal. At the height of her career, Callas behaved as though her salvation lay in her art, a risky strategy given the vagaries of her voice. Off the stage, her career benefited from idealized relationships with mentors, including Elvira de Hidalgo in Athens and, subsequently, the conductor Tulio Serafin and stage director Lucchino Visconti in Italy. Callas's struggle for completeness caused her to fuse her identity with Meneghini in the initial stages of their marriage, and later she did the same with Onassis during the nine years they lived together. Maria's search for completeness also contributed to her massive loss of weight, an attempt to mold her appearance in the image of Audrey Hepburn. But internal, psychological incompleteness cannot be filled by external factors alone, just as midlife crisis cannot be resolved by buying a fancy car or a lack of body esteem by invasive plastic surgery.

It is not that external events do not matter for our well-being or sense of self. Callas's life would have most likely turned out differently if her voice did not decline as precipitously as it did, if she had married Onassis, or if she weren't a rootless American-born Greek who established her career in Italy and ended up living in Paris. Nonetheless, Callas's rise to fame and her demise illustrate a crucial psychological insight: It is ultimately not what happens to us that defines our life, but what we make of it. To repeat the words of D. W. Winnicott: "if the artist (in whatever medium) is searching for the self, then it can be said in all probability there is already some failure for that artist in the field of general creative living [i.e., vitality and purpose in life]. The finished creation never heals the underlying lack of sense of self." True. But, highlighting one of the paradoxes of life, this doomed quest offers a royal road to artistic greatness.

INDEX

For the benefit of digital users, indexed terms that span two pages (e.g., 52–53) may, on occasion, appear on only one of those pages.

Plate 1 Maria Callas with her father George Kalogeropoulos, New York, 1946.

Plate 2 Maria Callas, in 1950, at the beginning of her Italian singing career (location and date unknown).

Plate 3 Maria Callas during her first visit to London to sing at the Royal Opera House, Covent Garden, November 1952.

Plate 4 Maria Callas on vacation in Venice (Italy) with her husband Battista Meneghini, circa 1952.

Plate 5 Maria Callas and Aristotle Onassis hosted by the journalist Elsa Maxwell in Venice, September 1957.

Keystone-France/Gamma-Keystone via Getty Images.

Plate 6 Maria Callas walking in Porto Fino (Italy) in July 1959 with Aristotle Onassis's wife, Tina (on the left), Winston Churchill's daughter, Sarah, and Antonella Agnelli, wife of the Italian industrialist Gianni Agnelli.

Keystone Press/Alamy Stock Photo.

Plate 7 Maria Callas and Aristotle Onassis dancing at New Year's Ball in Monte Carlo, January 1, 1960.

Keystone Press/Alamy Stock Photo.

Plate 8 Maria Callas with Antonio Ghiringhelli, General Manager of Milan's La Scala Theater, at the showing of Federico Fellini's film *La Dolce Vita*, Milan 1960.

Ullstein bild via Getty Images.

Plate 9 Maria Callas with adoring crowds, 1965.

Pictorial Press Ltd./Alamy Stock Photo.

Plate 10 Maria Callas, Tito Gobbi (left), and Renato Cioni after their performance of *Tosca* at the Royal Opera House, Covent Garden, London, July 1965.

Keystone Press/Alamy Stock Photo.

Plate 11 Maria Callas with her friend the Italian director Pier Paolo Pasolini and her two poodles, Pixie and Djeddas, 1971.

Plate 12 Maria Callas and Giuseppe Di Stefano during her final concert tour, Berlin, May 1973.

AF Archive/Alamy Stock Photo.

Plate 13 Maria Callas with accompanist Ivor Newton during her final concert tour, Hamburg, October 1973.

Dpa picture alliance/Alamy Stock Photo.

Plate 14 Maria Callas arriving at the Royal Concert Hall, Covent Garden, for rehearsal, November 1973.

Keystone Press/Alamy Stock Photo.